TEACHING LITERACY IN KINDERGARTEN

TOOLS FOR TEACHING LITERACY

Donna Ogle and Camille Blachowicz, Series Editors

This highly practical series includes two kinds of books: (1) grade-specific titles for first-time teachers or those teaching a particular grade for the first time; (2) books on key literacy topics that cut across all grades, such as integrated instruction, English language learning, and comprehension. Written by outstanding educators who know what works based on extensive classroom experience, each research-based volume features hands-on activities, reproducibles, and best practices for promoting student achievement.

TEACHING LITERACY IN SIXTH GRADE
Karen Wood and Maryann Mraz

TEACHING LITERACY IN KINDERGARTEN
Lea M. McGee and Lesley Mandel Morrow

INTEGRATING INSTRUCTION: LITERACY AND SCIENCE
Judy McKee and Donna Ogle

TEACHING LITERACY IN SECOND GRADE
Jeanne R. Paratore and Rachel L. McCormack

TEACHING LITERACY IN FIRST GRADE
Diane Lapp, James Flood, Kelly Moore, and Maria Nichols

TEACHING
LITERACY
in Kindergarten

Lea M. McGee
Lesley Mandel Morrow

Series Editors' Note by Donna Ogle and Camille Blachowicz

THE GUILFORD PRESS
New York   London

KH

© 2005 The Guilford Press
A Division of Guilford Publications, Inc.
72 Spring Street, New York, NY 10012
www.guilford.com

Printed in the United States of America

This book is printed on acid-free paper.

Last digit is print number: 9   8   7   6   5   4   3   2

Library of Congress Cataloging-in-Publication Data

McGee, Lea M.
    Teaching literacy in kindergarten / by Lea M. McGee, Lesley Mandel Morrow.
        p. cm. — (Tools for teaching literacy)
    Includes bibliographical references and index.
        ISBN-10 1-59385-152-9   ISBN-13 978-1-59385-152-1 (pbk.)
        ISBN-10 1-59385-153-7   ISBN-13 978-1-59385-153-8 (hardcover)
    1. Reading (Kindergarten).   2. Language arts (Kindergarten).
3. Literacy.   I. Morrow, Lesley Mandel.   II. Title.
LB1181.2.M34   2005
372.4—dc22

                                                    2004024045

1/4/10

ABOUT THE AUTHORS

Lea M. McGee, EdD, is Professor of Literacy Education at the University of Alabama. She teaches graduate and undergraduate courses in children's literature, beginning reading and language arts, and foundations of language and literacy development. Dr. McGee is coauthor of three books: *Literacy's Beginnings: Supporting Young Readers and Writers* (4th ed., 2004, Pearson) and *Designing Early Literacy Programs: Strategies for At-Risk Preschool and Kindergarten Children* (2003, Guilford Press), both coauthored with Donald J. Richgels, and *Teaching Reading with Literature: Case Studies to Action Plans* (1993, Merrill), coauthored with Gail Tompkins. She has published dozens of articles and book chapters in a variety of journals, including *The Reading Teacher, Language Arts*, and *Reading Research Quarterly*. Dr. McGee is also past president of the National Reading Conference.

Lesley Mandel Morrow, PhD, holds the rank of Professor II at Rutgers University's Graduate School of Education, where she is also chair of the Department of Learning and Teaching. She began her career as a classroom teacher, then became a reading specialist, and later received her doctorate from Fordham University. Her area of research focuses on early literacy development and the organization and management of language arts programs. Her research is carried out with children and families from diverse backgrounds. Dr. Morrow has more than 200 publications, including journal articles, book chapters, and books, most recently *Literacy Development in the Early Years: Helping Children Read and Write* (5th ed., 2005, Pearson/Allyn & Bacon), *Literacy and Young Children: Research-Based Practices* (coedited with Diane M. Barone, 2003, Guilford Press), *Organizing and Managing the Language Arts Block: A Professional Development Guide* (2003, Guilford Press), and *The Literacy Center: Contexts for Reading and Writing* (2nd ed., 2001, Stenhouse). She is also past president of the International Reading Association.

SERIES EDITORS' NOTE

As teacher educators and staff developers, we have become aware of the need for a series of books for thoughtful practitioners who want a practical, research-based introduction to teaching literacy at specific grade levels. Preservice and beginning teachers want to know how to be as effective as possible; they also know there are great differences in what students need across grade levels. We have met teacher after teacher who, when starting to teach or teaching a new grade, asked for a guide targeted at their specific grade level. Until now we have not had a resource to share with them.

We also collaborate with staff developers and study group directors who want effective inservice materials that they can use with teachers at many different levels yet that still provide specific insights for individual grade levels. Thus the Tools for Teaching Literacy series was created.

This series is distinguished by two innovative characteristics designed to make it useful to individual teachers, staff developers, and study groups alike. Each Tools for Teaching Literacy volume:

> Is written by outstanding educators who are noted for their knowledge of research, theory, and best practices; who spend time in real classrooms working with teachers; and who are experienced staff developers who work alongside teachers applying these insights in classrooms. We think the series authors are unparalleled in these qualifications.

> Is organized according to a structure shared by all the grade-level books, which include chapters on:

- the nature of the learner at a particular grade level

- appropriate goals for literacy

- setting up the physical environment for literacy

- getting to know students with appropriate assessments and planning for differentiation

- a week in the grade-level classroom—what this looks like in practice with important instructional strategies and routines
- resources for learning

With this common organization in the grade-level books, a staff developer can use several different volumes in the series for teacher study groups, new teacher seminars, and other induction activities, choosing particular discussion and learning topics, such as classroom organization, that cross grade-level concerns. Teachers can also easily access information on topics of most importance to them and make comparisons across the grade levels.

The explosion of interest in kindergarten as a foundational grade for literacy development makes this volume especially timely and critical. Lea M. McGee and Lesley Mandel Morrow are two educators with a long history of research and professional development work in preschool and kindergarten classrooms. Their approach to kindergarten literacy is a seamless blend of best practices in early literacy with the most advanced thinking about early childhood education. Their chapters are rich in ideas detailing how a young child's literacy emergence can be supported at the same time social and cognitive development is enhanced—and in a playful and enjoyable way appropriate to the kindergarten learner.

DONNA OGLE
CAMILLE BLACHOWICZ

PREFACE

Kindergarten is a special time in a child's life. It is often the first year that children attend "real" school. Most of us have warm memories of our kindergarten experiences. We remember the stories the teacher read aloud, building with those enormous wooden blocks, and creating the most extravagant art projects. For me (L. M. M.) kindergarten will always be special for a second reason: I began my career teaching kindergarten almost three decades ago. However, things were different then. There was no intentional teaching of literacy skills. As a matter of fact, in some schools, it was forbidden to teach literacy. Some of what we did then looks the same now and should be, and some looks vastly different. In today's kindergarten classrooms, we still utilize blocks and dramatic play centers. We still recite favorite poems, we still teach finger plays, and we still construct art projects. We still teach using themes; we read stories and teach science and social studies related to those themes. However, in addition, kindergarten teachers are expected to provide far more instruction in reading and writing skills than we ever did before.

While we continue to have debates over what is and is not appropriate for young children, the research is clear: Young children can and do learn a great deal about reading and writing at age 5. Kindergarten instructional approaches remain playful; but nonetheless, they are systematic and intentional. Kindergarten teachers are careful to engage children in activities that preserve the joy of reading and writing. However, they are intentional in providing children with opportunities to learn the foundational knowledge that is so critical for beginning to read and write with success. Kindergarten teachers guide children into the wonderful world of literature and discovery; yet they also teach the alphabet, phonemic awareness, concepts about print, and oral language. This book is intended to help teachers become better at meeting the needs of the diverse learners they will encounter as they teach kindergarten and to help students learn the skills in ways appropriate for their age. Kindergartners can learn letters, numbers, colors, sight words, and to do some writing, but instruction must be handled in a way that will enhance their joy of learning. We hope that this book will help teachers to accomplish these goals.

CONTENTS

CHAPTER 1.   A Week in Kindergarten   1

CHAPTER 2.   Preparing the Environment for Literacy Instruction   24
              in Kindergarten

CHAPTER 3.   What Do Kindergartners Know about Reading and Writing?   43

CHAPTER 4.   Whole-Group Literacy Instruction   63

CHAPTER 5.   Small-Group Literacy Instruction   92

CHAPTER 6.   Differentiating Instruction to Meet the Needs of All Learners   115

CHAPTER 7.   Assessment   146

APPENDIX A.   Resources for Kindergarten Teachers   179

APPENDIX B.   Alphabet Letter Formation   193

APPENDIX C.   ELKA Alphabet Recognition Tasks   199

APPENDIX D.   ELKA Concepts about Print Tasks   207

APPENDIX E.   ELKA Phonemic Awareness Tasks   215

APPENDIX F.   ELKA Phonics Tasks   227

APPENDIX G.   ELKA Writing Task: Invented Spelling List and Scoring Rubric   237

APPENDIX H.   Comprehension and Vocabulary Task   239

References   241

Children's Literature   247

Index   251

CHAPTER 1

A WEEK IN KINDERGARTEN

I n this chapter we describe a kindergarten teacher and her children in action. The teacher we describe is very experienced, and her approach to teaching reading requires her to have dozens of little books that range in difficulty from a single word or two on each page to books with one or two sentences per page. Later in this book we describe other ways to teach reading and writing in kindergarten. The week we describe occurred in March, so the children have become very familiar with the classroom routine. They have already acquired many skills that are expected in kindergarten. We use the description of this classroom to introduce many of the critical components, materials, and routines of a kindergarten classroom. These are further explained in later chapters of this book. We recommend that readers revisit this chapter after reading this entire book.

INTRODUCTION TO THE KINDERGARTEN TEACHER AND STUDENTS

Suzanne Kazi* has been teaching kindergarten for the past 7 years. Recently she completed a master's degree and now is eligible for reading specialist certification. She teaches in a middle-income community. She has 22 students in her all-day kindergarten, including nine European American, six Asian American, five African American, and two Hispanic American children. Twenty percent of Suzanne's class speaks one of four languages at home: Spanish, Japanese, Hindi, or Mandarin Chinese. Thirteen students are boys and nine are girls. There is a full-time aide in the room who is assigned to one physically disabled student who is in a wheelchair.

Suzanne's philosophy of teaching emphasizes integration of the curriculum so that students can build connections between content areas. She purposefully inte-

*We wish to thank Suzanne Kazi for the contribution she made to this chapter.

grates her literacy skills development in reading, writing, listening, speaking, and viewing with her social studies and science themes as much as possible. Her small-group literacy instruction is explicit by emphasizing specific skill development.

Ms. Kazi has a special interest in using informational texts with her children. She recognizes that background knowledge and vocabulary are enhanced by using expository material. Moreover, she realizes that as adults we read informational text in a variety of forms such as how-to manuals, applications, instructions, and websites. She has also found through experience that at-risk students and boys are particularly drawn to expository or informational text.

Setting the Stage for Instruction: Suzanne's Classroom Environment

Suzanne's classroom is warm and inviting, with well-defined centers located around the room. The displays on the walls clearly reflect the theme being studied and show considerable evidence of the children's growing literacy development. Nearly all of the displays include charts that Suzanne has written with her children, samples of children's writing, or children's artwork. In the whole-group area (a large carpeted space), Suzanne has placed an easel with chart paper for the morning message, a calendar, a weather chart, a temperature graph, a helper chart, a daily schedule, her classroom rules, a hundreds chart used to count the days in school, a pocket chart, and a word wall.

Suzanne's largest center is the literacy center. The literacy center has a rug for independent reading and is also used for whole-class meetings. The area includes lots of space for storing books. One set of shelves holds books organized in two different ways. There are baskets of books leveled for difficulty that coordinate with Suzanne's small-group reading instruction. For example, students reading in the green basket during small-group instruction know that books in the green basket are ones they can read independently. Other shelves hold baskets organized by themes and authors, such as dinosaurs, sports, alphabet books, and books by Dr. Seuss or Eric Carle. Suzanne rotates books in the baskets monthly. She also rotates theme and author books. Colored stickers on both the books and the baskets assist students in returning the books to the correct basket. Student-made class books and stories are displayed in their own special basket. Books about the current theme are displayed on a special open-faced shelf.

The *literacy center* is stocked with flannel-board characters, a flannel board, puppets, and props for storytelling. There is a rocking chair for the teacher and other adults to sit in while they read to the class. The children use the rocking chair to read independently and to read to each other. The listening area in the literacy center has a CD/tape player for listening to stories. There is a good selection of manipulative materials for learning about print. These include magnetic letters, puzzle rhyme cards, and letter chunks on small tiles for making words.

The *writing center* is an extension of the literacy center. This consists of a round table for small groups of children to meet with the teacher. There are shelves stocked with many types of paper (lined and unlined), a stapler, markers, crayons, colored pencils, dictionaries, alphabet stamps, and ink stamp pads. A word wall in the writing center features each of the letters of the alphabet taped on it horizontally. When the children learn a new word, Suzanne writes it on a card and tapes the card under the letter it begins with on the word wall. Children use the word cards when they need a spelling or to practice reading. During instruction children may be asked to think of words that begin with the same letter and sound as a word on the word wall or to think of words that rhyme with a word on the wall word. Suzanne places her students' names on the word wall and adds high-frequency sight words that kindergarten children are expected to learn.

Suzanne's *science center* provides a home for the class guinea pig, rabbit, and hermit crab. Equipment in this center includes magnets, objects that sink and float, and plants. Suzanne adds materials to match the themes she is teaching, and always provides new hands-on experiments for students to complete.

The *dramatic play center* includes typical kitchen appliances and furniture such as a stove, a refrigerator, a table and chairs, with empty food boxes that display print. Changes are made to the area to reflect the themes being studied throughout the year. This center is frequently converted into a restaurant where children can take orders, read menus, and check their bills. The restaurant helps with learning about multicultural food and customs. This year the class has had Italian, Chinese, Mexican, Portuguese, and Japanese restaurants, and a Jewish deli.

The *block center* includes wooden blocks of all sizes and shapes and other toys for construction such as Legos. There are toy trucks, cars, trains, buses, people, and animals in this area. There are labels that designate where the different toys go, such as trucks, cars, people, and so on. There are 5" × 8" cards and tape for labeling structures created by the children. There are several signs written in invented spellings (e.g., PLZ SAV) on buildings under construction and signs naming finished structures. Children sign their names on the labels.

Located near the sink is the *art center*, which contains an easel, a table, chairs, and shelves for materials. Suzanne has her easels opened three times each week. On the shelves are scissors, markers, crayons, and paper of many colors, types, and sizes. There are collage materials such as cotton balls, doilies, foil paper, wallpaper samples, and paste.

The *math center* contains math manipulative materials for counting, adding, measuring, weighing, graphing, and distinguishing shapes. There are felt numbers to use on the felt board, magnetic numbers to use on the magnetic boards, numbers to sequence in a pocket chart, and geometric shapes such as squares, triangles, cylinders, rectangles, and so on.

The children sit at circular tables; there are five tables with four to five children at each table. In a quiet corner of the room there is a horseshoe-shaped table, which Suzsanne uses for small-group instruction. Shelves located next to the table have materials needed for small groups such as letters of the alphabet, rhyming cards, leveled books, sentence strips, index cards, white boards, markers, and word study games.

Center Management

Suzanne uses her centers daily—5-year-olds learn best when they are manipulating materials such as those found in the centers. To ensure that students work at two specific centers a day, Suzanne has designed a contract on which she indicates the centers where children are expected to work daily. The contract includes the name of each center and an icon representing the center. These same labels and icons are repeated at the actual centers. When children complete work in a center, they check it off on their contracts. The completed work from a center is placed in a basket labeled "Finished Work." At the end of each day, Suzanne discusses and reviews with the children completed work from the centers and assigns their centers for the next day. Any incomplete work, or work that indicates a child needs help with a concept, is placed in the "Unfinished Work" basket. During the day time is set aside for completing unfinished work. When children complete their two centers daily they can work at any other centers they choose. Thus, children have a combination of required activities in centers assigned by Suzanne and self-selected activities in centers of their own choice.

Assessing Students to Determine Instructional Needs

In order to provide instruction to meet the varied levels of reading and writing of her students, Suzanne spends considerable time assessing them with formal and informal measures. In September, January, and June, she assesses students' knowledge about concepts of print and books, phonological and phonemic awareness, ability to recognize and write letters of the alphabet, knowledge of letter–sound relationships, ability to read sight words, listening comprehension, and writing ability. She plans instruction based on the needs she identifies. As children begin to read conventionally, Suzanne takes monthly *running records* for each child who has reached this level of reading. The running records assess the types of errors or miscues that children make, the decoding strategies they use, and their progress. Suzanne writes anecdotal notes about student behaviors that indicate both progress and points of difficulty. She collects samples of children's writing and anecdotal notes, dates and analyzes them, and places them in student portfolios. Suzanne also observes students for social, emotional, and physical development.

Small-Group Reading Instruction

Suzanne has developed a schedule that allows her to work with small groups of children for reading instruction. With the assessment information she collects, she places students with similar needs together for small-group instruction. As she works with students, she takes careful notes regarding their progress in literacy and adjusts the members of her various groups as needed. While working with small groups, Suzanne provides instruction in phonological awareness, identification of letters, letter–sound relationships, knowledge about books and print concepts, vocabulary, listening comprehension, oral language, and writing. She presently has four small groups and meets with each group three times a week. On Fridays she attends to any special needs that come up during the week. Suzanne finds that she needs to meet with her students who are struggling more often than with other groups and frequently does this on Friday.

Suzanne's Daily Schedule

8:45   When children arrive at school, they do the following:
- Carry out their jobs.
- Make entries in their journals.
- Complete unfinished work, practice skills needing extra attention.

9:00   The group meets as a whole for the morning meeting
- Morning greetings are shared.
- Poems are read in choral fashion.
- The calendar and weather are discussed.
- The number of days left until school ends is counted.
- The schedule for the day is reviewed.
- The morning message is read and added to.
- The students engage in singing and movement activities.
- The teacher reads a book using shared reading techniques.

9:30   Small-group reading instruction and center activities

10:30   Snack and play

10:50   Writing block (interactive writing, minilesson, and writing workshop)

11:45   Play/lunch/nap

1:00   Math

1:40   Theme-related activities, centers, and reading aloud

2:15   Creative arts, music, gym

2:50   Closing circle
- Reading aloud
- Sharing and reviewing activities of the day
- Discussing what was learned today
- Planning for tomorrow

A TYPICAL WEEK IN SUZANNE'S CLASSROOM

During this week Suzanne and her children are studying dinosaurs (Appendix A presents a list of resources for teaching a dinosaur theme, including narrative and information books for reading aloud, leveled books for children to read, videos, audiotaped books, and Internet sites). In Suzanne's classroom reading, writing, listening, speaking, and math activities are integrated throughout the dinosaur theme. However, Suzanne also meets individual needs in small-group reading instruction. On Monday she organizes activities for the week. In the next section we describe the routine activities as they occur on Monday; in subsequent sections we describe other activities that occur throughout the week with less detail. Although we may not discuss every routine included in Ms. Kazi's schedules, these routines occur daily.

Monday: Setting the Stage

When Children Arrive at School

It is 8:45 on Monday morning and quiet chatter begins to fill Suzanne's classroom as her students arrive. Classical music plays in the background as children complete their morning routines. Children move their nametags on the attendance board from the side labeled "Not Here" to "Here" and place their name stickers into the "Buy Lunch" or "Buy Milk" can. Several children cluster around the easel, where they work together to read the morning message Suzanne has written and discuss the question of the day. The morning message is predictable to help children not yet conventionally reading to decipher its meaning. Today's message says: "Good morning, kindergartners. Today is Monday, March 8, 2004. We will have art today. Do you like dinosaurs?   <u>Yes</u>   <u>No</u>."

Suzanne placed a picture of a dinosaur above the question to assist students with reading the word *dinosaurs*. She also wrote each sentence in a different color to represent different ideas to think about. Students are used to being asked "Yes" or "No" questions and respond with tally marks under the words "Yes" and "No." The students check the helper chart for their jobs, such as feeding the animals, watering the plants, or recording the temperature and day's weather on the weather graph. The *zoo keeper* reads the list posted by the animal cages to make sure he or she has completed all his or her tasks. The pictures placed next to each step help him or her read the chart and remember what to do.

Students know it is time for writing their *weekend news* in their journals. Suzanne greets each student as she circulates among the writers, gently reminding some children to use spaces between words, and suggesting that others use classroom tools such as the word wall to spell needed words. As she listens to completed entries, she has the opportunity to chat with the children about their weekend. When the 2-minute warning bell rings, several children are already in the meeting area on the rug in the literacy center, reading books, alone or with a partner. Those still writing begin to put away their materials and place their unfinished work in the "Not Finished" basket. They will be able to complete their entries later in the day during center time. Once the student shakes the tambourine announcing morning meeting, everyone gathers and forms a circle on the carpet.

The Morning Meeting

"Good morning, Emily," Suzanne begins, as they shake hands around the circle. Because they are beginning a new month, March, they echo-read a poem called "March" from *Chicken Soup with Rice* (Sendak, 1962a). Suzanne has written the poem on chart paper. At the end of the month the children will illustrate personal copies of this poem, and it will be placed in their *Poem Books*, along with other poems used throughout the year. As the *calendar person, weather reporter*, and *schedule person* lead the class in these activities, Suzanne records the attendance and lunch count, which the *messenger* takes to the office.

Suzanne leads the class in reading the *morning message* together. The children discuss the results of the tally of the day's question on the message, "Do you like dinosaurs?" For those who said no, they tell why they don't like dinosaurs. For those who said yes, they discuss why they like them. Suzanne leads a discussion related to the morning message about the end marks or punctuation marks at the end of each sentence. The period and question marks are named, explained, and circled.

Suzanne has a new poem for the theme being studied that is hanging on another chart called "I'm a Mean Old Dinosaur" (Pruett, 1991). Suzanne reads the poem to the class and tracks the print with a pointer. After the first reading, the children echo-read the poem with their teacher. Suzanne covers a different word in each sentence of the poem with a Post-it. She reads a sentence and then the students echo-read the sentence through. They say the word *blank* for the covered word. They go back to the beginning and read until the first covered word.

SUZANNE: When I get all *blank* I just growl. What word could be placed in the blank space? Think what might make a dinosaur growl.

STUDENT 1: When he gets all mad.

SUZANNE: When I get all mad, I just growl. Does that make sense?

CLASS: Yes.

SUZANNE: Does it match what you know about dinosaurs?

STUDENT 2: Well, some dinosaurs get mad, but maybe not all of them.

SUZANNE: So it does make sense?

STUDENT 4: Yes it makes sense, but it could be hungry too.

Suzanne writes the words *mad* and *hungry* on separate 5" × 8" card and proceeds in the same manner until the class has four words on cards that could fit into that sentence. The words they come up with are *mad, tired, hungry, sad*.

> SUZANNE: Words need to make sense in the sentence and they need to match the letters in the words we are reading.
>
> STUDENT 3: You have to look at the letters.
>
> SUZANNE: Right. Let's check the first letter and see which word matches.

They check *mad*, but none of the letters match; they check *tired*, but none of the letters match; they check *hungry* and all the letters match. The class continues with filling in the words left out on the chart. When all the words are figured out, the teacher echo-reads it with the children again. Before center time, Suzanne puts on some music and tells the children to walk around the room acting like dinosaurs.

Center Time

Suzanne spends a few minutes reviewing the center activities and describing new activities placed in the centers for the exploration of dinosaurs. Centers have materials that are in place over a period of time, and they are enriched with activities that reflect the current theme. A description of what has been added to each center related to the dinosaur theme follows.

➢ *Writing center.* Dinosaur-bordered writing paper, dinosaur-shape books, a dinosaur dictionary, a dinosaur-shaped poster with words about dinosaurs.

➢ *Literacy center.* Fiction and nonfiction dinosaur books, dinosaur books with accompanying CDs, a dinosaur vocabulary puzzle, a dinosaur concentration memory game, a teacher-made dinosaur lotto game.

➢ *Computer center.* Eyewitness Virtual Reality: Dinosaur Hunter (DK Multimedia, 1998) for printing dinosaur stationery, post cards, posters, and masks, and for visiting a virtual museum exhibit about dinosaurs.

➢ *Science center.* Small skulls and old animal bones are displayed, along with a magnifying glass and rubber gloves to examine the bones (children are encouraged to draw what they think the entire animal may have looked like), and there are dinosaur pictures to sort into meat eaters and plant eaters, and other pictures to be sorted into "walked on two feet" and "walked on four feet." There are recording sheets for all activities.

➢ *Math center.* Measuring tools in a basket and sheets to record the measurement of various plaster bones of dinosaurs, dinosaur counters, little plastic dinosaurs to fill an estimation jar, a basket containing 50 little dinosaurs numbered from 1–50 to put the dinosaurs into sequential order.

➢ *Blocks center.* Toy dinosaurs, trees, bushes, and some dinosaur books are placed in the block center.

> *Art center.* Dinosaur stencils and dinosaur stamps are added to the art center. There are clay models of dinosaurs and many pictures of dinosaurs to help students make their own sculptures.

> *Dramatic play center.* The dramatic play area is transformed into a paleontologist's office. Chicken bones are embedded in plaster of paris blocks, students use wood carving tools and small hammers to remove the bones while wearing safety goggles, paper and pencil for labeling the bones, and trays to display findings, dinosaur books, and posters of fossils and dinosaurs.

After Suzanne reviews center activities, her students look on their contracts and go off to do their *have-to* activities. The activities that must be done often target skills that students need practice in, such as matching pictures with letters to reinforce letter–sound knowledge. When they complete their *have-to* activities, children may select any center such as the block center, dramatic play center, or art center. As they leave a center, the children check off that center on their contract.

Small-Group Reading Instruction

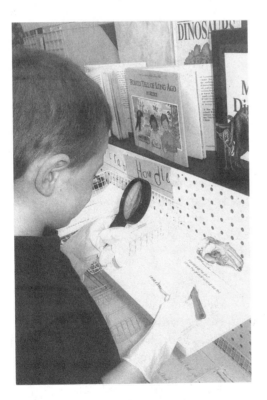

PHOTO 1.1. Examining dinosaur artifacts in the science center.

The first group that Suzanne sees is reviewing a book that they have read before, *We Went to the Zoo* (Sloan & Sloan, 1996). It is a simple patterned text with repeated words and phrases with some slight variations in the pattern. Suzanne provides a guided book introduction as children look through the book, stopping to talk about each page. During the book introduction, she asks students to find the words *saw* and *many* since these words caused some difficulty on the first reading. They also discuss the names of the animals in the book. As the group reads, Suzanne notices that one student makes no errors as he fingerpoint reads and finishes quickly. She makes a mental note to think about moving him to a different guided reading group. After the children finish reading, Suzanne asks everyone to turn to page 7. " I noticed that James read, 'We saw the . . .' and started to read *po-* for *polar bear*, but

PHOTO 1.2. Writing about dinosaurs in the science center.

then he used the first letter and read *bear* instead. He remembered that the words have to match the letters."

While the children were reading Suzanne was able to do a running record on one child. She noted that this student read "seals" instead of "otters" and said "pander bears" instead of "bears." Suzanne decides that tomorrow she will help this child to pay more attention to the print in the words as he reads.

Suzanne's next group will be reading the book *Who Can Run Fast?* (Stuart, 2001). The group has worked with this book before. To review they echo-read the book with the teacher. In the lesson that follows Suzanne will help her children to become more independent readers. She will teach them how to figure out unknown words by using the meaning of a sentence and by looking at the letters in the words. They begin with a game called "Guess the Covered Word," an activity they used while reading "I'm a Mean Old Dinosaur" during the morning meeting. This time the covered word in the sentence "I can *blank* fast" is the word *run*. The children are encouraged to select a word that makes sense in the sentence and then to look at the letters in the word to see which is the correct word. Words generated for the missing word were *walk, eat, hop, sleep,* and *run*. After successfully determining the correct word, the children are reminded that when we read, it must make sense and have the letters of the word we selected. Suzanne explains that this is what good readers do when they are reading alone and trying to figure out words. The activity is repeated in other sentences throughout their book.

The next group will read *Family Work and Fun* (Sloan & Sloan, 1996). In this lesson Suzanne will focus on looking at ending sounds to figure out words. Suzanne has written "I am *go* to the store" on the chart. She reads the sentence and the children quickly point out that it does not sound right. Suzanne writes a second sentence: "I am *going* to the store." The children identify the difference in the two sentences, pointing to the words *go* and *going*. Suzanne reminds them how they have to look at the ends of words as well as the beginning of words when they are reading. They read the book with special attention to the word endings.

Snack and Play

By midmorning everyone needs a break. The snack is dinosaur animal crackers and what Suzanne is calling "dinosaur juice." When snack time is over, children look at books or use some quiet table toys if time permits.

Writing Workshop

The children gather for writing in the whole-class meeting area. Suzanne prepares them for a schoolwide activity: they will survey all the students in the entire school to find out what their favorite dinosaurs are. Suzanne uses a shared writing activity to draft a letter asking the teachers and children in the school to participate in the dinosaur survey. She begins by reviewing the format of a letter, which was introduced during a previous unit on the post office. They discuss how to begin a letter and how to end a letter. Suzanne works with students to compose the text on chart paper. Then the class reads the finished letter together. Suzanne will type the letter and distribute it to each classroom; the original shared writing chart will be posted on the cafeteria door.

Next, Suzanne introduces the writing activity for the week. The children will be writing informational texts about dinosaurs. They are to select the one dinosaur they like the most and mention as many facts about that dinosaur as they can. They brainstorm what dinosaur they want to write about, and discuss facts they already know. Tuesday they will begin to browse through dinosaur books for information and start to write. Children will write facts and draw pictures. When the activity is completed at the end of the week, Suzanne will take everyone's illustrated fact sheets and make them into a class book.

Play, Lunch, and Nap

If weather permits, the children play outside. If not, play is in the gym or the classroom. Lunch is in the cafeteria, and children take naps on rugs in the classroom after lunch. Most of the children do sleep. At the beginning of nap time, Suzanne plays an audiotape of the story *Dinosaurs before Dark* (Osborne, 1992).

Math

A specific math curriculum (a core program) is followed in Suzanne's kindergarten. While Suzanne teaches from this curriculum daily, we describe here only the theme-related literacy activities that Suzanne added to her math curriculum. Today the class gathers in the meeting area to brainstorm a list of as many dinosaurs as they can name. Using the index of a dinosaur encyclopedia to verify spelling and locate a picture of each dinosaur, Suzanne writes the names on a large chart. After reviewing the list of 10 dinosaurs that they knew, children are asked to vote for their favorite dinosaur, while a student records the votes using tally marks for counting. Six dinosaurs received the most votes and their names are circled with a red marker. These dinosaurs are Allosaurus, Iguanodon, Spinosaurus, Stegasaurus, Triceratops, and Tyrannosaurus. These dinosaurs will be used in the schoolwide survey of favorite dinosaurs.

Special Theme Activity and Center Time

Suzanne has planned a themed art activity that the class will participate in during the week. Everyone will contribute to a mural and construct a habitat environment for dinosaur sculptures the children will be creating with the art teacher. To introduce the mural and habitat activity, Suzanne explains the details to everyone. Children talk about a piece of the mural they would like to work on, such as trees, vines, a cave, a river, plants, or a dinosaur. Suzanne writes the children's names on a chart with the item they would like to draw with markers.

One-third of the students remain on the carpet to work on the mural. These children huddle around books depicting plants and trees from the time of the dinosaurs. Animated discussions take place as each child draws food, shelter, water, and other elements necessary to sustain dinosaur life. The remainder of the children use this time to complete unfinished journal writing or center work. If they have completed all their work, they can select any center activity they wish. This is a playful time of the day, and children build with blocks, play in the dramatic play area, do an art project, explore in the science area, or look at books.

Art, Music, Gym

At this time of day the class goes to a special teacher for either art, music, or gym. Suzanne has coordinated with these teachers about the theme being studied, so the art teacher is working on papier-mâché dinosaur sculptures with the children, the music teacher has found some great dinosaur songs and one about habitats as well, and the gym teacher has thought of some movement activities to help the students really walk and run like dinosaurs.

Closing Circle with Read-Aloud

At closing time students clean up the classroom and gather in the meeting area for their closing circle and a read-aloud. Today Suzanne has chosen an informational book in big-book format titled *Discovering Dinosaurs* (Sokoloff, 1997) to read aloud. This book will provide children with more facts about dinosaurs that they may use in their writing and for the mural habitat they will create. Before she reads the book, she points out some of the features of this informational book. For example, there are labels on figures, captions describing pictures, headings introducing new topics, and technical vocabulary written in a bolder and bigger font than the rest of the words. Suzanne knows this book will introduce children to a topic not yet discussed in class: differences between dinosaurs that were plant eaters and meat eaters. After reading, Suzanne helps children list the characteristics of plant-eating and meat-eating dinosaurs on a shared writing chart. Finally, she and the children review the activities of the day and those they liked best, and they plan for Tuesday.

Tuesday: Learning More about Dinosaurs

Tuesday's schedule remains the same as on Monday. Children enter the classroom, begin their morning routines, and write in their journals.

Morning Meeting

The morning message says, "Good morning, kindergartners. Today is Tuesday, March 9, 2004. What is your favorite dinosaur?" Suzanne has listed the six dinosaurs the class selected as their favorites on Monday, and placed a picture by each dinosaur's name. An animated debate breaks out as the children use tally marks to record their vote. Not surprisingly, many journal entries begin "MI FAVT DINOSR IZ. . . ." Dinosaur-related conversations continue as the children gather for morning meeting.

The shared-reading book Suzanne has selected is *Dinosaurs, Dinosaurs* (Barton, 1989). Together she and the children talk about the title, the author, and the illustrations. The students predict what the book will be about. After a guided book introduction, when the class discusses the pictures in the text, the students confirm their predictions. Students are reminded that good readers use what they know about a topic to help them read. Suzanne reviews what they have already learned about dinosaurs listed on a chart from the day before. She begins reading *Dinosaurs, Dinosaurs.* Her goals are to build vocabulary and enhance knowledge. She has chosen a few spots in the story where the students will discuss the content further to accomplish these goals. At the end of the book there is discussion about new information learned. To support this discussion, Suzanne planned to write and illustrate new words from the book that are important to the study of dinosaurs such as *armored plates* on a chart. For example, she turned to a page in the text that illustrated a dinosaur with a horn. Children used their hands to make a horn on their heads and they discussed how dinosaurs used their horns. Suzanne wrote the word *horn* on a chart and drew a horn next to it. They continue to explore the meanings of other words in the book about dinosaurs such as *carnivore, habitat,* and *extinct.* Next Suzanne prepares children for their center time. Center activities are the same today as on Monday. Contracts are distributed and center time reviewed. Now Suzanne can take her first reading group.

Small-Group Reading Instruction

With her students engaged in center work, Suzanne calls her first group (one she had not met with the day before) to the small-group instruction table. This group is focusing on identification and pronunciation of the letters and sounds of f, w, and j. The children in this group were having difficulty with these letters in their reading and writing. Most of the students in this group are English language learners. Suzanne helps them with their oral language and vocabulary development during small-group instruction.

The students begin by identifying the pictures in a deck of prepared cards. The key pictures *fish*, *wagon*, and *jar* are introduced and placed on the table. Suzanne turns over the next card, which is a *fan*. She says "fan" with each of the key pictures to determine which has the same sound as "fish" and which words don't. She says "*fan–fish, fan–wagon, fan–jar.* I think that *fan* begins with the same sound as *fish*," placing the picture of the fan under that of the fish. When the deck is all sorted, the words on the cards in each sorted group are said together. The cards are shuffled and the students work together to complete the sort again.

Suzanne asks the children if there are dinosaur words that begin with the letters they are talking about. One child mentions dinosaur *jaws* for *j*, since they have such very big jaws. Another child says, "Dinosaurs waddle when they walk for the letter *w*." The group can't think of a word for *f*. Suzanne says, "*Ferocious* would be a good one for *f*." The children agree. Homework involves another sorting activity with the same letters. The students are given a sheet to take home with pictures to cut apart of items beginning with *f*, *w*, and *j*, and then to paste into their word study notebooks. Students are told to look in magazines and the newspaper for one more picture for each of the three letters to paste in their notebook. The children place their word study notebooks in their mailboxes to remember to take them home. Suzanne makes notes regarding individual student progress with this task.

The second group (one she met with on Monday) has just begun studying short-vowel ending patterns: *-ag, -at,* and *-an.* They will work on several tasks to help them with these patterns. First there are word–picture card sorts. There is a guide word and a picture for the top of the column and then words and pictures to sort in the columns. The guide words are *bag,* for the *-ag* pattern, *pan,* for the *-an* ending, and *hat,* for the *-at* rime. After the sorts are completed the children are to write one word for each rime.

Next is a building-word activity. Students have the three vowel rimes and several initial consonant cards to build words. Suzanne models the activity. To create the word *bag* she uses an initial consonant *b* card and the word-ending card *ag.* She then leads the students in changing the initial consonant card to create other *-ag* words. Nonsense words such as *cag* and *pag* are accepted. The children work on building *-ag, -at,* and *-an* words and write them after they are created. The last activity is to look in the book they are reading and try to find *-ag, -at,* and *-an* words and write them down.

The last group Suzanne will meet with is working on color words. The book Suzanne selected for them is called *Colors at the Zoo* (Henderson, 1998). This book includes words that she feels need to be in the children's reading vocabulary. Because three color words in this book begin with the letter *b—blue, brown,* and *black*—before reading Suzanne says that an important reading strategy is to look at the ends of the words closely to distinguish between words with similar beginnings. Suzanne uses a guided book introduction, and children go through the book discussing the colors in the pictures. They count the number of colors that are named throughout the story and discover there are eight. The teacher reads one line at a time, then the children echo-read the line. When she comes to a color word, she pauses and lets the children fill it in. After the story they write the color words on a chart and Suzanne gives each child eight color words on cards. On one side of the card is the word written in the color it says. On the other side of the card the color word is written in black. The children read their cards to each other, first using the colored cards, and then the cards written in black. They write the words in their journals.

Writing Workshop

On Monday Suzanne introduced the writing activity for the week: writing and illustrating dinosaur facts. Suzanne wants children to select different dinosaurs to write about. Today she demonstrates writing an informational composition about a dinosaur that none of the children have selected. She writes a sentence that describes the color of the dinosaur, a sentence that identifies the dinosaur as a meat eater, and a sentence that describes the dinosaur as dangerous. She includes sentences describing how tall the dinosaur was and about the habitat it liked. She reminds the children that they should try to write at least two facts about their dinosaur in their composition. The children begin drafts of their fact sheets. This project will take the week to complete.

Math

The children were very interested in how tall and how short their six favorite dinosaurs were. Since they had a large collection of dinosaur books in the classroom, Suzanne looked through many of them to try and find where the information about dinosaur height was located. She found these facts in the book *The Visual Dictionary of Prehistoric Life* (DK Publishing, 1995). This book had dinosaurs listed in alphabetical order, so she is prepared to use this book for her math lesson. She asks the children, "If I want to find *Stegosaurus*, what letter will I look under? That's right, I would look under *S*. But there are a lot of dinosaurs under *S*. So I have to look at the next letter. What is the next letter in *Stegosaurus*?" They locate *Stegosaurus* and find its height, and Suzanne writes it on a chart. They look for information on the remaining five dinosaurs. Then Suzanne uses the information from the chart to construct a graph showing the dinosaurs from tallest to shortest.

Theme Activity and Center Time

Suzanne calls a different group of children to work on the special theme activity, constructing a mural and habitat. Other children complete unfinished activities from the morning and then select centers in which to play. A quick look into the centers in the room shows Suzanne that a group of children are creating "The Dinosaur Restaurant." They are taking orders for dinosaur pizza, dinosaur burgers, and dinosaur drinks. In the block center a group of children continue work on their dinosaur zoo. They are using varied blocks to create spaces for plastic dinosaurs. A fight between a stegasaurus and a triceratops is role-played. The children decide that these two dinosaurs should be separated into two different cages.

Art

Suzanne accompanies the children to art today to see their progress with the papier-mâché dinosaurs. Yesterday they made balloon and cardboard tube frames of the dinosaurs. Two parents came to help during art. Today they will begin the papier-mâché phase.

Closing Circle with Read-Aloud

Suzanne has selected to read *Mary Anning and the Sea Dragon* (Atkins, 1999), a book about a young girl who is one of the first female paleontologists, to read aloud at closing time. This book is fairly complex, but Suzanne knows that her children like learning new words. After reading, the class talks about all the different kinds of work Mary Anning did in her job. They discuss whether children in the class would like to be paleontologists when they grew up. The children review the activities of the day and discuss what will happen tomorrow before going home.

Wednesday: The Dinosaur Unit in Full Swing

Morning Meeting

Today's morning meeting begins with the poem in a big book introduced on Monday, "I'm a Mean Old Dinosaur" (Pruet, 1991). As the children choral-read the poem, Suzanne uses a pointer to help the children follow the words from left to right across the page. After reading, the class counts how many sentences there are in the poem and record that number. They then count the number of words in each sentence and record that number. The children use highlighter tape to point out the periods and questions marks.

> SUZANNE: Let's put magic tape on the end marks or punctuation at the end of the sentences so we can see them really well.
>
> STUDENT 1: There's no period.
>
> SUZANNE: No period? Isn't there supposed to be a period at the end of a sentence?
>
> STUDENT 2: That's not the end of the sentence.
>
> SUZANNE: It's not? Where does it end?
>
> STUDENT 3: Maybe the next page?

When they turn the next page they discover that the period is there. After putting highlighting tape on the end-of-the-sentence marks for the entire poem, the class comes to the consensus that one line of words is not necessarily a sentence. Suzanne models how a reader drops his or her tone of voice and stops at a period. Everyone joins in reading the text, as they practice what they just learned. She reminds the students to look for end marks on pages they look at throughout the remainder of the day.

Center work is reviewed before children go off to work. Today a grandfather has come to be a helper to work with students on their informational texts about dinosaurs. He is in the writing center ready to help with ideas or spelling.

Small-Group Reading Instruction

Suzanne noticed that most of the children in one of her reading groups were not participating in the shared reading of "I'm a Mean Old Dinosaur." Therefore she repeated the activity in their small-group meeting. Using the word chart as they had done earlier, Suzanne echo-reads the text with the children as she points to the words as they read. After echo reading, the children choral-read the poem.

Evidence from running records over the past week indicated that the children in Suzanne's next reading group were ready for a longer and more difficult level book. Suzanne chose *Five Little Monkeys Jumping on the Bed* (Christelow, 1989) because she knew that the pattern of sentences and the familiarity of the text would assist students in reading through a longer story. During the book introduction, Suzanne notes to herself that all but one child is familiar with the rhyme. Suzanne cautions the children to finger-point read carefully and to look at the letters in each word to keep up with the sentence pattern because the sentences change patterns throughout the book.

In her next group Suzanne concentrates once more on helping children to figure out words independently. They have worked on this before, but Suzanne knows how important it is to repeat strategies that children need to learn over and over again. She models the strategy in which words have been covered to try and figure them out through the context of the sentence and the letters in the words.

Suzanne would like to tie the theme and small-group instruction together using books about dinosaurs. She has found this difficult to do with most of the readers in her class because the text in the books about dinosaurs and other topics is usually too difficult.

Writing Workshop

Since most of the children have completed drafts of their factual dinosaur compositions, they are ready to edit them. To help her young writers, Suzanne has chosen three areas to focus on in their miniwriting lesson. She decided upon these areas as a result of reading the children's writing journals. Suzanne prepared a worksheet to help guide her children during and after the minilesson. The sheet includes three icons: one icon reminds students to use spaces between their words, another indicates that there must be facts in the story, and the final icon reminds the children to use at least four colors and lots of details in their illustrations.

Suzanne puts a sentence on the board: "Dinosaurs lay eggs to have babies." The children identify this as one fact about a dinosaur. Then they count how many words they hear in that sentence and agree that they should see six words written on the paper. They discuss the need for spaces between words so they can see all six words. Suzanne models how to put one finger space between each word and two finger spaces between each sentence. Then she reminds them that when they draw a picture for this fact, they must include a specific dinosaur, a nest, and eggs in their illustration. She discussed how to find pictures in the dinosaur books in the classroom to help with details of what dinosaurs, nests, and eggs look like.

Closing Circle with Read-Aloud

The read-aloud that Suzanne has selected for Wednesday is called *Patrick's Dinosaurs* (Carrick, 1983). This story is about a young boy who imagines he sees dinosaurs everywhere, after his brother tells him all about them during their visit to the zoo. After Suzanne reads to the class, they discuss the story. It is obvious that the children are making connections between themselves and the story. Many children recall times when they imagined that they saw things that were not really there.

Thursday

Morning Meeting

The morning meeting on Thursday begins as Suzanne says, "As we read our poem today, I want you to listen for rhyming words." Suzanne uses her pointer as the class reads the "March" poem again. Many hands are waving in the air before they even finish the poem as they anticipate what will happen next. Suzanne will ask the class to use highlighter tape to identify the rhyming words. The six rhyming words are highlighted on the chart.

Today's shared reading will focus on finding facts in informational text. Suzanne reads *Dinosaurs, Dinosaurs*, which she read earlier in the week. When she reads she asks the children to listen for facts about dinosaurs and elements in the book that make it informational. She tells the children that we also call informational books "nonfiction."

After reading Suzanne asks, "How can you tell that *Dinosaurs, Dinosaurs* is an informational, nonfiction book?"

STUDENT 1: There aren't characters who have a story to tell.

STUDENT 2: It is about real things.

STUDENT 3: It teaches us things.

After the discussion Suzanne makes a web that includes the facts in the text. She draws a circle on a chart with the word *dinosaurs* written in the center. Then she draws lines radiating out from the center circle. Next she draws smaller circles connected to each of the lines radiating out from the larger circle. As children recall facts about dinosaurs, Suzanne writes the words in one of the smaller circles. After writing the web, Suzanne helps the children read the words written in the web: *big, dangerous, scary, vegetarians,* and *meat eaters.*

Small-Group Reading Instruction

Suzanne meets with her first group; this group continues to work on short-vowel patterns that rhyme. Suzanne selects the word *can* and asks the children to think of words that rhyme with it that have the same vowel pattern: *-an.* The children say *man, fan, tan, ran, pan, Dan,* as she writes them down on the chart. Suzanne writes:

> *I like Dan.   He is a nice man.*

She asks the children to think of sentences that begin with "I like Dan" and then a second sentence that rhymes with the first. The children think of the following:

> *I like Dan.   He is a nice man.*
> *I like Dan.   He has a fan.*
> *I like Dan.   He has a pan.*

Suzanne asks the children to copy two sentences about Dan that rhyme that they like the best after reading group. She places the sentences in the literacy center for these children to use as one of their *have-to* activities for the day. Next the group reads a little book that has many words with the *-an* pattern throughout. After reading, the children sort rhyming words they used earlier this week, they build new words by adding consonants to the *-at, -an,* and *-ag* rime endings, and they search for words in a group of specially selected books that have these patterns.

Suzanne meets with her second group. They are reading *Things That Go* (Mayes, 2002). Suzanne is still working with this group on looking at the letters in the word and the meaning of the sentence to figure out unknown words. She guides a book introduction to build some background knowledge about the book. They read through the book again, playing the game "Guess the Covered Word." The sentences in the book have been written on the chart for the first reading so Suzanne can track the print from left to right and cover up a word for the children to figure out. The class reads the sentence together and then goes back to figure out what the covered word is. They predict by using the meaning or context of the sentence, then they look closely at the first letter of the word to see if the word matches their predictions. By now the children are getting quite good with this strategy. Suzanne knows that this is an indication that this group of children are ready for more challenging reading skills, such as learning to build new words from familiar rhyming words.

In the next group Suzanne will read the story *A Dinosaur Day* (Thomson, 2000) to the children so they can practice finding facts in informational text.

Everyone is given a sheet of paper with "Triceratops" and "Tyrannosaurus" written at the top. The children have copies of the book and follow along as Suzanne reads. She tells the children to listen for facts about triceratops and tyrannosaurus. As she reads, Suzanne stops frequently to discuss new vocabulary words. She makes comments and asks questions to make sure children in this group understand the sequence of events. After listening to the reading, the children recall one fact they remember. Suzanne helps them to expand the amount of information they recall and helps them use the technical vocabulary found in the book. She helps the children recall on which page of the book their fact is found. She rereads that page, and shows each child where the fact is located in the book. Children draw a picture related to their fact. Some children copy the fact or other vocabulary words on their drawing. After drawing and writing, the children share their facts with each other. Suzanne plays a quick alphabet recognition game with the children as they complete their drawings.

Writing Workshop

The children have worked on their dinosaur compositions over the week. During writing workshop time, Suzanne has modeled placing one finger between each word, and has explained using the word wall and alphabet chart to help with spelling. Today Suzanne continues to circulate around the classroom, assisting children as they put the finishing touches on their fact sheets. Most children spend time illustrating their completed compositions. Suzanne reminds children to use the editing worksheet she introduced the day before. She reminds them to put actual details related to their facts and to use at least four colors in their illustrations. The children refer to their dinosaur book collection to help them with their pictures.

At the end of writing workshop some children share their writing. One typical report is presented in Figure 1.1. This composition contains three sentences and uses invented spellings that always include a beginning and an ending phoneme and sometimes have vowels. While some of the letter–sound associations this child used in her invented spellings are not conventional (y for the /w/ in the word *was*), they do demonstrate that she is able to hear many phonemes. Because of extensive modeling that began in September, students made the following types of comments about each other's work: "I noticed that you have

T-REX YZ 35 FET TL.
(T-Rex was 35 feet tall.)
HE YX A MET ETR.
(He was a meat eater.)
HE YZ MEN.
(He was mean.)

FIGURE 1.1. Dinosaur facts.

a lot of detail in your sentences," "You did such a good job in getting a lot of facts to write down."

Theme Activities and Centers

Children have collected the votes on favorite dinosaurs from the entire school and are counting the responses for each of the six dinosaurs. Papier-mâché sculptures of dinosaurs are being painted, and a group of children are working on the mural and habitat. Some children are working on their compositions about dinosaurs. Suzanne works with one or two children in centers and calls some children to the literacy center to play a rhyming word game.

Closing Circle with Read-Aloud

For today's read-aloud Suzanne selected *How Big Were the Dinosaurs?* (Most, 1994). This book is an informational text. Before reading Suzanne reminds the students about characteristics of informational text again. She tells children that informational text is also called "nonfiction" because everything is real instead of make-believe. After reading the book she asks the children why the book is an informational book.

> STUDENT 1: I think it was make-believe because the pictures are drawings. If it was an informational book there would be real pictures that we take with cameras.
>
> STUDENT 2: But they can't have real pictures because dinosaurs are dead. We don't have anymore. What is that word? They are _____?
>
> SUZANNE: You mean "extinct."
>
> STUDENT 3: Every page taught us about a different dinosaur.
>
> STUDENT 2: Yeah. There was no story, it was all things about dinosaur information.

Friday

As children enter the classroom, Suzanne checks with each of them to determine whether they have completed all their assigned work. By the time the children are called to the morning meeting, many children have completed the remaining work in their unfinished folders.

Morning Meeting

Suzanne spends time at this morning meeting reviewing activities completed during the week. The class choral-reads "I'm a Mean Old Dinosaur" and identifies the words that rhyme. Suzanne brings back the book *Dinosaurs, Dinosaurs*. After reviewing the facts, the class echo-reads the informational text. Next the class rereads the web they created about dinosaurs, and they add a few more words to it.

Small-Group Reading Instruction

On Friday, Suzanne assesses her students' progress and reviews the work each group has accomplished. Her first group reviews the initial consonants *f*, *w*, and *j* that they have worked on this week. She asks the students to write those letters at the top of a column. As she shows them picture cards, children point to the letter indicating the beginning sound. Some students are still having trouble identifying the sounds of *w* and *y* so Suzanne records that they need more work on these letter–sound relationships next week.

With her next group she checks on their ability to use the skip and predict strategy. Each child is given a chance at predicting a covered word in a sentence. Each child is successful at guessing some words that make sense in the sentence, and then selecting the correct word using the first letter clue.

When she meets with the third group, Suzanne checks to see how well they can read color words. Colors are a part of Suzanne's high-frequency word list for kindergartners to learn by sight. In January, Suzanne began introducing two high-frequency words at the beginning of each week during morning meeting or in small-group instruction. On Friday the children are assessed and the words are sent home for practice. The students in this group recognize most of the color words. They still confuse black, blue, and brown, and Suzanne discusses how they have to look all the way through a word and especially at its end to figure out some color words She give them the three color words printed on separate 5" × 8" cards to take home and practice.

Writing Workshop

Before binding the informational compositions written by the children into a class book, Suzanne leads a discussion about a title for the class book. She tells children that a good title helps predict what the book will be about. She shows them a book about dinosaurs, and asks if "The Elephants Went Walking" would be a good title. After the giggles subsided, the children agree that since the class book is about dinosaurs, then the title should to be about dinosaurs. Three titles are suggested for the book and Suzanne writes them on a chart. The children vote and the title is decided: "Kindergarten Dinosaur Information Book." Suzanne makes a cover and staples each of the children's compositions together to make the book.

Math

Suzanne has created a graph that summarizes results of the school vote for favorite dinosaurs. Each child colors a copy of the graph to display around the school for others to see the results of the favorite dinosaur contest.

Theme Activities and Centers

The children select centers of their choice while one small group of children works with Suzanne to set up their mural and arrange their habitat. The children place their papier-mâché dinosaurs into the habitat they created. This display is placed on the windowsill with the mural they painted hanging on the windows. Suzanne works with all the children in small group to complete the habitat. When it is finished, the entire class discusses the project and admires their work.

Closing Circle with Read-Aloud

Instead of a new read-aloud on Friday afternoons, Suzanne's class choral-reads poems from their three-ring binders. These poems have been chanted many times during the past several weeks. Children select a poem, locate it in their three-ring binders, and chant along with Suzanne as she reads aloud.

It's the end of a long, busy week. Before the children leave, Suzanne and the children take time to mention the helpful things children did during the week (they give their friends a thank-you) and reflect on what they have accomplished in the morning meetings, small-group reading instruction, writing workshop, math, art, centers, and themed activities. The class plans for the week ahead; they will continue their work on dinosaurs. They will invite several classes of students to visit them next Friday to see their dinosaur display, hear children read their informational compositions, and hear the entire class choral-read poems.

SUMMARY

Suzanne's kindergarten is playful and includes intentional instruction. Children have the opportunity to explore and experiment, and they have explicit instruction. They are expected to complete work assigned to them during small-group instruction or during whole-group lessons. However, they also have choices in the selection of activities during two times of the day. Much information is introduced during whole- and small-group lessons, and much information is repeated and reviewed all week long. Children's individual needs are met during small-group reading instruction, writing workshop, and center time. Reading and writing are integrated in content-area learning. Children in Suzanne's classroom read and write during math and as they learn scientific information about animals. Her classroom is arranged so that children have access to a plentiful supply of materials, books, and equipment. We present an extensive list of materials helpful to kindergarten teachers including a list of materials Suzanne uses in her dinosaur theme in Appendix A. These materials include stories, informational books, big books, poems, alphabet books, language play books, websites, and other media resources.

CHAPTER 2

PREPARING THE ENVIRONMENT FOR LITERACY INSTRUCTION IN KINDERGARTEN

The success of any program depends to a large extent on how it is organized, designed, and managed. Without carefully planning and preparing the environment, organizing lessons, and managing daily routines, even the best of teachers would have a difficult time. This chapter focuses on preparation of the physical environment, including selecting and placing materials in the classroom, organizing and managing routines during the school day, and planning a schedule for a kindergarten day. The classroom's arrangement and routines set the stage for a successful instructional program. Children learn what materials are included in the classroom, where to locate the materials, how they may be used, and how to return the materials to their appropriate storage areas. An imperative in kindergarten is to keep children occupied with activities that are playful, entertaining, and—most of all—productive for learning. When children are occupied in successful learning experiences that reinforce and extend their learning, they are eager to participate. The purpose of this chapter is to describe a classroom environment that allows teachers to spend their time *teaching* rather than *managing* children.

WHY DOES THE CLASSROOM ENVIRONMENT MATTER IN KINDERGARTEN?

Historically, philosophers and theorists who have studied early childhood development have emphasized the importance of the physical environment in learning and development. Pestalozzi (Rusk & Scotland, 1979) and Froebel (1974) described real-life environments in which young children's learning could flourish. Both discussed preparing manipulative materials that would foster literacy development. Montessori (1965) developed guidelines for creating a carefully prepared classroom environment that promotes independent learning, and she recommended that every material in the environment have a specific learning objective. Piaget (Piaget & Inhelder, 1969) found that children acquire knowledge by interacting with the world or the environment. He suggested that ideal settings for young children to learn should involve real-life situations, and that children need materials with which to explore and experiment. Dewey (1966) believed in an interdisciplinary approach; in his view, learning takes place through the integration of content areas. He believed that storing materials in subject-area centers encouraged interest and learning.

Classrooms designed to provide a literacy-rich environment and optimum literacy development will offer an abundant supply of materials for reading, writing, and oral language. These materials will be housed primarily in a large and extended literacy center. However, literacy materials should be placed in all other centers in the room to encourage the functional use of reading and writing (e.g., by making a graph in the math center or by reading a book about animal prints in the science center). Materials and settings throughout the classroom will be designed to emulate real-life experiences and to make literacy meaningful to children (e.g., the classroom will include at least one dramatic play area such as a restaurant, in addition to the usual home-living area). Materials for all dramatic play activities will be selected so that they are connected to children's experiences and knowledge, and will be functional so that children see a need and a purpose for using literacy. Dramatic play center themes such as home living or barber/beauty shop should be familiar to children.

Paying careful attention to a classroom's visual and physical design contributes to the success of an instructional program. Preparing a classroom's physical environment is often overlooked in planning instruction. Teachers and curriculum developers tend to concentrate on instructional and management issues, but give little consideration to the visual and spatial context in which teaching and learning occur. They direct their energies toward varying teaching strategies while the environment remains unchanged. The environment needs to be arranged and rearranged to coordinate with and support program activities; otherwise, instruction will not be as successful as it could be (Weinstein & Mignano, 2003).

When purposefully arranging the environment, teachers acknowledge the physical setting as an active and pervasive influence on their own activities and attitudes, as well as on those of the children in their classroom. Appropriate physical arrangement of furniture, selection of materials, and the visual aesthetic quality of a room contribute to teaching and learning (Loughlin & Martin, 1987; Morrow, 1990; Morrow & Tracey, 1996; Morrow & Weinstein, 1986). For example, even by itself the design of spatial arrangements affects children's behavior in the classroom. Rooms partitioned into smaller spaces facilitate verbal interaction among peers, fantasy, and cooperative play more than do rooms with large, open spaces.

Children in carefully arranged rooms show more productivity and greater use of language-related activities than do children in randomly arranged rooms (Moore, 1986; Reutzel & Wolfersberger, 1996).

Studies that have investigated the role of literacy-enriched dramatic play areas based on themes being used in the classroom have found that they stimulate increased language and literacy activity and also enhance literacy skills (Morrow, 1990; Neuman & Roskos, 1990, 1992). Morrow (1990) has also found that having story props to use in retelling or dramatic play improves children's story compositions and story comprehension, including their recall of details and ability to sequence and interpret.

Preparing Literacy-Rich Physical Environments

Research that has investigated the physical design of classrooms strongly suggests that by purposefully arranging the space and materials teachers can create physical environments that exert an active, positive, and pervasive influence on instruction. Educators must think of their classrooms as places to project a visual atmosphere that communicates a definitive message. The following sections describe the visual presentation of a literacy-rich physical environment to motivate reading and writing.

Print in the Classroom

Literacy-rich classrooms are filled with functional print that can be easily seen. When observing in such classrooms, we see labels on materials or constructions and signs communicating functional information and directions, such as "Quiet Please" and "Please Put Materials Away after Using Them." There are charts labeled "Helpers," "Daily Routines," and "Attendance," and a "Calendar" (Schickedanz, 1993). There are labels to identify learning centers and to identify each child's cubby. A notice board placed prominently in the room can be used to communicate with the children in writing. Shared writing charts and morning messages are used to display new words generated from themes, recipes used in the classroom, and science experiments conducted. Word walls display high-frequency words learned, new spelling words, sight words, and words that feature phonics elements being taught. Teachers make use of the print in the classroom with their students to ensure it is noticed. Children are encouraged to read and use words from the classroom print in their writing (Ritchie, James-Szanton, & Howes, 2003). Word walls include children's names and thematic words along with high-frequency words that the children are learning in their reading and need for writing. The words on the word wall are used by the children as they read and write independently.

The outdoor environment should also accommodate literacy development. In addition to the usual playground equipment, new materials that reflect unit instruction add to the interest of outdoor play. Where climates are seasonal, for example, flowers should be planted in the spring; rakes provided in the fall for leaf gathering; and pails, shovels, and other digging and building equipment provided in winter for snow play. Creative materials such as crates, boxes, plastic containers, boards, ropes, and balls give children incentives to play creatively. Materials such as these generate language during play and in class discussions, and provide information for writing experience charts and class books.

The Classroom Literacy Center

The literacy center, which includes the library corner, a writing area, and a letter-and-word study area, should be the focal point in the classroom. Immediate access to literature and writing materials increases the number of children who participate in literacy activities during the school day. Each of the three areas in the literacy center needs to be obvious and inviting but also should afford privacy and be clearly defined. Each area should accommodate four or five children comfortably. The center says to children that as teachers we value literacy by making it an important part of our classroom. The materials should range in difficulty to meet individual needs and the different developmental levels of the children. Each set of materials has its own place and is to be respected. The literacy center includes materials for reading, writing, oral language development, and developing word-study skills.

The Library Corner

The library corner houses books by category using a coding system that helps children identify books by author, genre, level, or theme. Coding introduces the idea that books in regular libraries are organized systematically for easy access. Some shelves in the library corner should be open-faced to display book covers, thus calling attention to their content. Teachers should use open-faced shelving to feature books about themes being studied and should rotate new books in every few weeks. Other books can be stored on shelves in plastic tubs and labeled by genre or by author. Teachers store leveled books in plastic tubs that are labeled by level of difficulty. To ensure that there is something for everyone in the center, teachers include five to eight books per child representing different genres of children's literature and different levels of difficulty. They stock multiple copies of popular books because children enjoy reading the same book together.

Teachers furnish the library area with a rug and pillows. Elements of softness such as stuffed animals belong in a library, especially if they are related to books available in the corner—a stuffed rabbit next to *The Tale of Peter Rabbit* (Potter, 1902), for instance. Children enjoy reading to stuffed animals or simply holding them as they look at books. This area is where children read for pleasure, read to other children, or present stories to the class that they have written. Teachers provide a cozy private spot for reading. Teachers have used large cartons from household appliances, painted or covered with contact paper, into which children can crawl to read. Near the library corner and in the literacy center, teachers include a rocking chair representing the *Literacy Chair of Honor*, where the teacher and others read aloud to children as they sit in a large carpeted area.

Posters and other bulletin board displays that celebrate reading should be used to decorate the area. Teachers can get posters from the Children's Book Council (12 West 37th Street, 2nd Floor, New York, NY 10018; www.cbcbooks.org) and the American Library Association (50 East Huron Street, Chicago, IL 60611; www.ala.org).

Teachers will provide materials for active involvement in storybook reading and storytelling, with storytelling props such as a felt board with story characters, puppets, and headsets for listening to taped stories. These materials enhance comprehension; moreover, children are frequently required to engage with activity props to retell stories as *have-to center* activities. Techniques such as using a felt board and story characters for storytelling and preparing puppet presentations build children's knowledge of story sequence and structure. Using objects to retell facts from information books strengthens vocabulary and classification skills. Listening to books on CDs or tapes is helpful for English language learners because they provide a model for spoken English. They are also enjoyed by children who are not yet reading conventionally; they can follow along in the text while listening to a fluent reader.

Books are not difficult to accumulate. They can be purchased inexpensively at yard sales or flea markets. Teachers can borrow up to 20 books a month from most public libraries, ask for book donations from parents, and hold fundraisers for book purchases. In addition, children's paperback book clubs offer inexpensive books and free bonus books with bulk purchases. Children's magazines and newspapers belong in the classroom library, even if they are not current. For the cost of mailing and shipping, some publishers and local magazine agencies will donate outdated periodicals to schools.

To ensure her or his students' continued interest, the teacher introduces new books and materials in the library corner frequently. Approximately 25 new books should be introduced every 2 weeks, replacing 25 that have been there for a while. In this way, "old" books will be greeted as new friends a few months later. When teachers recirculate books, it compensates for a limited budget.

Books from the library corner should be available for students to check out and take home for a week at a time. Teachers will need to devise a method for checking books out of the classroom library to take home and read. The check-out system should be simple. There should be a specified time each week for checking books out so that the date, child's name, and book title are recorded. Some kindergarten children have been taught to check out books themselves by copying titles and recording dates on 5" ×8" cards filed under their own names. Other youngsters enjoy keeping track of books borrowed and read by recording titles and dates on index cards held together with a key ring. Another method for checking out books is a loose-leaf notebook with a separate page for each child to record books he or she takes out and returns.

Books in the Library Corner

Books and other materials selected for the library corner should appeal to a variety of interests and span a range of difficulty levels. It is advisable to stock multiple copies of popular books because children enjoy reading a book a friend is reading (Morrow, 1985). Several types of children's literature should be represented. Picture storybooks are the most familiar children's literature. *Picture storybooks* have texts that are closely associated with their illustrations. They are available on a wide range of topics, and many are known for their excellence. The *Caldecott Medal* is awarded annually to the illustrator of an outstanding picture storybook. Many of these books have become classics and their authors renowned—Dr. Seuss, Ezra Jack Keats, Tomie dePaola, Maurice Sendak, and Charlotte Zolotow, to name just a few. Every child should have the benefit of hearing some of these books read. Quality picture storybooks will include a setting, a well-defined theme, episodes closely tied to the theme, and resolution to the story. Quality literature includes a rich vocabulary and sophisticated syntactic structures in the text.

Informational books are nonfiction selections that explain, tell how to, or describe the steps in a process. Many adults choose to read nonfiction, so we need to provide children with experience listening to this type of text. Informational texts can be related to an abundance of topics, such as foreign countries, communities, dinosaurs, and famous people. They include not only books but pamphlets, magazines, instructions, and menus. These functional texts broaden children's background information, help them to explore new ideas, and often stimulate a deep interest in a particular topic. Quality informational texts have a definitive structure including description, sequence, compare and contrast, cause and effect, problem and solution, and exemplification.

Picture concept books are appropriate for the very young child. Most picture concept books do not have story lines, though they often have themes, such as animals or toys. Each page usually includes a picture identified by a printed word. Many concept books are made of cardboard, cloth, or vinyl to withstand rigorous handling. Alphabet and number books are also considered picture concept books.

Traditional literature includes nursery rhymes and fairy tales, the familiar stories that are part of our heritage and originated in the oral tradition of storytelling. We often mistakenly assume that all children are familiar with *Goldilocks and the Three Bears* (Izawa, 1968) and *The Three Little Pigs* (Brenner, 1972), yet many youngsters have not been exposed to these traditional stories. Children who do know the stories welcome them as old friends.

Realistic literature is a category within picture storybooks that deals with real-life problems. *Tight Times* (1983) by Barbara Hazen, for example, describes how a family handles the problems that arise when the father loses his job. He tries to explain the situation to his son so he will understand when he calls it "tight times." Books in this category deal with issues that many children face, such as bedtime fears or problems that arise when a new baby comes into the family. These books can touch on very sensitive issues, such as divorce, drugs, alcohol, and death. Many can be read to the entire class if they address issues that everyone shares. Teachers should use discretion as to what is read to the whole class. They can recommend specific titles to families of children who face difficult issues.

Fantasy is the genre that deals with make-believe; such books involve events that could never happen in the real world. These books may have animal characters that talk and act like humans such as Peter in *The Tale of Peter Rabbit* (Potter, 1901) or characters that can do magical or extraordinary deeds. *Officer Buckle and Gloria* (Rathman, 1995) involves a dog who can act like he is being electrocuted, has slipped and fallen, or has sat on a thumbtack as Officer Buckle explains safely rules such as don't go swimming during an electrical storm, wipe up spills, and never leave a thumbtack where you might sit on it.

Fables and folktales retell many of the myths and traditional stories that are available in picture-book style for the younger child. Many of these stories originate in other countries and cultures and therefore broaden a child's experience and knowledge base.

Poetry is too often forgotten in collections of children's literature at home and in school. Many themed anthologies have been compiled for young children, and they are an important part of the literacy center. Novels or *chapter books* are longer books with chapters. Teachers begin reading chapter books to young children in kindergarten to expose them to this genre. Children are often quite attracted to them and eager to begin to read them. *Biography* is another genre appropriate for young children. There are simple biographies of historical figures, popular figures in sports, and figures on television.

Big books are usually large versions of smaller picture storybooks or original picture storybooks in a large format. They are oversized books that rest on an easel in order to be read. The purpose of the big book is for children to be able to see the print as it is being read, to make the association between oral and written language, and to see how the print is read from left to right across the page.

In addition to these categories of books, young children enjoy joke and riddle books, craft books, cookbooks, participation books—which involve them in touching, smelling, and manipulating—books in a series built around a single character, and books related to television programs appropriate for their age. As mentioned, magazines and newspapers should also be choices for reading in the library corner. They provide an easy nonthreatening format, locally related topics, and multicultural material. Newspapers and magazines appeal to parents as well.

Children particularly enjoy literature that is predictable because it helps them understand the story line more easily and enables them to read along with the individual reading to them. *Predictable literature* contains rhyme; repetition; catchphrases; conversation; familiar sequences, such as days of the week or numbers; cumulative patterns, in which events are repeated or added on as the story continues; stories about familiar topics; familiar or popular stories; uncluttered illustrations that match the text; and stories that have well-developed story structures (setting, theme, plot episodes, and resolution).

A list of children's books in a variety of genres, book clubs, and children's book awards can be found in Appendix A.

The Letter- and Word-Study Area

The literacy center includes an area for letter and word study. Manipulatives that help children learn letters of the alphabet, rhymes, and sound–symbol relationships of consonants, digraphs, and long and short vowels should be included in a special section of the center. These manipulatives come in the form of magnetic letters, puzzles, bingo games, and board games, to name just a few. Word-study activities include making words and sorting words based on letter patterns to help build independent readers. Teacher-made materials can also be used in this center. Teachers place many materials in the letter- and word-study area after using them for instruction. For example, they place pocket charts with familiar poems read during morning meeting in this area for children to match words during center time. Or they place rhyming sorting games used in small-group instruction for children to sort independently.

The Writing Area

The writing area includes a table and chairs and an abundance of materials to encourage writing: colored felt-tipped markers, large and small crayons, pencils (both regular and colored), chalk, a chalkboard, and paper in a variety of sizes, kinds, and colors. Teachers include unlined plain paper or newsprint of many different sizes. They provide index cards so that children can record their *very own words*, high-frequency words, or word patterns they may need to practice. A *writing folder* for each child can be kept in a large box. Computers should also be situated in the writing area. Teachers need quality software for children to practice the skills they have learned and electronic books. Book-making materials include paper, a hole punch, a stapler, and construction paper. Blank books prepared by the teacher and children can be keyed to special occasions and completed by youngsters. Teachers display children's writing on a bulletin board. Equally valuable are notice boards on which messages can be exchanged among classmates or between teacher and students.

Literacy Materials in Other Centers

A print-rich kindergarten includes many centers in addition to the literacy center. These centers are related to the content children will be learning. They have materials for children to learn about the content as well as materials to read and write about that content. Kindergarten literacy-rich environments include the following centers and materials:

➤ *Science.* Aquarium, terrarium, plants, magnifying glass, class pet, magnets, thermometer, compass, prism, shells, rock collections, stethoscope, kaleidoscope, microscope, informational books and children's literature reflecting topics being studied, and blank journals for recording observations of experiments and scientific projects.

➤ *Social studies.* Maps, a globe, flags, community figures, traffic signs, newspapers with current events, artifacts from other countries, informational books and children's literature reflecting topics being studied, and writing materials to make maps, graphs, class books, or individual books about topics being studied.

➤ *Art.* Easels, watercolors, brushes, colored pencils, crayons, felt-tip markers, various kinds of paper, scissors, paste, pipe cleaners, scrap materials (bits of various fabrics, wool, string, etc.), clay, playdough, food and detergent boxes for sculptures, books about famous artists, and books with directions for crafts.

➤ *Music.* Piano, guitar, or other real instruments; CD and/or tape players, and tapes and CDs of all types of music; rhythm instruments; songbooks and photocopies of sheet music for songs sung in class.

➤ *Mathematics.* Scales, rulers, measuring cups, movable clocks, stopwatch, calendar, play money, cash register, calculator, dominoes, abacus, number line, height chart, hourglass, numbers (felt, wood, and magnetic), fraction puzzles, geometric shapes, math workbooks, children's literature about numbers and mathematics, and writing materials for conducting surveys, creating graphs, and composing books related to mathematics.

➤ *Block area.* Blocks of many different sizes, shapes, and textures; toy people, animals, cars, trucks, and specific items related to themes being studied; paper and pencils to prepare signs and notes; and reading materials related to themes.

➤ *Workbench.* Wood, corrugated cardboard, hammer, scissors, screwdriver, saw, pliers, nails, glue, tape, and worktable. Drawings of possible projects and simple directions should also be included. The center can house books made from photographs of children's constructions with written captions.

➤ *Outdoor play.* Sand, water, pails, shovels, rakes, gardening area and gardening tools, climbing equipment, riding toys, crates, playhouse, balls, tires, and ropes. Outdoor play spaces can be converted into a car wash, a drive-through window, or a circus. Children can construct signs, play with money, and pretend to be car-wash attendants, fast-food workers, or circus performers.

Dramatic Play in Kindergarten

A familiar center in kindergarten classrooms is the dramatic play center. It includes dolls, dress-up clothes, several play telephones, stuffed animals, a mirror, food cartons, plates, silverware, newspapers, magazines, books, a local telephone book, a class telephone book, cookbooks, notepads, cameras and photo album, a table and chairs, a broom and dustpan, and child-size kitchen furniture such as a refrigerator, a sink, an ironing board, a couch, and storage shelves. Dramatic play provides children with critical learning experiences. Children learn to solve problems, role-play real-life experiences, cope with situations that require sharing and cooperation, and extend their oral language and awareness of how literacy is used in real life. Dramatic play provides children with the opportunity to interact with one another and their teacher. They touch, smell, taste, listen, and talk about what they are doing. They explore and experiment with the materials and engage in creative, imaginative, problem-solving, decision-making experiences.

Dramatic play provides endless possibilities for literacy development as children pretend to read and write with the real items placed in the dramatic play center. The materials and activities typical of dramatic play areas stimulate considerable language, and the addition of new props and materials provides the opportunity for continued growth. Dramatic play provides realistic settings and functional reasons for using print. New units in social studies and science trigger opportunities to add print materials that stimulate reading, writing, and oral language. A unit on community helpers—a topic familiar to early childhood teachers—invariably leads to a discussion of firefighters, police officers, supermarket clerks, doctors, nurses, mail carriers, and office workers. The mention of any of these community helpers is an opportunity to add associated literacy materials to the dramatic play area.

Role-playing supermarket, for instance, is aided by the addition of food and detergent containers, a toy cash register, play money, notepads, a toy telephone and directory, store signs, a schedule of hours, advertisements, and posters for food and other products. Teachers or aides might visit a nearby supermarket to note for the classroom kinds of print materials that are used there, and to ask for outdated signs and posters. Store managers readily give away such materials when they no longer need them. Among materials for dramatic play about supermarkets, definitely include a bookshelf full of magazines and books "for sale." All these materials help children engage in conversation as they role-play a store manager, a clerk, or a shopper. They read posters, books, signs, and magazines and write shopping lists, orders, and new signs when they are needed.

Themed Dramatic Play Centers

The dramatic play area, which is usually arranged to resemble a home, can be changed or extended to create theme dramatic play areas such as a grocery store, a beauty shop, a gas station, a business office, or a restaurant. When new themes are studied, the teacher adds materials appropriate for reading and writing related to the theme. Following are some ideas for the design of specific themed dramatic play settings that promote literacy through play:

> *Newspaper office.* Include telephones, directories, maps, computers, paper, pencils, and areas that focus on sports, travel, general news, and weather.

> *Supermarket or local grocery store.* Include labeled shelves and sections, food containers with their labels left on, a toy cash register, a toy telephone, computers, receipts, checkbooks, coupons, and promotional flyers.

> *Post office.* Can be used for mailing the children's letters and needs to include paper, envelopes, address books, pens, pencils, stamps, toy cash registers, computers, and mailboxes. A mail carrier hat and bag are important for delivering the mail by reading names and addresses.

> *Airport.* Can be created with signs posting arrivals and departures, tickets, boarding passes, luggage tags, magazines and books for the waiting area, safety messages on the plane, and name tags for the flight attendants. A computer is used to get onto the Internet to make plane reservations.

> *Gas station and car repair shop.* Can be designed in the block area. Toy cars and trucks can be used for props. There can be receipts for sales, road maps to help with directions to different destinations, auto repair manuals for fixing cars and trucks, posters that advertise automobile equipment, and empty cans of different products that are sold in gas stations (Morrow & Rand, 1991a).

Organizing for Dramatic Play

Teachers limit the dramatic themes they place in the classroom during a time period. Teachers prepare a dramatic play area matched to the theme being studied. They change the dramatic play theme when introducing a new theme. For materials to be used for literacy to their fullest potential, teachers need to use props that are natural and from the child's own environment. The materials in the setting created must serve a real function and be familiar to children. The materials in dramatic play areas should be clearly marked and be accessible. Initially, teachers need to guide the use of materials. Keep in mind that encouraging children to play in themed dramatic play centers is a time for literacy to be initiated by the children themselves naturally in the setting provided (Neuman & Roskos, 1993) rather than a time for the teacher to be teaching skills. All levels of literacy development should be accepted, and reading or writing attempts should be recognized as legitimate literacy behaviors.

Managing Work in Centers

Besides preparing the classroom centers, the teacher also plays an important role in modeling the use of materials before they are ever put into the center so that children are familiar with them. It is crucial that children are familiar with the center materials and possible activities before they go to use them on their own. The teacher helps children get activities started, and participates along with the children in their activities when they need assistance. The goal for this period is for the children to be self-directed in the activities they undertake.

At the beginning of the school year, some teachers start center time in a structured fashion. They assign groups of children to particular centers for a specified amount of time. Children are expected to stay in the center and to accomplish two or three tasks. As kindergartners learn to function independently, they are given opportunities for decision making; children themselves select which center they will visit and decide which activities in the center they will complete.

Management of center time is crucial for its success. Students must know their possible choices, the activities in which to participate, the rules that guide participation concerning the selection of materials, and what is going to happen in groups or when working alone. Children can help generate the guidelines and rules for working independently. Some rules that are important during center work include:

> Speak in soft voices.

> Put materials in their proper places.

> Put completed work in a designated spot.

> Share materials.

> Take turns.

> Listen to your friends when they talk.

> Offer help to others you are working with if they need it.

Planning Furniture Arrangement: A Floor Plan

Well-organized classrooms have centers that are partially separated from each other by furniture that is used to house center materials. Centers should be labeled and their materials stored on tables, on shelves, in boxes, or on a bulletin board. Each piece of equipment in a center should have its own designated spot so that teachers can direct children to it, and children can find and return it easily. Early in a school year, a center need hold only a small number of items; new materials are gradually added as the year progresses. The teacher should introduce the purpose, use, and placement of each item as it is added.

The classroom floor plan in Figure 2.1 illustrates this type of learning environment for a kindergarten classroom. As shown on the floor plan, the art center is placed by the sink for easy access to water. In this same area are children's cubbies for storing individual work. Because the working needs of a kindergarten classroom are better met by table surfaces than by desks, children will need to use cubbies to store their individual belongings.

In addition to generating a rich literacy atmosphere and an interdisciplinary approach, the room presented in Figure 2.1 is designed to cater to different teach-

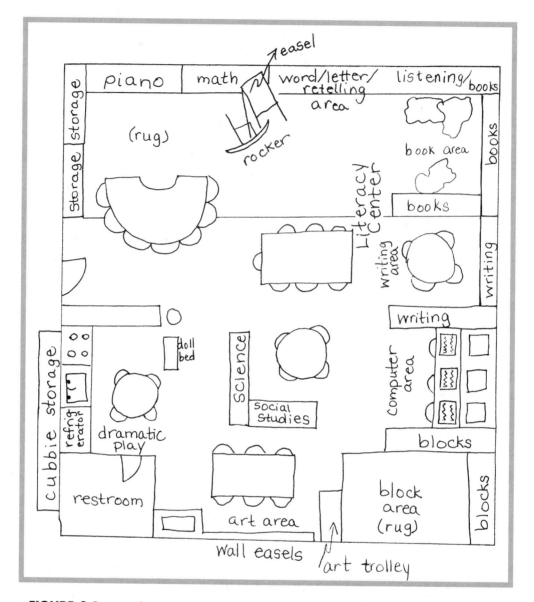

FIGURE 2.1. Kindergarten floor plan.

ing methods, organizational strategies, and grouping procedures so that the individual differences among the children can be accommodated. Each of the centers provides space for independent or social learning, exploration, and self-direction. The tables provide a place for whole-class instruction, as does the open area between the music center and the literacy center. This area has a rug on which children can sit. The teacher's conference table is a place for individual learning or small-group lessons. All furniture is, of course, movable so that any other needed teaching arrangement can be accommodated. The centers are located to create both quiet relatively academic areas and places for more active play.

The literacy center, for example, which houses the library corner, letter-and-word study area, and writing area, is next to the math center. Because these areas generally house activities that require relative quiet, they are in close proximity. Alternatively, dramatic play, woodworking, and block play tend to be noisier activities, so they are placed at the opposite end of the room from the quiet areas. The art center can also be a noisy area and is set aside from the quieter sections of the room. The teacher's conference table is situated in a quiet area, yet allows the teacher a good view of the rest of the classroom. While the teacher is involved in small-group or individualized instruction at the conference table, the rest of the class is working independently. The table's location allows the teacher to see all the children even while working with just a few of them.

The contents of the various centers diagrammed in Figure 2.1 have been described earlier in this chapter. In addition to all the materials available in them, it is important that each has books and writing materials. The music center, for example, can include picture storybooks adapted from songs, such as Ezra Jack Keats's (1971) *Over in the Meadow*. In addition to looking at the book, children may copy words from the story. Social studies and science centers should hold informational books and children's literature that relate to the topics being studied. The art center might have books with craft ideas and books featuring the work of great artists.

Kindergarten Environments in Action

As examples of the critical role a well-designed environment plays in kindergarten, we now describe two kindergarten classrooms in action. In the first classroom, Ms. Heyer's kindergarten is learning about workers in the community. While discussing news reporters, the children decided they would like to have a news office in the dramatic play area where they could publish their own newspaper. Their teacher helped create the center, where they placed writing paper, telephones, phone directories, and a computer. There were pamphlets, maps, and other appropriate reading materials for the different sections of the newspaper, such as sports, travel, weather, and news. Children frequently played in this center, pretending to run a newspaper, write feature stories, broadcast the weather, and interview celebrities. The teacher capitalized on the children's enthusiasm and taught minilessons during writing workshop on how to write various parts of a newspaper. As part of the teacher-directed writing lessons and play in the newspaper center, the class completed their first newspaper. Ethan was in charge of delivering the paper. He had a newspaper delivery bag, and each paper had the name of a child on it. As the delivery person, Ethan had to match the names on the papers to the names on the children's cubbies. Later, when the kindergartners read their newspapers, they shared them with great enthusiasm. Each child had contributed something to the paper—for example, a drawing, a story, or a group poem.

The second example comes from an observation that one of the authors of this book made in a second kindergarten classroom as the children interacted in the literacy center. Due to the teacher's good modeling and management, her students' center time was extremely productive.

I (Lesley Mandel Morrow) visited Ms. Lynch's kindergarten the last day of school. I had been working with this teacher and her children for an entire school year. Ms. Lynch and I shared a sense of pride while observing the children during their literacy center time. We saw some children curled up on a rug or leaning on pillows in the literacy center with books they had selected themselves. Louis and Ramon were squeezed tightly into a rocking chair, sharing a book.

Marcel, Patrick, and Roseangela snuggled under a shelf—a "private spot" filled with stuffed animals—where they took turns reading. Tesha and Tiffany were on the floor with a felt board and character cutouts from *The Gingerbread Man*, alternately reading and manipulating the figures: "Run, run as fast as you can! You can't catch me, I'm the Gingerbread Man!"

Four children listened on headsets to tapes of Maurice Sendak's (1962) *Pierre*, each child holding a copy of the book and chanting along with the narrator, "I don't care, I don't care."

Tyrone had a big book that he was able to read. He gave several other children copies of the same story in smaller format. Role-playing a teacher, he read to the others, occasionally stopping to ask who would like to read (Morrow, 1990, 1992; Morrow, O'Connor, & Smith, 1990).

A Schedule for the Kindergarten Day

The daily schedule in kindergarten must take into account the social, emotional, physical, and intellectual levels of the children. The environment should be prepared so that learning can take place in spontaneous ways, but with intentional instruction that will help children achieve their fullest potential. Young children cannot sit for long periods, so their schedule needs to vary. Whole-class lessons that require sitting and listening must be few and short. Children need large blocks of time for exploring environments. They need play situations, manipulative materials, learning centers, and outdoor areas. Activities that require sitting and listening need to be followed by ones that allow movement. Quiet times must be followed by noisier times. The teacher must include rich literacy experiences throughout the day.

In scheduling the school day, teachers include whole-class, small-group, and one-to-one settings for learning. There need to be teacher-directed experiences and activities that children participate in independently. Children should have opportunities for oral reading and silent reading from books and from their own writing. They need to have time for shared reading experiences and shared writing experiences. Time should be set aside for periods of guided reading and teacher-modeled writing, as well as for reading and writing independently. Children should have the opportunity to read and write collaboratively with peers and to perform in formal and informal settings the products of their reading and writing.

The sample schedules for half-day and whole-day kindergarten found in Figures 2.2 and 2.4 illustrate where and when specific opportunities to promote literacy can occur. The schedules provide a routine or structure for the day that seems to make children comfortable. Keep in mind that there is no one schedule for all classrooms.

Figure 2.2 presents a possible schedule for a half-day kindergarten. Children have numerous opportunities to engage in reading and writing in this schedule as well. First thing in the morning children sign in. *Sign-in* is when children write their names on a specially prepared sheet for attendance purposes (Richgels, 1995). One way to have sign-in is to assign children to groups, print all the names of the children in a list on a sheet (four of five children in each group works best), and place the sheet on a clipboard at a designated spot in the classroom. As chil-

8:30–8:45: Arrival at school, storage of outdoor clothing. Sign-in. Quiet activities.

8:45–9:10: Whole-group morning meeting including opening exercises such as calendar and weather, morning message, discussion of theme topic, singing and movement activities related to theme topic, daily news, and planning for the school day.

9:10–9:40: Whole-class lesson in language arts, mathematics, social studies, or science, varying from day to day, with an assignment to complete during center time.

9:40–10:00: Center time and small-group reading lesson for one group. The rest of the class completes work from the whole-class lesson; children work on individual contracts in small groups or at designated centers (literacy, social studies, science, or mathematics).

10:00–10:35: Free play. All centers open, including art, music, blocks, dramatic play, literacy, science, and social studies. Special projects may be set up at different centers, such as art or science. Teacher conducts one small-group reading lesson and may teach a small-group lesson in math.

10:35–10:50: Clean-up and snack.

10:50–11:10: Literacy center time. Children use materials from the literacy center (library corner, letter and word area, writing area) or other centers on special literacy projects set up in those locations. Teacher conducts one small-group reading lesson.

11:10–11:30: Outdoor play, if weather permits, or large-motor-skills games in the gymnasium.

11:30–11:55: Whole-group book reading including interactive read-alouds, shared book experiences, role-playing, and creative storytelling.

11:55–12:00: Summary of the school day. Dismissal.

FIGURE 2.2. Half-day program for kindergarten.

dren in that group enter the classroom, they write their name on the clipboard beside their printed names. An alternative is to have a clipboard and sign-in sheet for each child. One kindergarten teacher uses this procedure and encourages children to keep their sign-in sheet during opening exercises. Children copy words from the morning message, weather, and calendar (McGee & Richgels, 2004).

Figure 2.3 presents an example of a sign-in sheet a kindergarten teacher developed about midyear. By then children were very familiar with the routine of trying to read the question on the sign-in sheet and easily recognized the words *yes* and *no*. This teacher has used the question stem *Do you like* for the past 5 days, so the children are familiar with this pattern. In addition, she is using this activity to reinforce children's recognition of color words. During morning meeting, the teacher reads the sign-in question with the children, and then two "special helpers" gather the sign-in sheets to tally the number of *yes*'s and *no*'s. At the close of the day, these helpers report the numbers and present a graph they have prepared with the support of the teacher during the day.

After sign-in and other entering-the-room routines are accomplished, children move to the large carpeted area for morning meeting. They read a morning message, discuss the weather, and count days on the calendar. Then children go to centers or have a small-group lesson in reading. When not working in small groups, children complete reading and writing activities prepared for them in the literacy center or other centers in the classroom. They listen to books their teacher reads aloud (both for language arts and for content theme study).

Teachers who have half-day programs will need to work even more closely with parents to provide children with additional experiences in literacy at home. Teachers may want to advocate for a reading specialist in their building who will provide extra support for those children who are struggling. Teachers will also want to make activities in all centers more directly supportive of children's reading and writing in order to make the best use of the short half-day program.

Figure 2.4 presents an example of a possible full-day schedule. Full-day schedules allow for larger blocks of time and more time for learning through exploration and manipulation of materials during center activities. Literacy occurs throughout the day in this schedule. It begins as children enter the classroom and sign in. The morning meeting includes read-

Good Morning

Do you like red?

              Yes   No

Name: _____

Words: _____

_____

_____

_____

_____

_____

FIGURE 2.3. Kindergarten sign-in sheet.

ing the morning message, discussing the weather, and doing calendar activities. The teacher conducts a whole-class lesson that may include an oral language activity such as dramatizing a story. Then the children work in centers while the teacher conducts small-group lessons in reading. The teacher reads at least one book aloud and then conducts writing lessons before lunch. After lunch, children participate

---

8:30–8:50: Arrival at school, storage of outdoor clothing. Sign-in. Quiet activities such as reading books, playing with table-top toys, writing in journals, or completing unfinished work.

8:50-9:15: Whole-group morning meeting with opening routines such as calendar or weather, morning message, discussion of theme topic, singing and movement activity related to the theme, daily news, and planning for the school day.

9:15-9:40: Whole-class lesson, either in language arts or mathematics, varying from day to day, with an assignment to complete during center time.

9:40–10:20: Center time and small-group reading instruction for two groups of children. The rest of the class completes assigned work from the whole-class lesson or works on individual contracts at centers designated for use during this quiet period (literacy center, math, social studies, science).

10:20–10:45: Free-play/theme time. All centers are open, including dramatic play, blocks, and woodworking. Special art or food preparation projects are set up in the art center once each week for small groups independent of the teacher. Teacher may work with small groups in reading or math.

10:45–11:00: Clean-up and snack.

11:00–11:30: Interactive read-alouds, creative storytelling, repeated story readings, role-playing, shared book readings, use of big books.

11:30–12:15: Minilesson in writing and small-group instruction in writing. Other children have literacy center time. Children use materials in the literacy center (library corner, writing area, letter and word area), including "very own words."

12:15–1:15: Lunch and outdoor play, if time and weather permit. Otherwise, large-motor-skills activities in the gymnasium.

1:15–1:45: Whole-group lesson in science or social studies theme incorporating language arts, reading aloud, music, or art. Math is integrated where possible.

1:45–2:15: Center time (all centers are open or centers are designated for children's use). Special projects can be set up in any center for small groups to rotate through in a given week. Examples include science investigations, whole-class surveys, or special computer games. The teacher meets with a small group for reading instruction.

2:15–2:50: Whole-group circle time. Summary of the day's activities, planning for the next day, sharing of items brought from home that are related to study units, performance of work created by children, songs, and adult story reading.

2:50–3:00: Preparation for dismissal. Dismissal.

FIGURE 2.4. Full-day program for kindergarten.

in special social studies–or science-theme activities that involve reading and writing. Children work in centers while the teacher conducts another small-group lesson in reading. The day ends as the teacher reads another book or poem aloud.

It is critical that teachers establish a routine early in the school year beginning on the first day of school. Children need instruction in how to go to centers, what to do in each center, and how to get back to the carpet or tables. The more teachers follow a consistent schedule, the easier it is for children to be productive and independent learners. If teachers are to be able to conduct small-group lessons with children, children must become independent workers in activities that are more than busy-work. Children need to engage in activities that will extend their learning rather than merely keep them occupied. Teachers will carefully move materials used in small-group lessons out into centers where children can use them again and again to reach fluency. Adding new materials to centers that have been used in instruction is highly motivating to children. They eagerly seek out letter cards to build words or reread sentences from the pocket chart when they are presented with these opportunities.

SUMMARY

Programs that motivate early literacy development require literacy-rich environments that recognize the need for an integrated approach to literacy learning and awareness of individual differences and developmental levels. These classrooms are arranged in centers designed for particular content areas. Centers contain materials specific to topics currently under study along with general supplies and resources. The materials are usually manipulative and activity-oriented. Each subject-specific center includes literacy materials as well: things to read, materials with which to write, things to listen to, and things to talk about. These materials create interest, new vocabulary and concepts, and a reason for participating in literacy activities. All centers are designed so that children can use them independently or in small groups without teacher supervision. With each new theme studied, additional books, posters, artifacts, music, art projects, dramatic play materials, and scientific objects are added to create new interest. Teachers establish a classroom schedule and demand that children adhere to classroom rules. The daily schedule allows sufficient opportunities for children to explore materials in the classroom centers, and for teachers to present planned intentional instruction in reading and writing.

CHAPTER 3

WHAT DO KINDERGARTNERS KNOW ABOUT READING AND WRITING?

This chapter is divided into three parts. In the first part, we describe five areas of foundational knowledge that all kindergartners are expected to develop in order to be successful readers and writers in first grade and beyond. We also describe at least one informal assessment that teachers can use at the beginning of the year to determine the level of foundational knowledge that each child brings to school. In the second part, we describe kindergartners as they talk with their teacher during a storybook read-aloud. We examine children's responses to their teacher's questions to demonstrate the way that kindergartners think about and react to books. In the final part, we look at the types of writing that we can expect in kindergarten. We describe how teachers can use children's writing to assess children's alphabet knowledge, phonemic awareness, awareness of structures of genre, and understanding of the variety of functions that writing serves. This chapter is intended to give teachers an indication of the range of literacy behaviors they might expect in kindergarten and to demonstrate how kindergartners learn.

CONVENTIONAL FOUNDATIONS OF READING AND WRITING EXPECTED IN KINDERGARTEN

All kindergartners learn fundamental literacy skills like recognizing the alphabet letters and learning letter–sound relationships. Some kindergartners, as we saw in Chapter 1, learn how to use letter–sound knowledge to read new rhyming words and actually begin reading conventionally. However, at the same time that kindergartners are learning the foundations of reading and writing, they also use unconventional strategies to engage in reading and writing events. They pretend to read favorite storybooks by memorizing the text nearly word for word, and they use scribbling to pretend to write grocery lists in their dramatic play. Later, they learn to spell—but their spelling is invented and not conventional (see Figure 1.1). Effective kindergarten teachers expect and encourage this mixture of conventional knowledge and unconventional reading and writing. They help children learn the foundational skills kindergartners must learn, but they also value and encourage children to use unconventional strategies to read and write independently. The classroom environment we described in Chapter 2 is specifically designed to help children practice foundational skills taught by the teacher, and to engage in playful reading and writing in dramatic play and other centers.

In order to determine the foundations that need to be learned in kindergarten, researchers have posed the question: What do kindergartners need to know so that we can predict with a high degree of certainty that they will be successful readers and writers in first grade? These researchers (summarized in Snow, Burns, & Griffin, 1998) have discovered that kindergartners need to have knowledge in five foundational areas of literacy development. They must have:

1. Alphabet knowledge
2. Phonological and phonemic awareness
3. Understanding of letter–sound relationships and the alphabetic principle
4. Concepts about print and books
5. Oral comprehension and vocabulary

Alphabet Knowledge

Most children are aware of alphabet letters before entering kindergarten. We do not mean that they necessarily recognize or identify the letters by name. Rather, children intuitively know that print "says." They know that the printed word on the golden arches "says" *McDonald's*. Some children acquire this basic understanding when they are as young as 2 or 3 years old as they talk about the word *Cheerios* on their box of cereal or the word *Barbie* on the box of their new doll. As children are taught to recognize the alphabet and write their names, they begin to differentiate among those squiggly marks that we call "alphabet letters." For example, some young children recognize the letter *M* as "Mom's letter" rather than as *M*. While these children may not be able to identify the letter *M* by name, they are aware of particular letters and know that particular letters have particular meanings. *G* is "Grandpa's letter" and *K* is "Kristen's letter" (McGee & Richgels, 1989). That is, before children learn to identify letters by name, they learn to pay attention to different letters that are uniquely meaningful to them.

During kindergarten it is expected that all children will learn to recognize the upper- and lower-case alphabet letters accurately and quickly. In fact, the most successful readers and writers are often those children who enter kindergarten already recognizing most alphabet letters. However, those children who learn alphabet letters during kindergarten may also begin reading successfully in first grade. Teachers can easily assess children's alphabet knowledge by presenting children with the upper-case and lower-case letters printed or typed on cards or on a sheet of paper (Appendix C presents an alphabet recognition task that teachers can use for this purpose). They can create a class profile that shows at a glance which children have learned which letters. Teachers write the upper-case letters across the top of the sheet and the names of the children down the left side of the sheet. For each child, they check off the letters that child correctly identified. Teachers can use the back of the sheet for lower-case letters.

Successful kindergartners must also learn to write recognizable alphabet letters with some fluency. Kindergartners are still developing the motor control to be able to write completely conventional letters, and their sense of orientation is still evolving. Therefore, alphabet writing in kindergarten includes some letter reversals and unconventional letter formations. Still, learning the alphabet is a hallmark of kindergarten instruction.

Most children learn to write their first alphabet letters as they learn to write their names (Bloodgood, 1999). Thus, children's ability to write their signatures is also part of kindergarten. Many children enter kindergarten already writing their names in a recognizable form, while other children do not. As an example of what can be expected in alphabet and name writing, Figure 3.1 presents Mercedes's signature as she wrote her name at the end of September, October, and November. The changes in her signature reflect the kinds of changes that can be expected in children's letter and name writing in kindergarten.

In September Mercedes was able to write every letter in her first name (quite an accomplishment for someone with such a long name!). The form of all the letters is recognizable—although some have unconventional forms, especially the letter s. The different sizes of the alphabet letters are also typical of kindergarten writing and signal developing motor control. By October Mercedes's signature has already changed considerably. The letter formations are much more recognizable and are more uniform in size. The letter s is in conventional format, and Mercedes has switched from writing an upper-case

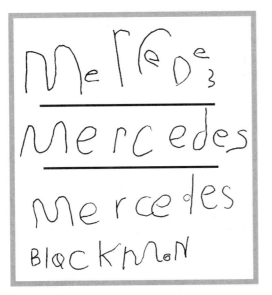

FIGURE 3.1. Mercedes writes her name in September, October, and November.

D to a lower-case one. This signature shows considerable gains in motor control. In November Mercedes was willing to write both her first and last name. While her first name does not look as conventional as it did in October, this is to be expected when she has taken on the much more demanding task of remembering and writing *Mercedes Blackmon*—16 letters! Many children may not make as much progress as Mercedes did at the beginning of kindergarten. Yet all kindergartners are expected to write their first and last names by the end of the school year.

A good assessment of alphabet and name writing is to collect children's signatures from a sign-in procedure over the first few weeks or months of kindergarten. The *sign-in procedure* occurs when children sign their names on a special chart for attendance purposes as they enter the classroom (see Chapter 2). For assessment purposes, as we demonstrated with Mercedes's signatures, teachers collect and date sign-in sheets daily. Teachers usually select one sign-in sheet each week or month to keep for documentation purposes. After collecting samples, teachers examine each child's name writing for changes in alphabet formation, growing awareness of upper- and lower-case letters, and gains in motor control.

Phonological and Phonemic Awareness

Phonological awareness is a term that encompasses many different concepts related to hearing sounds in the environment as well as sounds in spoken language. Children demonstrate phonological awareness when they march to the beat of music, use their voice to emphasize the rhythm in poetry, and clap syllables in spoken words. All of these activities require at least an intuitive awareness of syllables. However, being able to respond to syllables is not strongly related to later reading or writing skill. The first level of phonological awareness that matters is at the level of onset and rime (Anthony, Lonigan, Driscoll, Phillips, & Burgess, 2003). An *onset* is every letter in a word that appears before the word's first vowel. The *rime* is the vowel and every other letter that follows. For example, the word *hat* consists of the onset *h* and the rime *at*. The word *flat* consists of the onset *fl* and the same rime *at*. The word *splat* consists of the onset *spl* and the rime *at*. The word *at* has no onset but includes the rime *at*.

Awareness of onset and rime indicates that children can segment speech sounds that are smaller than a syllable. Syllables are easy for all young children to hear and segment and they naturally can seem to do this. However, being able to hear and segment sounds smaller than a syllable is much more difficult; thus children need considerable experience listening to rhyming poems, songs, and books before becoming conscious of rhyme (Anthony et al., 2003).

During kindergarten it is essential that children move from merely enjoying reciting rhyming poems or nursery rhymes to a conscious awareness of *rhyming words*. However, developing this conscious awareness of rhyming is difficult for some children. Many children enter kindergarten without being able to separate the sounds in a spoken word from the meaning of that word. One kindergartner playing a rhyming word game exclaimed: "No, that can't be. Pants and ants *never* go together." He got up to demonstrate ants in his pants!

Being able to identify whether two words rhyme (Do *car* and *star* rhyme? Do *cat* and *dog* rhyme?), to find a rhyming word that matches a target word (Match the pictures of a *tree* and a *key* when given pictures of a *tree*, a key, and a *road*), and to produce a word that rhymes with a target word (Say *mall*, *fall*, and *tall* when given the word *ball*) are all phonological concepts expected to be mastered in kindergarten.

Phonemic awareness requires children to detect and manipulate the smallest speech sounds in words: *phonemes*. This concept is demonstrated when children can identify whether two words have the same beginning phoneme (whether two words start with the same single sound—for example, does *car* begin like *cat* or *tick* begin with the same sound as *baby*?), match words based on beginning phonemes (matching the pictures of *moon* and *monkey* when given the pictures *moon*, *monkey*, and *soap*), and produce a word with the same beginning phoneme as a target word (saying that *jump*, *jet*, and *jar* begin with the same sound as the word *jacket*). These three phonemic awareness abilities are also expected to be developed in kindergarten. They are the easiest level of phonemic awareness that children are expected to acquire; they require children to hear initial sounds—the single phoneme at the beginning of words.

Yet kindergarten children must go beyond hearing and manipulating beginning phonemes; they must be able to hear and say (i.e., segment or isolate) both the beginning and the ending sound in a word (Morris, Bloodgood, Lomax, & Perney, 2003). For example, they should be able to say that *turtle* begins with /t/ and ends with /l/. In many kindergarten reading programs children also are expected to hear middle phonemes. When children first are able to segment or isolate a single phoneme from the rest of the spoken word, this signals that children are ready to learn *phonics*, the relationship between letters and sounds or phonemes (Johnston, Anderson, & Holligan, 1996).

Phonics and the Alphabetic Principle

"Phonemic awareness" and "phonics" are often confused. *Phonemic awareness* never includes alphabet letters—it only involves hearing the phonemes in spoken words. *Phonics*, on the other hand, is the knowledge of how letters are associated with particular sounds or phonemes. Phonemic awareness is part of phonics—children must be able to hear and produce phonemes in order to match sounds with letters.

Kindergartners who know at least a few alphabet letters and can segment a few phonemes are usually taught *consonant letter–sound associations*. These are the most consistent letter–sound relationships in English. For example, the letter *t* is almost always associated with the phoneme /t/, whereas the letter *a* is associated with many different phonemes including the sounds found in the words *apron*, *apple*, *all*, and *about*.

Some children enter kindergarten already knowing some letter–sound associations; they may have attended preschools where these skills were taught. Some children discover letter–sound relationships all by themselves. Children who have strong alphabet knowledge and who have parents who encourage them to write notice that their mouths, lips, teeth, and tongue are in the same places when they say the name of an alphabet letter and when they say the beginning of a word. When children say the letter name *B* and the word *baby*, their lips are tightly pressed together. This discovery allows children to spell words using their own invented spelling: *B* spells *baby*. Children who have learned a few letter–sound correspondences can also be encouraged to spell in the same way (Morris & Slavin, 2003).

Figure 3.2 presents Carly's spelling. Her teacher asked her if she would be willing to write and Carly agreed to try. Her teacher asked her to write *bed* (Carly wrote *B*), *ship* (Carly wrote *G*), *when* (Carly wrote *Y*), *lump* (Carly wrote *l*), and *train* (Carly wrote *G*). Each of these spellings shows either knowledge of the conventional letter–sound association or a relationship between manner of articulation (i.e., the position of mouth, tongue, teeth, and lips as well as the use of voice and air) and the letter name. Carly spelled the word *bed* with the conventional letter–sound association. However, she spelled *ship* with *G*, an unconventional but reasonable letter choice (Richgels, 2001). When saying the word *ship*, speakers push a stream of air through partially clenched teeth. When saying the letter name *G*, the same stream of air is briefly a part of the letter name pronunciation. Carly's use of the letter *Y* to spell the word *when* can also be explained by manner of articulation. When saying the letter name *Y*, the lips are rounded just as they are when saying the word *when*. Carly spelled the word *lump* with the conventional letter–sound association. Again, she used manner of articulation to select the letter *G* to spell *train*. When saying the word *train*, speakers slush air through their mouths just as air is slushed when saying the letter name *G*.

Carly's writing demonstrates more than her letter–sound knowledge; her willingness and ability to spell words with letters that have a reasonable association with phonemes demonstrates the beginning of the alphabetic principle. The *alphabetic principle* is the realization that letters in written words are systematically related to sounds in spoken words. Conventional reading and writing cannot happen unless children grasp the alphabetic principle. Simply memorizing some letter–sound associations does not guarantee that children will discover the alphabetic principle. However, knowing letter–sound associations is a critical component of the alphabetic principle.

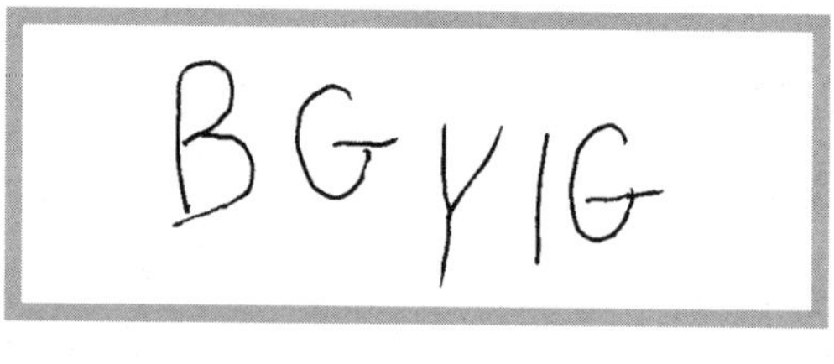

FIGURE 3.2. Carly spells *bed, ship, when, lump,* and *train*.

Children in kindergarten are expected to use the alphabetic principle in kindergarten in many ways. One way includes using letter–sound understandings to spell words. Teachers do not expect kindergartners to spell conventionally, although some kindergartners learn the conventional spellings of a few high-frequency words such as the words *the, mom, for, and, do,* and *you.* Figure 3.3 presents Cierra's spellings when she was asked to write *bed, ship, when, lump,* and *float* in the spring of kindergarten. Her spellings demonstrate that she has strong phonemic awareness—she can segment and detect the beginning, middle, and ending phoneme in all the words. Her spellings also show that she knows every word has a vowel, although only two of the vowels she used in her spellings were the conventional short-vowel letter–sound associations (*ship* was spelled as *tip* using the conventional short-*i* vowel; *lump* was spelled as *lup* using the conventional short-*u* vowel). Cierra's spelling also reflect the kinds of instruction provided in kindergarten: how to segment and detect three phonemes in single-syllable words and the short-vowel letter–sound relationships.

A second way kindergartners are expected to use the alphabetic principle is to build and read new rhyming words (see examples in Chapter 1). For example, teachers write the word *cat* on a wipe-off board, tell children they have just written the word *cat,* and then wipe off the letter *c.* Teachers tell children they will add a new letter and build a new word for children to read. Teachers might add the letter *b.* They demonstrate how to read the new words by first saying the sound associated with the letter *b* and then demonstrating how to blend the rime *at* to the phoneme /b/. Teachers continue demonstrating and inviting children to build and read new rhyming words. They might wipe off the letter *b* and add the letter *f.* Again they demonstrate reading the word by first identifying the sound associated with the letter *f* and blending that phoneme with the rime *at.*

Kindergarten teachers can assess children's phonemic awareness and application of the alphabetic principle in several ways. They might ask children to spell a few words. At the beginning of the year most kindergartners will loudly announce they can't spell. Teachers can also read aloud a poem or nursery rhyme, pausing for children to supply rhyming words. After reading the poem, they

FIGURE 3.3. Cierra spells *bed, ship, when, lump,* and *float.*

can invite children to remember the rhyming words and think of new words that would rhyme, noting which children participate and which do not. Because phonemic awareness and the alphabetic principle are so important in kindergarten, we recommend early and systematic screening and monitoring of these abilities. These assessments are described in Chapter 7 (and presented in Appendices E and F).

Concepts about Print, Books, and Words

Children's concepts about print, books, and words include awareness of *book orientation*—for example: knowing that print rather than pictures are read, books have fronts and backs, pages have tops and bottoms, pages are read from front to back, and turning each page one at a time. Children also learn *print directionality* concepts including that the left page is read before the right page, and that reading begins at the top left line of print and proceeds across that line of print before the return sweep to the left of the second line of print. Children acquire *letter and word concepts* such as that words are composed of letters, some words are long and others are short, and punctuation marks tell readers where to stop or pause (Clay, 1993b).

Children demonstrate their early book orientation concepts as they look through a favorite book. Almost all kindergartners hold books correctly and turn the pages from front to back as they look at a book on their own. Many kindergartners can show a book's front, back, top, and bottom, and demonstrate that left pages are read before right pages. Fewer kindergarten children show directionality concepts of tracking (pointing) from left to right with a return sweep. Yet being able to *track print*—that is, to point across a line of print from left to right—while saying the words of a favorite story is a critical skill that must be developed in kindergarten. This is often referred to as *pretend reading*. Children memorize the text of a favorite book, and say the text as they look at each page, often sweeping their finger across the lines of text. Fingerpoint reading represents a more advanced level of pretend reading. In *fingerpoint reading*, children say the memorized text and point word for word across a line of text as they attempt to point to a written word matched one-to-one with a spoken word (Ehri & Sweet, 1991). This is the critical skill children must acquire.

Kindergarten teachers can assess children's concepts about print and books by helping children memorize a simple text (such as *Brown Bear, Brown Bear, What Do You See?* [Martin, 1967]) and then inviting them to read the book aloud. As children read teachers can observe the coordination between what children say and where they point in the book. Many kindergartners do not point at print even when they are invited to do so. Others sweep across print without regard for matching voice with finger. A few children at the beginning of kindergarten attempt to match print with speech, but all children must learn to fingerpoint read during kindergarten (Morris et al., 2003).

Pretend reading also allows teachers to assess children's concept of a word.

Children who attempt to fingerpoint read are beginning to realize that printed words are separated by spaces. By paying attention to their pointing and to the words they are saying, children can track print to find a target word. Teachers can invite children to find the word *bear* or *you* in the title of *Brown Bear, Brown Bear, What Do You See?* Children who can use tracking to find particular words have developed a concept of the written word. Again, this concept is critical for kindergartners to develop; its development precedes conventional reading development (Morris et al., 2003).

Oral Comprehension and Vocabulary

Learning to sit still, to listen intently to a book read aloud, to answer questions, and to make comments are important foundational reading skills. These behaviors signal that children are comprehending or understanding what is being read aloud. Listening to books is a critical avenue for learning new vocabulary words as well (Wasik & Bond, 2001). Vocabulary and comprehension development have a reciprocal relationship: the more children hear books read aloud, the more words they acquire. The more words that children know, the more complex books and stories that they are able to understand. During kindergarten, all children must learn hundreds of sophisticated vocabulary words and increase the level of complexity of the books they can understand and enjoy. Having a rich vocabulary and being able to understand complex books paves the road for later quick advances in reading achievement.

One way teachers can assess children's vocabulary and oral comprehension is to ask them to retell a familiar story (Morrow & Smith, 1990). Teachers select a complex story or informational book with some sophisticated vocabulary words that might not be in the everyday spoken vocabulary of 5-year-olds. Teachers identify 5–10 of these words to emphasize during reading by giving a definition or pointing out a detail in the illustrations that would explain the word. Teachers read the book aloud, emphasizing the vocabulary, and inviting children to make comments and answer a few questions (see Chapter 4 for a description of effective read-aloud techniques). Then teachers read the book again the following day, now inviting children to perhaps add dramatic motions to the story. Finally, teachers read the book a third time. One by one children are asked to retell the story (many teachers use a tape recorder for this purpose; but other teachers use a retelling checklist, a technique discussed in Chapter 7).

Figure 3.4 presents Harmone's retelling of *Owl Moon* (Yolen, 1987). This retelling only includes two details from the story: the main characters (the man and the boy) and the overall action (they went looking for a bird). It includes none of the sophisticated vocabulary of the story such as the words *owling, Great Horned Owl, clearing, meadow,* or *forest.* Figure 3.5 presents Justin's retelling. He also identifies the main characters (a girl and her daddy) and some of the critical events of the story (they went into the woods, they saw the owl, the owl flapped his wings, and

> A man and a boy went looking for a bird.

FIGURE 3.4. Harmone retells *Owl Moon* (Yolen, 1987).

they went home). Justin made one cause–effect connection (they went into the woods *to look for owls*). While he did not use the elegant phrasing of the story—"the owl pumped its great wings"—Justin did get the meaning of the word *pumped* when he said that "the owl flapped his wings." These are fairly typical retellings for kindergartners who have not had much experience retelling stories and where children are not looking at the book.

Many children refuse to retell stories. When asked to retell, Ke Onta responded, "I don't know, I can't do it." However, he was willing to pretend to read the story. His pretend reading is presented in Figure 3.6. This pretend reading is more like a description of the book's illustrations than a retelling. Nonetheless, it demonstrates that Ke Onta clearly understood more about the story than his "I don't know" suggested. He remembered that the moon was important in the story, that the story mentioned several different sounds the characters heard as they went owling, and that the shadows of the dad and child were different. He also remembered the part about shining the flashlight right on the owl and going home. Just like Harmone and Justin, his pretend reading lacked the sophisticated vocabulary in the story.

Learning to retell stories and information books with some detail and to use some of the sophisticated vocabulary in books is an important part of kindergarten. With experience kindergartners' retellings of both stories and informational books include more information, take on more of the complex sentence structures found in books, and include some sophisticated vocabulary. Teachers can ask children to retell stories or information books and examine the detail and vocabulary to gain an idea about children's oral language and comprehension development.

> The girl and her daddy went into the woods to look for owls. They saw the owl. He flapped his wings, and they went home.

FIGURE 3.5. Justin retells *Owl Moon* (Yolen, 1987).

Walking to the moon

Whoo whoo

He heard a lot of noise

Yours big and mines little. I got to catch him.

Whoo whoo

Walk there

It was dark there

We were almost there

Whoo whoo

Then they said whoo

Then they showed his flashlight at him so he could see his face. Police have a flashlight to shine in the car.

Then he showed his face again.

They went back home. The end.

FIGURE 3.6. Ke Onta pretends to read *Owl Moon* (Yolen, 1987).

STRATEGIES FOR READING

Young children learn many strategies that allow them to participate in a familiar reading event: listening to books their teachers read aloud. Some children enter kindergarten already having acquired these strategies because they have had many experiences listening and talking as adults read aloud. These children are easy to recognize; they sit still and listen attentively. They frequently and spontaneously make comments (being active during listening by talking about interesting characters or events is an effective reading strategy!) or ask questions about the illustrations or text (asking questions to clarify information is another good reading strategy!). They answer questions often without raising their hands when teachers pose them.

Other children have not had many experiences with listening to books read aloud or have not been invited to talk during book read-alouds. They are easy to spot as well. They do not immediately settle down and look at the book expectantly. It is as if they do not realize that something really interesting is about to happen—they will need to learn that books are funny and entertaining and challenging. Teachers expect to teach young children many strategies for participating effectively in book read-alouds (Hargrave & Senechal, 2000). Children learn these strategies unconsciously as their teacher asks questions and models thinking aloud about books. We next describe some of the strategies that children learn in kindergarten that help them participate effectively in book read-alouds.

Levels of Thinking and Comprehending

Reading is never successful until readers understand what they read because comprehension is the ultimate goal of reading. Yet comprehension is complicated. What do we mean by "comprehension"? Understanding the gist of a story? Being able to recall all the details of a story as well as to summarize it? Being able to interpret a story and tell what it means beyond the mere events in the story? All of these are aspects of comprehension, or what we might call "levels of comprehension or thinking." These levels include *literal recall*, which is being able to recall what was stated in the words or shown in the illustrations of a book. *Inferential thinking* is being able to predict upcoming events, make inferences about something only implied in the book's words or illustrations, or draw conclusions. *Evaluative and critical thinking* involve making judgments about the actions of characters or the turn of events (McGee & Richgels, 2004).

Using Levels of Thinking to Talk about Books

Being able to recall the literal events, draw inferences, and make evaluative or critical judgments are strategies that children learn as they participate in book read-alouds and as they comprehend. Figure 3.7 presents portions of a conversation that a group of children had as their teacher, Ms. K, read the book *Me and Neesie* (Greenfield, 1975) aloud. In this story, the main character, Janelle, has an imaginary friend, Neesie, who does everything that Janelle does. Janelle not only plays with Neesie, but also insists that she have a place at the dinner table. Janelle's mother and father tolerate Janelle's insistence that Neesie really exists. However, when Aunt Bea visits, Janelle's mother gets Janelle to promise that she will not mention Neesie. However, Aunt Bea's actions cause Janelle to reveal Neesie's existence. Janelle's imaginary friend ultimately does disappear in the story after Janelle's first day in school when she meets new, real friends. *Me and Neesie* is a complex story because Neesie, the imaginary friend, is always present in the illustrations. However, the story text makes it clear that no other character sees Neesie even though she is portrayed in all the illustrations.

In order to help children develop strategies for understanding this complex story, Ms. K planned to stop reading the text to ask a question at three critical points in the story. The conversation presented in Figure 3.7 occurs at one of those critical points. It begins right after Aunt Bea thinks Janelle is seeing a ghost and starts swatting the couch to get rid of it. Ms. K planned to ask a question to help children make inferences. Ms. K read the story text:

"Did I get it Janelle?" Aunt Bea asked, "Did I get it?" Mama couldn't talk. She was holding her forehead, "Oh, oh. "

Then Ms. K paused and asked, "Why do you think her mom was going 'Oh, oh.' "

The children came up with two inferences about the mother's feelings. First, one child suggested that her mother is mad because Aunt Bea beat on the couch. This is a reasonable inference, although obviously not the one implied in the story. Then other children noted that she is sad because Janelle broke her promise. Ms. K is satisfied with these two inferences, so she begins reading the text again.

Figure 3.8 presents the conversation that occurred at another critical point in the story when Ms. K paused to ask another question. In the story Janelle comes home from her first day of school and she cannot find Neesie. Again, Ms. K wanted

Ms. K:	Why do you think her mother was doing that?
Child:	I know!
Child:	Because she was beating up the couch . . .
Ms. K:	How do you think the mother is feeling?
Child:	Sad.
Child:	Mad!
Ms. K:	Mad?
Child:	I know why.
Child:	Angry.
Ms. K:	Angry?
Child:	It was like, 'cause she was like the other, the girl called Neesie, broke her mother's promise. Oh, she broke her promise.
Ms. K:	So you think that's why she's sad?
Children:	She's sad.
Child:	She's sad because she told her not to.

FIGURE 3.7. Children discuss why Janelle's mother is sad in *Me and Neesie* (Greenfield, 1975).

the children to use the strategy of making an inference, so she stopped reading and asked: "I wonder why she couldn't find Neesie? Where's Neesie?" The children's answers demonstrated considerable confusion between the characters Janelle and Neesie, so Ms. K lead a discussion about the meaning of the word *imaginary* in order to clarify the story's characters and actions. Once the children clarified that the imaginary person, Neesie, is gone, they began to make inferences about why she is no longer at Janelle's house. The children suggested two possible inferences: that Neesie is off at school trying to find Janelle, and that Neesie might have moved away.

These two portions of a book conversation demonstrate children's struggle to comprehend, their willingness to explore vocabulary meanings, and their ability to use higher level thinking strategies. Ms. K's children had gained literal meaning of the story; they remembered that Aunt Beas beat on the couch. They also made inferences when they concluded that Janelle's mother was sad because Janelle broke her promise. It is important for kindergarten teachers to assess how well their children enter into these kind of book conversations and use strategies to clarify and expand their understanding of books. Teachers might tape-record a portion of a book conversation and listen to determine which children answer questions, the level of thinking particular children demonstrate, and whether children

Ms. K:	Neesie is gone. I'm wondering why she can't find Neesie. Where is Neesie?
Child:	She's gone.
Ms. K:	Where? Where did she go?
Child:	She went home.
Child:	She went to that other person's house.
Ms. K:	What other person?
Child:	That girl's Janelle (*pointing to book illustration*)?
Ms. K:	Yes, this girl's Janelle, right here (*pointing to book illustration*). In the picture that's Janelle.
Child:	Oh!
Child:	That's the pretend person?
Ms. K:	The who?
Child:	That's the imaginary person?
Ms. K:	No, she, Janelle, cannot find her friend Neesie. I'm asking why?
Child:	Neesie went to school to find her.
Child:	Maybe she came home earlier.
Child:	Maybe she moved and she doesn't see her anymore.
Ms. K:	I'm still curious why Neesie isn't there any more.
Child:	Maybe Neesie thought she wasn't her friend no more.
Ms. K:	Why would Neesie think that?
Child:	Because she went to school and she might have thought she had a good time and she was at home.
Ms. K:	Did you hear what Ethiopiah said? Maybe Neesie thought that Janelle wouldn't be her friend anymore. Now let's talk about this. Was Neesie a real person?
Children:	No! — Yes!
Child:	Janelle thinks she is a real person to her because other people don't.
Ms. K:	What do we call that kind of a person when they're not really real?
Child:	Imaginary.
Ms. K:	What does that word *imaginary* mean?
Child:	Fake.
Child:	Spirit.
Child:	Sometimes you have to use your imagination.

cont.

FIGURE 3.8. Children discuss why Neesie is gone in *Me and Neesie* (Greenfield, 1975).

Ms. K:	Who used their imagination?
Child:	Neesie. No, um, Janelle.
Ms. K:	Janelle. And what did her imagination do?
Child:	It helped her with her friend.
Ms. K:	Her friend, right. And what kind of a friend was it?
Child:	An imaginary friend.
Ms. K:	Why did Janelle have an imaginary friend in the first place?
Child:	She was probably lonely.
Child:	And she didn't have no friends around her.
Child:	She got real friends.
Ms. K:	She got real friends, didn't she? Where did she get real friends?
Child:	At school.
Child:	Maybe she went away in her mind.
Ms. K:	Because Neesie came out of Janelle's (*pause*) . . .
Child:	Body.
Child:	Mind.
Ms. K:	Maybe she went back in her mind.

FIGURE 3.8. *cont.*

demonstrate understanding of vocabulary words. This will provide an indication of children's use of strategic thinking about books.

KINDERGARTNERS WRITE

Writing is also a critical activity in kindergarten for accelerating children's literacy growth (Whitehurst & Lonigan, 2001). Children pretend to write as they play in the home living center or other dramatic play centers, they write in the writing center, and they write as part of instructional activities with their teacher. We have already discussed that one of the foundational skills children must acquire in kindergarten is being able to write alphabet letters. Here we discuss children's willingness to compose messages designed to meet specific purposes. Kindergartners, of course, cannot write conventionally, but they can dictate a composition for their teacher to write during shared writing (see Chapter 1 for examples of shared writing). They can pretend to write and read their writing, and they can, eventually, invent spellings to write independently as did many of Suzanne's children (see Figure 1.1).

Pretend Writing in Kindergarten

Many kindergarten children are willing to pretend to write, especially when they engage in dramatic play with appropriate props. Figure 3.9 presents a grocery list that Micah wrote as he played with two other friends in the home and grocery store dramatic play centers in his classroom. His teacher stocked both the home center and the grocery story center with lots of props to suggest reading and writing including pads of paper with pencils, telephone message pads at each center near telephones, grocery store coupons, grocery ads from newspapers, and checkbooks in wallets and purses. Micah read his list to the teacher: "apples, crackers, bouquet, pig, cake, candy." While his writing is unconventional, Micah did read one word for each line of text that he wrote. It is also interesting that he included a pig in his grocery list! Stocking a dramatic play center with lots of props for reading and writing provides teachers with many opportunities to learn about their children's use of writing strategies such as Micah's strategy of reading a word for a line of written text. Teachers can observe in the dramatic play center to watch the different ways children pretend to use print. For example, children can pretend to write messages, lists, or invitations.

Teachers can also observe as children write in the writing center and invite them to read what they have written. These observations provide many opportunities to discover children's awareness of linearity, alphabet letters and features, and the match between written and spoken texts.

Writing Different Genres

Another way that kindergartners write is by copying or asking for spellings. Figure 3.10 presents one kindergartner's story composition. She told the story to a parent volunteer who began to write; Marie announced that she would write it herself and asked the volunteer to spell the first word. Marie continued to write her entire story as the volunteer spelled each word. Notice that Marie wrote her words in a list-like format. This is likely because she was emphasizing her awareness of words rather than a

FIGURE 3.9. Micah writes a grocery list (*apples, crackers, bouquet, pig, cake, candy*).

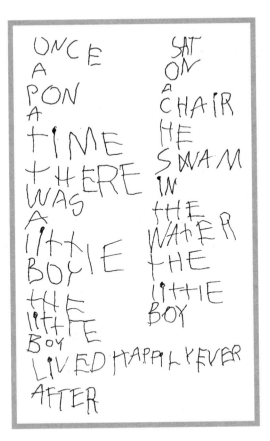

FIGURE 3.10. Marie's story.

lack of awareness of the linear nature of story text. The last line of her story was written in linear format. Also note the Marie used more upper-case than lower-case letters. While this writing sample provides a great deal of information about Marie's foundational knowledge (she knows and can write alphabet letters and is aware of words), it also provides information about Marie's unconscious awareness of the elements found in particular genres of literature.

Genres are the different kinds of literature we read aloud to children including ABC books, nursery rhymes, stories, and informational books. Each genre has it unique components and language uses. *Narratives*, or stories, have characters who have problems. They attempt to solve their problems as they encounter obstacles. A climax is reached just prior to the ending of the story where the problem is usually solved. Authors of stories use figurative language and sophisticated vocabulary to engage our senses. Marie's story actually barely qualifies as a story because it lacks the essential component of a problem. Instead Marie's character acts in a random way (he sat on a chair and swam in the water). However, Marie does include the formulaic story opening ("once upon a time") and closing ("he lived happily ever after").

In contrast, *information books* have very different genre elements than do stories (Donovan, 2001). Information books explain rather than merely describe phenomena of the social, physical, or natural world. They are written in the timeless present tense (rather than in the past tense as are stories) and include a topic presentation (often in the title or beginning sentence), description of attributes (e.g., descriptions of what animals look like, what they eat, or where they live), characteristic events (such as how animals capture their prey or care for their young), category comparisons (e.g., comparing two different kinds of animals), and a final summary in which all the information that has been presented is stated in a more general way. Information books often present superordinant vocabulary terms, cause-and-effect relationships, sequence of events, and comparison and contrast of ideas. Many of these relationships are not directly stated, but must be inferred. While information books may not include all of these genre elements or language characteristics, they will include several of them.

Teachers can help children compose information text during shared writing (see Chapter 4). The following is a shared-writing text a small group of children composed with their teacher:

Gatherers

Gatherers are people who go in search of food.

They get berries and apples from trees.

Teachers will notice that this composition includes a topic (Gatherers) and two descriptions of attributes of gatherers (they go in search of food and they get berries and apples from trees). The text includes general characters (Gatherers, they) rather than a specific character and uses the timeless present tense (they *are* people) as is expected in the information genre. These children obviously are not aware of their use of the information text genre, just as Marie was not aware of her use of the story genre. Nonetheless, they have heard their teachers read stories and information text enough so that they unconsciously are able to use the differing language structures in each of these genres (Duke & Kays, 1998; Purcell-Gates, McIntyre, & Freppon, 1995).

Independent Writing

At the beginning of kindergarten many children are not writing independently other than in pretend writing during dramatic play. However, by the end of kindergarten all children are expected to write independently using invented spelling with at least the *boundary phonemes* (first and last phonemes) spelled with reasonable letter–sound matches (Morris et al., 2003). Figure 3.11 presents two compositions Kristen wrote, one at the middle of kindergarten and the other at the end of kindergarten. The first composition was completed with her teacher's help during

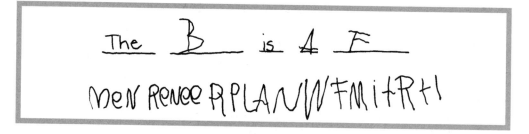

FIGURE 3.11. (top) Kristen composes during winter of kindergarten (*The bunny is a fish*). (bottom) Kristen composes at the end of kindergarten (*Me and Renee are playing with my turtle*).

kid writing (we describe this technique in Chapter 4). The teacher first helped Kristen say the sentence she wanted to write and then drew a horizontal line for each of the words. The teacher helped Kristen write the words she could, and wrote herself words that she believed were beyond Kristen's ability. For words she believed that Kristen could spell, the teacher said the word slowly, emphasizing and then segmenting the beginning phoneme. Kristen spelled the word *bunny* with B and the word *fish* with F. Her teacher told her the word *a* was spelled A and Kristen wrote it. The teacher wrote the word *The* and the word *was*.

Kristen's first composition included five words, of which she spelled two words. This sample demonstrates that Kristen is a beginning invented speller (also called "late emergent speller"; see Bear, Invernezzi, Templeton, & Johnston, 2004) because she occasionally uses letter–sound relationships to write a salient phoneme in words. She was able to select an appropriate consonant letter for a salient phoneme in two words with the strong support of her teacher. The teacher did much of the phonemic awareness work by segmenting the beginning phoneme for Kristen.

Figure 3.11 also presents a composition that Kristen wrote with support at the end of kindergarten. She wrote this sample one day when a parent volunteer sat with Kristen and several other children at the writing center. The teacher had just taught a lesson demonstrating how to listen all the way through words to detect three or four sounds, especially long-vowel sounds. Kristen asked the volunteer to help her spell. The volunteer suggested that Kristen could write herself by listening to the sounds in the words. Then he said the first word, *me*, very slowly, while elongating its two phonemes. With this support Kristen spelled the word *me* conventionally (probably by listening to the sounds rather than by actual memory of the conventional spelling), spelled the word *and* with N, and knew how to spell her friend's name *Renee*. She spelled the word *playing* as PLAN, the word *with* as WF, the word *my* as Mi, and the word *turtle* as tRtl. This writing sample demonstrates that Kristen has made progress as a writer and a speller during kindergarten. She spells long vowels (in the words *playing, me,* and *my*), spells blends (*pl* in *playing*), and hears up to four phonemes in a word (in the spellings of PLAN and tRtl). This is a significant advancement over only spelling a beginning phoneme with single consonant letters as she did in the middle of kindergarten. She now would be considered a letter-name alphabetic speller (Bear et al., 2004) because she routinely uses letter–sound correspondences, including vowels, and occasionally spells consonant blends.

SUMMARY

A few children come to kindergarten already knowing many of the foundational skills of reading and writing. These children recognize many alphabet letters, can write both their first and last names, know some letter–sound associations, and may be able to use this knowledge to begin spelling words using invented spellings. They eagerly participate as the teacher reads aloud by making comments and answering questions, often drawing insightful conclusions. During small-group reading instruction, they quickly memorize text, learn some sight words, and use strategies to read other unknown words.

Unfortunately, many children enter kindergarten with very few foundational literacy skills in place. They identify only a few, if any, of the alphabet letters, are insensitive to rhyming words, and do not pretend to write during their dramatic play. They seem disinterested during storybook read-alouds and may wriggle and bump other children or attempt to play with toys as the teacher reads. Regardless of children's entry skills, all children are expected to reach high levels of achievement by the end of kindergarten. The purpose of this book is to provide information for teachers on appropriate instructional activities and routines that will guarantee that all children develop the critical foundational skills they need in order to be successful in first grade and beyond.

CHAPTER 4

WHOLE-GROUP LITERACY INSTRUCTION

T eaching kindergartners the foundations of reading and writing occurs in whole- and small-group instruction. In this chapter we describe four research-based reading and writing teaching routines that kindergarten teachers should use daily during whole-group instruction. These include interactive read-alouds, shared reading, shared and interactive writing, and kid writing (Feldgus & Cardonick, 1999). These whole-group literacy teaching routines allow teachers to read *to* children (interactive read-alouds), read *with* children (shared reading), write *for* children (shared writing), and write *with* children (interactive writing). More importantly, these routines provide opportunities for children to acquire strong literacy concepts within the contexts of actual reading and writing. These instructional routines allow children to read and write independently as they reread books their teachers have read aloud during shared reading and as they write on their own in kid writing.

READING BOOKS ALOUD

Reading books aloud is one of the most enjoyable of all literacy experiences. Each read-aloud in kindergarten should be planned so that children experience the joy of good literature. However, reading aloud also provides opportunities to teach many different literacy skills. In order to capitalize on the potential for teaching literacy knowledge and skills during book read-alouds, teachers use special reading techniques. There are two basic techniques for reading books aloud to young children: interactive read-aloud techniques and shared-reading techniques. These two kinds of reading techniques serve different purposes, use different materials, and require different activities. *Interactive read-aloud techniques* are used to help children acquire new vocabulary, use comprehension strategies, and explore the literary components of various genres of literature. These techniques are appropriate when reading more complex picture storybooks or informational books when the focus is on understanding the story or informational content of the book. Interactive read-alouds involve an active exchange between teacher and children. Teachers read, but they also make comments and ask questions. Children listen, but they also answer questions, make predictions, and offer responses in the form of comments, questions, and enactments (Sipe, 2002). Books read with interactive techniques are reread, and the focus on rereading is strengthening vocabulary, extending comprehension, and learning more about literary elements.

In contrast, *shared-reading techniques* are used to help children learn alphabet letters, rhyming words, or concepts about print and books. These techniques are appropriate when reading aloud predictable books such as nursery rhymes or poems when the focus is on learning how print works and understanding the connection between the words spoken while reading and the print. Shared reading involves children in a different kind of participation than in interactive read-alouds. Teachers read and children listen, but children also are encouraged to chant along with the teacher as she reads. Thus, children share reading aloud with the teacher. Children may also predict, answer questions, and offer comments that demonstrate comprehension; however, the major focus of shared reading is learning concepts about print, rhyming words or words with the same beginning sound, or letters and letter–sound relationships. Books read during shared reading are also reread frequently so that their texts are memorized by the children. Using both interactive read-aloud and shared reading techniques is important in kindergarten literacy instruction.

INTERACTIVE READ-ALOUDS

Interactive read-alouds are carefully planned so that children and teachers talk about a book before, during, and after it is read. During these discussions, teachers insert definitions of a few vocabulary words and listen carefully to children's comments and questions so that they can clarify misunderstandings and expand responses. Teachers also ask questions, but they are careful not to ask so many questions that interactive book reading merely becomes a question-answering activity.

Teachers should read at least one book daily using interactive read-aloud techniques. Books selected for interactive read-alouds should be challenging in terms of their content and vocabulary; therefore, they provide many opportunities for children to grapple with a book's content (Beck & McKeown, 2001). Teachers should gradually increase the complexity of books they select for interactive read-alouds, and select from a variety of genres including stories (folktales and fairy tales, realistic fiction, and fantasy) as well as information books (Pappas & Barry, 1997; Richgels, 2002).

Value and Purpose of Interactive Read-Alouds

Research has demonstrated that using interactive techniques during read-alouds allows children to develop several literacy concepts and skills. Through listening to stories read aloud, watching television and movies, and engaging in personal and family storytelling activities, children acquire concepts about the literary features that are included in all stories (van den Broek, 2001). They include literary features in their retellings of stories and information text they have been read (see Figures 3.4, 3.5, and 3.6 for retellings of a story). The features found in stories or narratives include characters, settings, problems, actions, and resolutions (Stein & Glenn, 1979). The basic building block of narratives is a goal-based episode that is initiated by a problem and resolved through goal-directed actions aimed at solving that problem—that is, characters set goals, which are often implied, in order to solve a problem.

Children also gain awareness of the literary features included in information books such as the use of timeless present verbs and generalized rather than specific characters (Donovan & Smolkin, 2002; Duke & Kays, 1998). Information books include a topic presentation, as found in the title of the book *Houses* (Jeunesse & Delafosse, 1995). Informational books may also include descriptions of various aspects of the topic (e.g., houses are made of stone, mud, and straw), characteristic events related to the topic (e.g., to build a home you buy land and get a permit to build), or comparisons of the topic to other topics (e.g., children can build pretend cardboard-box houses compared to adults who buy or build real houses). Children who have strong concepts of stories and informational genres comprehend better (van den Broek, 2001). Therefore, reading aloud books from a variety of genres and drawing attention to their literary features provides children with systematic comprehension instruction.

Research has also shown that interactive techniques increase children's vocabulary learning and their comprehension. Teachers increase vocabulary learning when they pause to insert definitions and when they gather and lead discussions about objects and photographs related to a book's vocabulary. Comprehension is extended when children answer questions requiring them to analyze and explain events in books (Dickinson & Smith, 1994; Hargrave & Senechal, 2000; Reese & Cox, 1999).

Therefore, teachers should have in mind three purposes for interactive read-alouds. Listening to books as they are read aloud using interactive techniques helps children:

1. Gain new vocabulary and concepts.
2. Develop strategies for comprehension.

3. Acquire understandings about the literary features of a variety of genres.

Interactive Read-Aloud Techniques

There are four components included in interactive read-alouds: book introduction, vocabulary-enhancing techniques, comprehension-enhancing comments and questions, and after-reading discussion.

Book Introductions

Book introductions vary depending on the genre being read. In planning an introduction to a storybook (including realistic fiction, fantasy, or folktales), teachers read through the book and identify the main characters and their problems and goals. For example, *Dora's Eggs* (Sykes, 1997) is a story about a hen who has laid eggs for the first time. She does not seem to realize that chicks will hatch from her eggs and she is envious of the other farm animals' babies because they can walk, tumble, and snuggle. Dora gets more and more despondent when none of the other animals will come to visit her eggs because they are too busy taking care of their own babies. Eventually, Dora's eggs hatch and she is very proud of her new babies. All the other farm animals admire her chicks. Dora's problem in the story is that she is unaware that her eggs will hatch into live baby chicks. This causes her to be jealous of the other animals and their babies.

Teachers use the characters' problems, their goals, and major events in the story as a guide to construct a three- or four-sentence introduction that will help kindergartners get ready to understand this particular story's problem and events. The introduction either explicitly states or strongly implies the main problems and goals in the story. For example, a good introduction for *Dora's Eggs* is: "In this story you are going to meet a hen who is laying eggs for the first time. Because she has never laid eggs before, she does not realize what is inside those eggs. She is very envious, that means jealous, of the other babies in the farmyard. Let's see what happens to Dora and her eggs."

In planning an introduction to an information book, teachers first decide whether they will read all or only a portion of the book. Teachers may read some books all the way through including concept books such as *Houses* (Jeunesse & Delafosse, 1995) or books that explain a phenomena such as *Why Do Leaves Change Color?* (Maestro, 1994). Or they might decide to read only a portion of longer and more complex books such as *Dinosaurs Everywhere!* (Harrison, 1998). Book introductions for information books should provide an overview of the major concept that is covered in the book or portion of the book to be read along with an introduction to critical technical vocabulary. For example, *Why Do Leaves Change Color?* explains the process by which leaves stop producing chlorophyll during the fall, which allows other pigments already in the leaf to be seen for the first time. A good introduction for this book is: "We are going to be learning about something inside a leaf that is called chlorophyll. Why don't you say that word with me. *Chlo-*

rophyll. Chlorophyll is the part inside of leaves that gives them the green color. Leaves are green because they have chlorophyll inside them. But leaves have something else hidden inside them besides chlorophyll, and that is the secret for why leaves turn a different color. Let's find out what leaves do when they are alive and why they die. It is just before leaves die that they turn a different color."

Vocabulary-Enhancing Techniques

Children's books provide a wealth of new concepts and vocabulary. To take advantage of the vocabulary-learning opportunities in books, teachers must be deliberate about selecting words to highlight and clarify while they read. Before reading the book aloud, teachers read through the entire book and select four to eight vocabulary words or phrases to explain during reading. Teachers select words and phrases that are slightly more sophisticated than the words found in children's spoken vocabularies. These words should be critical to the story and likely to be related to everyday experiences (Beck, McKeown, & Kucan, 2002). If the book does not include sophisticated vocabulary, teachers should insert some additional words into the story as they read aloud. Once vocabulary words and phrases are selected, teachers decide how to explain or clarify their meanings for young children. Teachers can clarify or expand word and phrase meanings in one of four ways:

1. Inserting a short phrase or sentence that defines or explains a word as they read the text.
2. Pointing to salient parts of the illustration that help clarify a word or phrase meaning.
3. Using dramatic gestures.
4. Using voice to demonstrate meaning.

It only takes a few moments to plan these activities, but the most effective read-alouds are ones in which teachers decide which of the vocabulary-enhancing techniques they will use and plan short definitions, where needed. For example, in *Henny Penny* (Galdone, 1968) teachers may decide to insert the words *foolish, ordinary, mistake,* and *sly* as well as to highlight the word *feast* which is included in the story text. To explain the meanings of *foolish* and *ordinary* the teacher could point to the illustration where Henny Penny is first running to tell the king the sky is falling and comment: "She is really foolish. She believes that the sky is going to fall down. Look at her running without really thinking. She is very foolish. If she would only look down at the ground, she would see that something very ordinary fell on her head. I'm going to turn back a page and point to the very ordinary, everyday thing that fell on her head. What was that ordinary thing?" After children identify the acorn, the teacher could turn ahead to the next page and further comment: "There goes that foolish hen who didn't stop to think. She is making a big mistake, isn't she?" On the last page of the story the fox and his wife and six baby foxes are smiling as they remember the wonderful feast they had that day. The teacher could pause after reading the sentence containing the word *feast* and simply insert a definition: "*Feast* means a big meal, a big dinner. They really did have a big feast!"

Comprehension-Enhancing Techniques

In order to help children more thoroughly comprehend books, teachers carefully plan comments and a few questions that will scaffold children's understanding of a few events or ideas that otherwise may be difficult for them to grasp. Planning where to stop and ask a few questions helps to keep children focused on talking about the ideas included in the book rather than inserting comments that draw attention away from the story (Beck & McKeown, 2001). First, teachers select a few points in the book (about three or four) that they think might by confusing to children or where children should be making important inferences. At these critical points, teachers plan to make explanatory comments and then ask one or two questions that will help children gain better understanding of the events or ideas or make important inferences.

For example, a critical event in *Henny Penny* occurs when Henny Penny and her friends meet Foxy Loxy, and he praises them for going to the king with their information. However, he informs them that he knows a shortcut. All good readers infer immediately that the birds are in danger because the fox really has no intention of helping them reach the king. The fox is tricking the birds into thinking he is helpful when he is really a threat to their safety. Good readers immediately predict that Henny Penny and her friends will fall into the fox's trap because they *are* rather foolish! Teachers should pause at this event in order to make sure that children do make those inferences and predictions. In order to make sure children engage in these comprehension activities, teachers make some comments followed by probing questions. For example, teachers might read the text and then pause to say: "I'm thinking that the fox is sure trying to be helpful. He is going to show Henny Penny and her friends a shortcut. That is helpful. But you know, I'm wondering about that. I'm thinking foxes are usually pretty sly. They are tricky. Do you think this fox is trying to be helpful or do you think he might be trying to tricky? What do you think the fox is thinking?" After listening to several children answer this question, the teacher might prompt children to predict what will happen next: "Do you think Henny Penny knows that Foxy Loxy is being sly? Will she follow the fox?"

Questions should be carefully crafted because different kinds of questions encourage children to use different comprehension strategies. *Comprehension strategies* are mental activities that readers use to think about events or ideas while they construct understandings about text. For example, effective readers connect information they hear in a book to prior information—information they already know. This mental action allows readers to elaborate on or call to mind additional information about the content that might not be stated directly in the story but which they know from their own experiences. If a book describes a boy riding in a car to school, children call to mind what they already know about going to school in a car. They can mentally picture getting in a car, buckling a seat belt, perhaps fighting with a sister or brother, and listening to the car radio. Calling to mind this mental information allows children to make inferences and judgments about characters and their actions. If the book states that the brother always gets to sit in the front seat, this might prompt a child to infer that the brother is older, bossier, and much resented.

Questions that prompt children to *infer* call for children to bring to mind information that is not directly stated in the text or shown in the illustrations. For example, children have to infer when they speculate on the unstated internal thoughts and feelings of characters. Questions such as "What do you think [character] is thinking?" or "I wonder why [character] decided to _____?" prompt children to infer character thoughts and motivations—why they act as they do. Being able to infer what characters are thinking and feeling is critical for understanding a story plot. Asking a few inference questions is important at the conclusion of first read-alouds, but they should be asked even more frequently during second, third, and fourth rereadings.

Another kind of question prompts children to anticipate or *predict* upcoming events in stories or informational text. Teachers ask children, "What do you think will happen next?" or "What will [character] do now?" Effective prediction questions are asked in the middle of the story. Once children begin to understand a character's thoughts and motivations, they can better predict what that character might do next. A special kind of prediction question is when children are invited to speculate on what characters will do beyond the story. For example, children can be invited to predict what the king might have said if Henny Penny had actually made it to the castle and told him the sky was falling.

Another comprehension strategy involves *explaining why* events occur or characters act as they do. Teachers ask questions that help children analyze a character's thoughts or feelings in relation to his or her actions; this kind of thinking is difficult for kindergartners but is critical for reaching higher levels of comprehension. Teachers prompt this kind of thinking by asking questions such as "I wonder why [character] wanted to _____?" These kinds of questions are most effective at the end of a story as a review of why characters acted in particular ways.

Discussion after Reading

After reading, teachers ask one or two questions to initiation a discussion in which children explain why events occurred as they did. This kind of analytical discussion, about *why* things happened as well as *what* things happened, is especially important in increasing children's vocabulary and comprehension (Dickinson & Smith, 1994). For example, teachers can ask children: "I'm wondering why Foxy

Loxy didn't just jump on those silly birds and eat them? Why did he try to fool them by telling them he knew a shortcut?"

After-reading discussions should also review the vocabulary words selected for focus (Beck & McKeown, 2001). Teachers can review the vocabulary in *Owl Moon* (Yolen, 1987) by using questions such as "Who can remember the words the author used to describe the snow in this book?" Or teachers can pause for children to supply important vocabulary words. For example, a teacher might say: "When the owl flew away, he (using the dramatic movement of flapping arms to prompt children's use of the word *pumped*) pumped his wings."

Reading a Book for the Second and Third Time Using Interactive Techniques

Good books are well loved; children want to hear them read again and again. Therefore, teachers should also plan to reread books frequently during whole- and small-group activities. When reading a book for the second or third time, teachers can take advantage of the children's familiarity with the book to increase the amount of conversation from children. In fact, the amount of children's participation during interactive read-alouds should substantially increase during the second and third rereadings. During second and third interactive rereadings teachers should actively monitor who contributes to the discussion to make sure all children have several opportunities to participate. In contrast, many children during the first reading may be silent as they attempt to understand the story. Reading books the second and third time allows children who are more reluctant to talk and especially English language learners a better opportunity to contribute to the book conversation before, during, and after reading.

During a second and third interactive read-aloud teachers introduce the book by guiding children to recall events of the story or important points of an information book. During reading teachers can continue to prompt for recall. After reading a page in the book, teachers can say, "Who remembers what happens next?" During second and third rereadings, teachers prompt children to make more comments, connections, and explanations by asking more questions requiring explanation and connections between the event in the books and children's experiences. Because the children know the story—for example, the story of *Henny Penny*—they are not distracted by talking about where they have seen acorns. Teachers will continue to emphasize the four to eight vocabulary words selected during the first reading by inserting the same definition or asking children to define the word. They may insert definitions for a few new vocabulary words not discussed during the first reading. Discussion after reading a book for the second or third time can focus on retelling favorite parts, identifying interesting words or phrases, making connections to children's lives or events in the community, or comparing events and characters to those found in other books.

Second and third rereadings should also focus on the special literary features of stories or informational books. Teachers can ask children to recall the main characters, identify the problem in the story, and notice changes in settings. They can help children summarize all the actions that were attempted in order to bring a resolution to the problem. Using words such as *characters, problem, setting, actions* and *events,* and *resolution* are important for helping children build a strong concept of story. Teachers can alert children to watch for captions in illustrations or labeled drawings as they reread favorite informational books.

Reading Informational Books Using Interactive Read-Aloud Techniques

There is an abundance of high-quality informational books that are appropriate for kindergartners. These books have limited text, some specialized and technical vocabulary, and engaging illustrations and photographs on topics of interest to children. However, teachers must be deliberate in seeking out these books to include in their interactive read-alouds. Many teachers select stories more frequently than information books, and most classroom libraries have fewer informational books than stories (Duke, 2000). Teachers can extend the number of informational books they include in interactive read-alouds by using these techniques as a part of social studies or science theme study. A list of appropriate information books for interactive read-alouds is included in Appendix A.

Because of their format, teachers can read informational books all the way through or can choose to read only a portion of the book. Regardless of how teachers read information books, their planning for these kinds of text should be just as thoughtful and deliberate as their planning for reading storybooks. Book introductions are carefully organized, vocabulary is selected and definitions are crafted, and questions are planned before reading. Because information books are often full of technical vocabulary, effective teachers are careful to select a few of these words, the ones central to understanding the concepts presented in the book, for attention. During reading, teachers can stop to define a term briefly and then reinforce the meaning of the technical word by asking questions. Teachers can use the same vocabulary-enhancing strategies discussed for use in reading storybooks aloud.

Many informational books explain phenomena—for example, how an earthquake occurs or why a spider spins a web. Events and ideas in these texts are connected to one another through cause-and-effect relationships that most often are not explicitly stated. Therefore, teachers need to make comments to clarify the ways in which ideas in a text are connected to one another (Smolkin & Donovan, 2002). Teachers should use words and phrases such as "because," "as a result," and "that causes." With informational books, teachers should stop reading frequently and summarize the information that has been previously presented. This continually reminds children of the sequence of events and the causes and consequences of these events. As they read, teachers should stop to define a term briefly and then reinforce how the text provides definitions: "This part of the text tells me the meaning of the word *chlorophyll*. Let me read it to you slowly."

Helping children explain a sequence of events after reading is critical when reading information books aloud. This activity reinforces children's awareness of the unique features of information text including its generic nouns (*penguins* vs. "Tacky the penguin") and timeless-present verbs ("swim in the water"). Teachers can carefully guide the retelling of information books and help children use the new technical vocabulary during their explanations, especially as a part of second or third rereadings.

As with all texts used in interactive read-alouds, informational books should be placed in the library corner for children's independent exploration. Placing books in a special location in the library corner along with a few props encourages children to visit the center and use the props to talk about the book or pretend to read it as they browse through the book independently. For example, one teacher put a copy of the book *Dinosaurs Everywhere!* (Harrison, 1998) along with several plastic dinosaurs in a special plastic basket she uses to house interactive read-aloud books. After books are read interactively, children can be invited to respond to books using art, writing, and drama either during whole-group activities, center time, or in small groups. Teachers can place special materials in a variety of centers to encourage children's responses to specific books. For example, teachers can put small bottles of puffy paint to make webs in response to *The Very Busy Spider* (Carle, 1984) or sponges and paint to respond to *One Potato: A Counting Book of Potato Prints* (Pomery, 1996) in the art center. Teachers can put a variety of leaves and nuts in the science center for children to sort and examine with a magnifying glass after reading *Autumn Leaves* (Robbins, 1998) and *Why Do Leaves Change Color?* (Maestro, 1994). They can place a scarf, a woolen hat, snow boots, a flashlight, and a stuffed owl in the dramatic play center to encourage dramatizations of *Owl Moon* (Yolen, 1987). A variety of stuffed animal and doll replicas of book characters are commercially available that teachers can place in the library corner to encourage further responding to books.

SHARED READING

Comprehension is always the ultimate objective of reading; however, some books are more easily understood by children and do not require extensive vocabulary- or comprehension-enhancing techniques. Many books are intended to draw attention to language rather than to content. Alphabet books fit this category. These books do present new vocabulary and content—for example, kindergartners learn to connect their prior experiences with fruit to learn about mango and kiwi—but alphabet books appropriate for kindergarten focus attention on letters and objects rather than on complicated events or processes. Nursery rhymes and other books with rhythm and rhyme are also examples of books that are easily understood and draw attention to language over content. For example, teachers are more likely to encourage children to recite the rhyme and to identify rhyming words when reading *Humpty Dumpty* than they are to ask a question about why Humpty Dumpty fell off the wall.

Repetitive or pattern books are another kind of book that children easily understand due to their repeated words, phrases, and events. These books encourage children to chime right in and repeat the interesting language of the text. Books such as alphabet books and predictable books elicit high levels of child interaction right from the very first reading. Teachers will read these kinds of books aloud using shared-reading techniques in order to capitalize on their potential for teaching alphabet recognition, rhyme, or concepts about print.

Value and Purposes of Shared Reading

Reading alphabet books is one way that children learn about alphabet letters (Murray, Stahl, & Ivy, 1996). Alphabet books most useful for kindergarten instruction have a page for each letter, the letter is prominently displayed, and there are only a few illustrations of familiar objects for each page. The objects in the illustrations should begin with the letter's most basic letter–sound association (Murray et al., 1996). Vowels can often be problematic in alphabet books. For example, a picture of an automobile for the *A* page is not helpful to teach the two most basic sounds associated with that letter (long /a/ and short /a/). Unusual objects are also not helpful. For example, one alphabet book features an opossum on the *O* page, and each time a child read this book he said, "*O* is for *mouse*" (Yaden, Smolkin, & Conlon, 1989).

Reading nursery rhymes and books with alliteration and rhyme also plays a critical role in children's acquisition of phonemic awareness. Children who know many nursery rhymes learn to read easier and more successfully than children who know few (Maclean, Bryant, & Bradley, 1987). Reading nursery rhymes or rhyming poems is usually included in lessons intended to teach awareness of beginning or ending phonemes (Byrne & Fielding-Barnsley, 1991).

Researchers have also demonstrated how shared reading, and a related type of reading called "fingerpoint reading," support children's concepts about print, especially their concepts about letters and words (Ehri & Sweet, 1991). *Fingerpoint reading* occurs when children attempt to point to printed words one by one, left to right across the page, while they recite from memory a predictable text. Not all children in kindergarten can fingerpoint read, although they get better at it during the year (Morris et al., 2003). At first children memorize the text (this is called *memorized pretend reading*), but they do not point at the printed words. They merely sweep across a line of text with their hands without even attempting to point to individual words (Ehri & Sweet, 1991). Later they do point to individual words, although they do not match the words they have pointed to with the actual words they are saying. Children who learn to fingerpoint read demonstrate higher levels of concepts about print and phonemic awareness (Morris et al., 2003).

Therefore, the purposes of shared reading techniques are to help children:

1. Recognize alphabet letters and associate sounds with letters.

2. Develop phonemic awareness skills such as identifying rhyming words or words with the same beginning sound.

3. Acquire concepts about print including book orientation, print directionality, and concepts about letters and words.

4. Learn to fingerpoint read.

Books Used in Shared Reading

Most teachers think of shared reading as the kind of reading teachers do when they read from enlarged versions of texts (big books or charts on which a poem or song is written). The book or chart is positioned so that children can see the text as it is read aloud. As children become familiar with the text, they are encouraged to chant it along with the teacher (Morris et al., 2003). However, shared-reading techniques can also be used when teachers are reading from regular-sized books. For example, teachers can use shared-reading techniques when reading alphabet books aloud or books with many rhyming words. Shared reading is not defined by the size of the book being read. Instead the technique of reading, either interactive or shared, is determined by the purpose of the read-aloud. Teachers can read from big books when their purpose is to build vocabulary and comprehension; however, they will use interactive techniques. Many big books are too complex for shared reading, and are better suited for interactive read-alouds. Teachers can also read from big books when their purpose is to develop concepts about print. These will be simpler books with less text to facilitate children's ability to track the print. The common element in shared reading, whether reading from big books or from regular-sized books, is that children are invited to read the text along with the teacher (which is not the case in interactive reading).

Teachers will select alphabet books, books with language play, predictable books, and appropriate big books to use in shared reading. Children need to be able to see the alphabet letters in alphabet books, but do not necessarily need to view the text. Thus, regular-sized books can be effective for shared reading when the letters are large, although big-book alphabet books can also be used. Similarly, children do not need to see the text in order to gain the benefits of a shared reading of a book with language play. When the intention is to develop phonological or phonemic awareness (e.g., identifying rhyming words or finding two words that begin with the same phoneme), children only need to listen. Therefore, teachers can use regular-sized books, but again, big-book formats could also be used. In contrast, when teachers intend to teach concepts about print, big books or enlarged charts must be used. Children must be able to see the text and observe as their teacher points to words left-to-right across the page.

Shared Reading Techniques for Reading Alphabet Books

Appendix A provides an extensive list of alphabet books that can be used in shared reading. Publishers also sell sets of 26 books wherein each book features one letter. Each page of these little books provides an illustration of an object beginning with that letter. Having at least one set of these little alphabet books is a critical tool for all kindergarten teachers. They can be used to focus on the name and shape of the letter as well as to introduce and reinforce letter–sound relationships.

When reading alphabet books aloud teachers pause after reading a page to make explicit the connection between the words, letters, and phonemes presented on that page. After reading a page of text in an alphabet book, teachers say, "The letter N tells your mouth to get ready to say /nnnnnn/ at the beginning of the word *nnnnnnnose*" (Murray et al., 1996). Notice that teachers say the letter name, isolate the phoneme associated with the letter, and emphasize that phoneme as they pronounce the word. Next, children should be invited to say the letter name, its phoneme in isolation, and its pronunciation in words. Teachers do this by modeling and inviting children to imitate. As teachers reread alphabet books many times, they gradually reduce the amount of support they provide children. They can pause before pronouncing the phoneme in isolation for children to recall and produce it on their own without imitating the teacher. Teachers then observe children to identify those children who can do this (and provide them with praise for doing so) and children who will need additional practice during small-group instruction.

To summarize, the shared-reading techniques for reading alphabet books aloud require teachers to read each page of the alphabet book while inviting children to chime in and say the text of that page along with the teacher. The teachers pause at the end of each page. They draw attention to the relationship between the letter name, its sound, and the sound in words on that page by saying a phrase like "The letter L tells my mouth to get ready to say /lllll/ at the beginning of the word *lemon*." They invite children to repeat the name of the letter and its sound and to pronounce words beginning with that letter and sound that are presented on that page of the book.

Shared Reading Techniques for Reading Language Play Books

Appendix A provides an extensive list of language play books appropriate for kindergarten including illustrated copies of Mother Goose rhymes, books with rhyming words, and books with alliteration. Shared-reading techniques for calling attention to rhyming words or words with alliteration also occur after reading a page of text. Teachers follow a four-step sequence to explicitly teach rhyme in literacy-focused read-alouds:

1. Before reading the book, teachers *define rhyming words* ("Rhyming words are words that sound alike at the ending of the words") and alert children that the book they will read will have many rhyming words: "You will hear some rhyming words as I read this book. After I read we will talk about them."

2. As they read the book, teachers pause *after* reading a page with two rhyming words, look at the children, and *identify the rhyming word pair* by saying something like: "I heard two rhyming words: *lake, cake*. They sound alike, *lake, cake*. You say the two rhyming words." If the page of text includes more than two rhyming words (*sheep, jeep, steep*), teachers will only identify two words. During the first reading of a rhyming-word book, teachers scaffold children's identification of rhyming word pairs by explicitly stating the two words and then inviting children to say them. Later, children may add the third rhyming word as teachers reread the book on another day. Kindergarten teachers who have children who already know rhyming words can skip this step. However, children who have not yet acquired this concept may need the step of imitation in order to develop the concept.

3. As teachers reread the rhyming book on the next day (the second reading of a language play book should occur the day immediately after the first reading), they pause after reading a page. On the second rereading teachers will provide less scaffolding of children's identification of rhyming words by *pausing after saying the first of the rhyming words*. The teacher will say something like: "I heard two rhyming words. *Lake* [pause for children to say *cake*]. Yes, *lake* and *cake* rhyme." Teachers pause after saying the first rhyming word to allow children an opportunity to supply the second rhyming word on their own.

4. On the third and subsequent rereadings of the book, teachers read a page and pause after reading the page. Now they provide even less scaffolding for children to identify the rhyming word pairs. They immediately *invite children to identify both rhyming words* by saying something like: "I hear two rhyming words," and then they pause for children to say *lake*, and *cake*. Teachers can extend this activity by inviting children to produce other rhyming words for the pair of words they have identified. At first many children may make up nonsense words. This is to be accepted and even encouraged. For example, teachers can challenge children to think up as many rhymes as they can for a single word such as *cake* and demonstrate coming up with *bake* and *pake*.

The same four-step shared-reading technique used to read rhyming books aloud is effective for reading books that have alliteration. However, teachers should take children one step further. Once children can supply two words with the same beginning sound (e.g., *fur, feet*), teachers should introduce children to segmenting or saying the beginning phoneme in isolation. First teachers can demonstrate for children how to isolate "the first little bit of sound" they hear in the two alliterative words: "I am going to say just a little bit of those words, the sound I hear at the beginning. It is *ffff* [/f/]. Now you say that sound. *Ffff*. Yes, I hear *fff* at the beginning of *fffur* and *fffeet*."

To summarize, the first step in shared reading is to read the text page by page and encourage children to chime in saying the text. Then teachers pause at the end of a page that has a rhyming word pair or a pair of words that begin with the same letter. They say, "I hear two words that rhyme [or begin with the same sound]," and invite children to identify those words. Over several readings of the same book and after children can identify rhyming words, teachers quickly invite children to make up additional rhyming words not in the book.

Shared Reading of Big Books and Charts

When the purpose of shared reading is to build concepts about books and print, teachers read from big books, pocket charts, or charts. These are displayed on an easel or hung from a stand so that children can see the printed text as it is read aloud. Big books and charts of poems or songs are appropriate for shared-reading activities only when

- ➢ The print consists of two or three lines of text per page (teachers cannot demonstrate the return sweep without two lines of text).

- ➢ Words are printed in fonts large enough for children to see easily.

- ➢ Word spaces are large and prominent.

- ➢ Some words repeat in the text.

- ➢ The text is short and easily remembered by children.

Appendix A provides a list of 50 big books (although some of these are more appropriate for interactive read-alouds than for shared reading).

Developing Concepts about Print

As teachers read from the enlarged print of a big book or chart in shared reading activities, they demonstrate many concepts about print (Clay, 1993b). Early on, teachers develop book orientation concepts by pointing out or inviting children to show the front and back of books, top and bottom of pages, and how to turn to the next page. They demonstrate how to open the book to the title page and then to locate the first page of the story. They also demonstrate print directionality concepts by pointing out that they read the left page before the right page. As they read, teachers use a ruler or pointer to sweep across the lines of print from left to right. Teachers make explicit that they will begin reading at the left on the top line of print, read across that line, and return to the left on the next line of print.

Shared-reading techniques used to develop these concepts are a mixture of introducing the book, reading aloud, inviting children to read along, and stopping to talk about the print concepts or inviting children to discuss them. To introduce books, teachers may invite children to predict what the book might be about, to point to the title of the book, and to tell what an author and illustrator does. Teachers can read the title page and perhaps invite children to count the number of words in the title. They can capitalize on a book's predictability to invite children to make predictions as they read aloud. The first time teachers read a book during shared reading, they talk about a concept they want to teach before starting to read (e.g., title page, author, dedication). Then they read the book, inviting some predictions or talking about some unfamiliar events in the story. The second time teachers read the book, they read all the way through, inviting children to read along. While they read, they refer to the concept about print previously taught or teach another one. Teachers might invite children to find words that begin with a particular letter, words or letters that repeat, or punctuation marks. Teachers can use transparent highlighter tape to highlight these concepts.

Teachers can make interactive charts to extend children's work with a poem or song. For example, a favorite song often written on a chart for shared reading is "A Hunting We Will Go." One line of this song is "We'll catch a little fox and put him in a box." Teachers often want children to substitute new words for *fox* and *box*, such as "We'll catch a little *cake* and put it in the *lake*." To make the chart interactive (and allow words to be substituted), teachers make small transparent pockets where the words *fox* and *box* would appear on the chart by taping a small rectangle of overhead transparency on the chart. Then as children think up substitutes, teachers write the words on the cards and slip them in the pockets. Or teachers may simply put the song on a pocket chart and have children substitute words.

After reading a big book or chart several times, teachers prepare pocket chart extensions. Pocket chart extensions allow teachers to demonstrate more complex concepts about words and letters. *Pocket charts* are large commercially available charts with transparent horizontal pockets that hold sentence strips. To prepare for shared reading using pocket charts, teachers create several sentence strips on which they have written several lines of text from a familiar song, poem, or predictable book. The first few sentences in a text make good selections for pocket chart shared-reading activities. For example, teachers may select the text "Rosie the hen / went for a walk / across the yard" (divided into three phrases) from the book *Rosie's Walk* (Hutchins, 1968). This sentence is printed on three sentence strips. Each word in the phrase is separated with large word spaces, and the strips are placed in three pockets of the pocket chart.

To prepare children to use shared reading of the pocket chart, teachers read *Rosie's Walk* several times using shared-reading techniques. Then teachers introduce the pocket chart and tell children that the words on the chart are from the beginning of *Rosie's Walk*. Next, teachers read the pocket chart several times while using a pointer to point under each word as they read. Children are invited to join in and read the sentence as the teacher points. Teachers are careful to provide interesting practice for children to reread the text—for example, by inviting children to whisper-read it, have only girls read it, or have only boys read it. It is critical that children become very familiar with the short text so that it is nearly memorized. Then children are given opportunities to point to the words as other children repeat the sentence (teachers usually need to guide children to point to the correct word as the sentence is spoken). Teachers can also invite children to use their hands to isolate just one word on the pocket chart, to match letters and words written on cards with letters and words on the pocket chart, or to find long and short words. Table 4.1 summarizes the concepts about print that teachers can teach during shared reading using both big books and charts and the pocket chart.

Fingerpoint Reading

Fingerpoint reading occurs when children say a memorized sentence while pointing to each word in the sentence. It is important that teachers not confuse fingerpoint reading with actual or conventional reading. In fingerpoint reading children are relying on memory and their concepts about print to match their voices with their eyes and hands. However, when children can fingerpoint read accurately, they often begin to recognize and actually learn to read by sight some words—especially such frequently repeated words as *the, was, is, he,* and *she.* Teachers can support this new reading ability by challenging children to use fingerpoint reading to locate target words in the text of a pocket chart. For example, children can be asked to read the *Rosie's Walk* sentence to locate the words *hen, for,* and *yard.*

Charts of short poems or songs make excellent texts for fingerpoint reading. Charts used for more advanced fingerpoint reading should have six to eight lines of texts with large and exaggerated word spaces. This requires children to memorize longer pieces of text in order to be able to attempt to fingerpoint read. Figure 4.1 summarizes the activities that can be used with a pocket chart to facilitate children's fingerpoint reading.

Once pocket chart activities are introduced in whole-group lessons, they should be moved into the letter and word area of the literacy center. Children should be encouraged and occasionally required to read from the pocket charts, to match words and letters, or to copy words from the chart. One kindergarten teacher regularly hangs large charts on the wall next to a pocket chart. She invites children to copy words from the pocket chart onto the large chart. After showing children digital photographs of various graffiti she found in the school neighborhood (Orellana & Hernandez, 1999), her children decided to call this activity *pocket chart graffiti.*

SHARED AND INTERACTIVE WRITING

Shared writing is an activity in which teachers help children cooperatively compose a message that teachers write on enlarged charts. As teachers write the message negotiated with the children, they talk about what they are doing, such as moving

TABLE 4.1. Concepts about Print That Can Be Taught during Shared Reading

Orientation to books
    Front and back of the book
    Top and bottom of a page
    Title
    Title page
    Author
    Illustrator
    Dedication page

Directionality
    Left page is read before the right page.
    After the right page is read, we turn to the next left page.
    Text is read from left to right (using left-to-right sweep).
    Text is read one line at a time (using return sweep to next line of text).

Letter and word concepts (these can also be taught using a pocket chart)
    Words are separated by spaces.
    Words are made up of letters.
    Words begin with a particular letter.
    Words are long (they have many letters).
        We can count the letters in words.
        We can pull words from a pocket chart and place them on a graph (e.g, words with 5 letters, words with 4 letters).
    Words are short (they have just a few letters).
    Words can be repeated.
    Words can be matched by their letters.
        We can match words to word cards and check first and last letter.
    Some words begin with a capital letter.
    First word (in a line of text or a title) comes before others.
    Last word (in a line of text or a title) comes after all the others.
    Words can be counted.
    Sentences end in punctuation marks.
    Periods mean stop, commas mean pause, and question marks mean an asking voice.
    Words can be substituted.
        We can substitute new words in a sentence that would make sense.

Learning the text

Read and reread the text many, many times.

Use choral-reading techniques to have different children read different lines of text (use different colors of marker on each line of text).

Have children use very short pointers or their finger to point to each word (long markers used by teachers to read big books are too awkward for young children; they need to get their finger in the text).

If children have difficulty memorizing, use fewer lines of text.

Add challenge by having more lines of text.

Anticipate what will be read before actually reading (stop reading before a line of text and ask children to say what this line of text says).

Using fingerpoint reading to locate and identify words

Demonstrate holding finger in place for longer words (teach two- and three-beat words—words that you have to hold your finger for two or three beats).

Demonstrate using fingerpoint reading to identify a word (turn the word card over so that there is a blank space for the word; (point to a word in the first line of text; say, "I'm going to use my finger to figure out this word"; demonstrate starting at the beginning of the line, fingerpoint reading, stopping at the word, then saying it).

Have children use fingerpoint reading to identify all the words in the first line of text.

Have children use fingerpoint reading to identify words in several lines of text (teach children to start either at the beginning of the whole text or at the beginning of a line of text and track to identify the word).

Demonstrate how to find a word (say, "I want to find the word *walk*. I can use my finger to find it. I just read until I hear the word." Demonstrate starting at the beginning of the text, fingerpoint reading, and stopping at the word *walk*).

Using first-letter clue (phonics) to monitor fingerpoint reading

Demonstrate how to use a first-letter clue to confirm a word after it is identified (after identifying a target word, e.g., *walk*, say, "I want to check that this word is really *walk*. What would be the letter I would expect that word to begin with?," pause for children to say *w*, turn the word card over, and check the first letter).

cont.

FIGURE 4.1. Fingerpoint reading activities with the pocket chart.

Have children practice using the first-letter clue to confirm words after they are identified.

Demonstrate how to use the first-letter clue to confirm a word after it is located (after locating a word, say, "I'll use the first-letter clue to make sure this word is *walk*. I know *walk* will begin with the letter *w*. So I'll check to make sure the word I've located starts with that letter").

Have children use the first-letter clue to confirm words after they are located.

FIGURE 4.1. *cont.*

over to leave a space for the next word or listening to beginning sounds to identify which letter they will write. After the message is written, teachers help children reread the chart. Eventually shared writing merges into interactive writing in which children write some portions of the message and teachers write other portions.

Purposes of Shared Writing

Shared writing demonstrates a great variety of concepts about print including that writers communicate ideas that can be written, generate ideas for writing by talking, change ideas and refine their language, and consider sequence structures. Children learn that print is written from left to right and from top to bottom in lines of text, and that words are composed of letters (Parkes, 2000).

Shared writing can also be used to help children recognize and write alphabet letters. Before writing a word, teachers can tell children what letter they will write. After writing a word, they can have children name the letters in the word. Later, when children can recognize several alphabet letters and have some directionality concepts, shared writing can be used to demonstrate the *alphabetic principle* (i.e., the awareness that printed letters in words are related to spoken sounds in words), and thus help children learn letter–sound relationships. Teachers will pause before writing a word, say the word slowly, and then say: "*Pppudding, pppppudding*. What sound do you hear at the beginning of that word?" After children isolate the /p/ phoneme, they will ask, "What letter should I write for that sound?"

Shared-Writing Routines

Shared writing grows out of any experience that prompts writing. For example, after taking a walk, children can compose a list of some of the objects that they observed on their walk. After reading a book during interactive or literacy-focused read-alouds, children can make a list of the book's characters or some of the story's events. Or a shared writing text may simply be a record of something a character has said. Figure 4.2 presents a shared-writing chart written after an interactive read-aloud of the story *Warthogs in the Kitchen* (Edwards, 1998). After reading, the teacher merely asked children to remember some interesting things the characters did. Other children remembered interesting words. Once the children had a chance to contribute to the discussion, then the teacher wrote a shared list of five ideas that many of the children had mentioned during the discussion. After writing and reading the list presented in Figure 4.2, the teacher extended the lesson by focusing on alphabet letter recognition. She circled the letter *o* and invited other children to *Step Up* to the chart and circle another *o*. When all the *o*'s were located, she circled an *e* and invited children to find more examples of that letter. As shown in Figure 4.2, the teacher used *Step Up* to draw children's attention to the alphabet letters *o, s, e,* and *w.* During *Step Up* teachers can invite children to circle a letter they know, circle two letters that are alike, or circle a particular target letter.

Whenever possible, teachers should make shared writing functional. For example, children can use shared writing to compose a get-well card to a child or assistant who is ill. To prepare children for pretending to have a yard sale in a home center, teachers can read yard sale notes in the newspapers and then help children compose a yard sale ad for a pretend newspaper and yard sale signs for their pretend neighborhood. Composing together these kinds of printed texts usually found in the home, but not in school, allows children to draw upon their untapped literacy knowledge (Duke & Purcell-Gates, 2003). These printed texts can include grocery or to-do lists, gift tags, coupons, baseball trading cards, toy catalogs, brochures, greeting cards, newspapers, and calendars.

The most effective shared-writing experiences for kindergartners result in texts that are very short so that they are quickly composed and written. Teachers should help the entire group of children compose the message rather than taking dictation from individual children. Allowing each child to dictate a message takes too long and results in a text that is too lengthy. Lists of only a few words or phrases, such as writing a list of some of the animals found in a story or a few of the kinds of trees described in an information book, are more easily written and more effective for build-

FIGURE 4.2. Shared writing for *Warthogs in the Kitchen* (Edwards, 1998).

ing early concepts about print. Short texts allow children to remember more of what they have written, which is critical for helping children reread the message. As the year progresses, shared-writing texts can become longer and more complex.

While the message is being written, teachers draw children's attention to a variety of concepts about print. They can say: "Put your eyes up here. I am going to start writing right up here." As they write, teachers naturally demonstrate the left-to-right progression of letters in words. Teachers can emphasize words and spaces by saying: "I just wrote the word *happy*. Now I have to write the word *birthday*. I'll scoot my marker over a little to make a space before I start writing that word." Teachers can teach the concepts listed in Table 4.1 as a guide for making decisions about what to teach as they write a shared-writing chart.

After writing the message, teachers guide children in rereading the text by pointing to each word and inviting children to read along with them (as they do in shared reading). Each shared-writing chart should be read at least three or four times. This is quickly accomplished when the text is kept short, and children can easily memorize its message. A few children might be invited to point to the words during rereading as is done in fingerpoint reading. Shared-writing charts can be posted around the classroom for other children to fingerpoint read during center time.

Another extension of shared writing, called *Write On*, can be used to teach alphabet letter writing. During a Write On activity, the teacher invites each child to step up to the shared-writing chart, point to a letter printed on the chart, name it (teachers can help identify the letter where needed), and then write it somewhere on the chart. When needed, teachers first model writing the letter on a dry-erase board to support the child's attempt. Children with more advanced concepts can be invited to locate a word they would like to write on the chart. Again, these charts can be placed in the letter and word area of the literacy center for children to write on during center time.

Figure 4.3 presents a shared-writing activity in which the children dictated to the teacher the objects they used in a sorting activity (the teacher had a basket of objects beginning with /b/ and others beginning with /m/ for sorting). After the shared-writing chart was completed, the teacher invited children two at a time to step up and write other *B* words on the chart. In most cases the teacher spelled these words for the children (because this teacher knew that most of the children could not yet invent spellings). However, at least one child wrote a word using invented spelling (spelling the word *big* as BYG). When the Write On activity was completed, the chart was hung in the letter and word area of the literacy center where children were invited to continue writing during center time.

Interactive Writing

As the year progresses, kindergarten teachers can take advantage of children's growing competency in writing to "share the pen" during shared writing

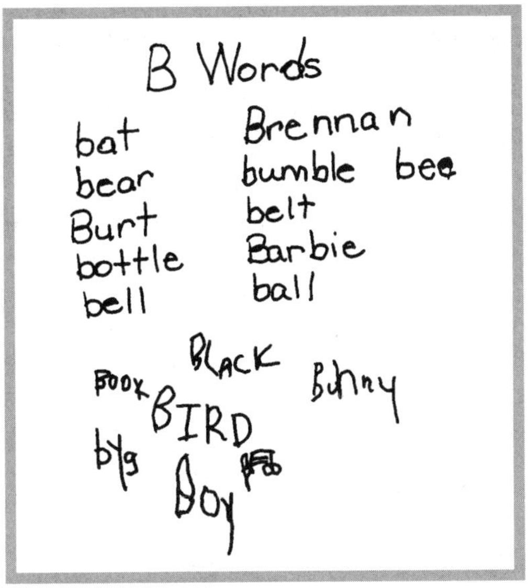

FIGURE 4.3. Shared writing and Write-On of B words.

(McCarrier, Pinnell, & Fountas, 2000). When teachers and children both contribute to the writing, shared writing becomes interactive writing. In *interactive writing* the children write portions of the text when teachers judge they can, and teachers write other portions that they know children will not yet know how to do. Children can write individual or groups of letters to spell portions of a word (when the whole word is unknown, but children do know letter–sound correspondences for parts of the word). Children might write the beginning or ending letter or write the ending of a word by using a familiar word family. Sometimes children write the entire word when they locate a spelling in the word wall or when they know the conventional spelling.

Two kindergarten teachers use this procedure daily to write an interactive calendar (Ritterskamp & Singleton, 2001). They prepare a large chart on a bulletin board or chalkboard to which squares of paper for each day of the month are paper-clipped. At the end of the day, children gather around the easel and the day's square of paper is clipped on ready for interactive writing. First the children recall important events of the day, and then they compose one sentence. Children are invited to write portions of words and whole words when they have located a spelling. The calendar entries are often reread as shared reading, and children refer to the calendar as a resource for spelling words during writing workshop.

KID WRITING

Kid writing (also called *guided invented spelling*; McGee & Richgels, 2003) is a systematic approach to helping children write independently (Bodrova, Leong, Paynter, & Hughes, 2001; Feldgus & Cardonick, 1999). Teachers model writing by demonstrating how to compose a short message and count the number of words in the message. They draw a line for each word they will write in the message. Then teachers demonstrate how to listen carefully to the sounds in each of those words. Children write letters for the sounds they hear in the words. Children reread what they have written, and teachers write the message with conventional spelling somewhere on the children's paper or on a sticky note attached to the paper.

Teachers end kid-writing lessons with a minilesson in which they teach a new concept about phonemic awareness, a new letter–sound relationship, or a new word family and how to use the word family to spell (rhyming words with the same spelling patterns such as the -et family including the words bet, jet, met, net, pet, and wet).

A form of kid writing called "scaffolded writing" has been successfully used in kindergarten classrooms (Bodrova & Leong, 1998). Researchers have shown that children gradually acquire an awareness of words within messages (by writing lines to represent the number of words that will be written) and then the ability to match one or two letters for phonemes in each word in the message.

Purposes for Kid Writing

Kid writing moves children from emergent writing into invented spelling. Emergent writing occurs when children pretend to write using mock letters, symbols, or letters. Their writing does not draw upon the alphabetic principle. On the other hand, invented spelling occurs when children write messages by carefully matching at least one letter with one phoneme in the words of their messages. When children invent spellings they demonstrate an awareness of the association between letters and sounds. Kid writing provides opportunities to teach letter–sound relationships useful for more sophisticated spelling. Later, in Chapter 5, we show how letter–sound associations (phonics) is taught for the purposes of helping children begin conventional reading. Thus, kid writing connects phonemic awareness and phonics in an authentic context for kindergartners—writing messages on their own.

There are three purposes that teachers keep in mind when conducting kid-writing activities:

1. They strive to increase children's phonemic awareness: their ability to hear individual phonemes and to segment beginning, ending, and middle phonemes in words.

2. They work to increase children's knowledge of conventional letter–sound associations: knowledge of consonant letter–sound associations, consonant digraph associations, and associations found in the spellings of familiar word families.

3. They attempt to increase children's awareness of the structures and language found in a variety of written text genres including, but not limited to, invitations, lists, graphs and charts, signs and labels, menus, alphabet books, counting books, and nonfiction accounts.

Kid-Writing Routines

To begin the kid-writing routine teachers demonstrate how to identify a topic to write about, draw a picture about that topic, and compose a message. Kid writing relies on children being able to compose a message and then hold that exact message in memory. Teachers demonstrate saying the message, then repeat it again. Then teachers write a line for each word in the message as they say the exact message one more time from memory. Next teachers demonstrate writing a variety of ways including emergent writing and invented spelling. Children learn that the lines for each word are "magic" (Feldgus & Cardonick, 1999). If children cannot think of any letters for the word, the *magic line* will just stand for the word. Therefore, the earliest form of kid writing consists of children drawing a picture, composing a message that remains constant throughout the activity, drawing a line for each word of that message, and then reading the message back from memory while pointing to each word line.

During the first day of kid writing teachers demonstrate using all three kinds of writing. For emergent writing they demonstrate stretching the word and saying it slowly, saying, "Um, I don't know any of those sounds so I'll choose some letters." Then teachers write one or two random letters. For writing using only the magic line, they demonstrate by saying, "I don't know a letter in this word, so I'll just let the magic line stand for it." For invented spelling, they demonstrate by saying the word slowly and stretching out the first sound in a word, then identifying an appropriate letter to spell that sound in the word. Then they demonstrate rereading their message by looking at the lines and remembering what they wrote. After the first day of kid writing, teachers continue to demonstrate stretching out words by saying them slowly enough so that children can hear prominent phonemes and write them on the magic lines.

Kid writing can be used as a whole-group activity but at the beginning it is easier to help small groups of children learn the routine. Children draw pictures, and the teacher sits with a group of children helping each of them compose a message. At first teachers will draw the lines for the words and help each child write letters on each line. They will have children reread their messages. Once children are familiar with this routine and know several consonant letter–sound relationships, children can draw their own lines for words and stretch out sounds in words for themselves. At the end of each kid-writing activity, the teacher provides a 5-minute minilesson. Minilessons focus on an aspect of writing that one child used that day (a new strategy for spelling that other children have not yet used) or information that many children needed help using during that day. Examples of topics for a minilesson include listening for sounds at the beginning and ending of words, listening for word families and using word family lists posted around the classroom to spell, and learning a new letter–sound relationship such as the spelling for the /ch/ phoneme.

As children become familiar with the routine, teachers can include kid writing in their daily schedule as journal writing. All the children have journals with several pages of unlined paper stapled together. Each day during journal time children get their journals, select topics, draw pictures, compose messages, draw lines for words in their messages, and then invent spellings for the words in their messages.

Teachers circulate among students helping them to compose, stretch out words, and reread. Because teachers cannot help all children during any one day's journal writing, they make a schedule that identifies which children will be helped during each day of the week. At the end of journal-writing time, teachers teach a minilesson.

Figure 4.4 presents a page of Darrell's journal. Darrell drew a picture of himself at the beach spreading out his towel. His teacher helped him to compose the message ("Me and my brother went to the beach"). After Darrell repeated the message, his teacher wrote eight lines, one for each word of the message. The teacher guided Darrell in restating his message again, pointing to each line as he said each word. Then the teacher directed his attention back to the first line and asked: "What is the first word you are going to write?" Darrell replied: "Me." His teachers said: "Say it slowly. What do you hear?" Darrell said the word somewhat slowly and his teacher demonstrated saying it even more slowly. Darrell heard first the /m/ phoneme and wrote M. Then his teacher asked: "Do you hear anything else?" She said the word slowly again. Darrell wrote e. His teacher continued to invite Darrell to say the word slowly and then demonstrated saying the word even more slowly. She encouraged Darrell to hear a second sound, and on most words he was successful. While he invented spellings for seven of the eight words in his message, he used the magic line to write one word, *the*.

Teachers use interactions with individual children during kid writing to help children stretch beyond what they can do on their own, as Darrell's teacher did. First, she let him attempt to stretch and spell. While she knew Darrell could sometimes hear the first sound in words on his own, he was more successful after hearing her stretch the word. She also encouraged him to hear another sound in the word, which she knew Darrell could not do on his own. With other children, the teacher encouraged children to listen all the way through a word for sounds. These children routinely spelled with boundary phonemes on their own. They needed a challenge of hearing nearly all the sounds in word in order to stretch beyond their current independent functioning.

Kid writing in journals may be further extended by making the journals more interactive. One kindergarten teacher frequently writes a response to children's journal entries (Hannon, 1999) in an activity she calls *dialogue journals*. She simply announced: "If you want me to write back to you in your journals, I will"

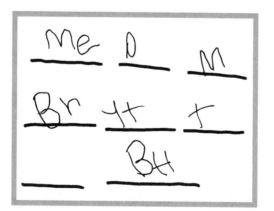

FIGURE 4.4. Darrell's kid writing (*Me and my brother went to the beach*).

(Hannon, 1999, p. 201). She took time to write a sentence or two back to children when they requested it.

As the year progresses journal-writing time can evolve into writing workshop (Behymer, 2003). During *writing workshop* teachers present a minilesson before children write. This minilesson can be used to demonstrate some aspect of a genre teachers expect children to use in their writing. For example, children can learn how to write informational books (see Chapter 1 for a description of using writing workshop to write informational books about dinosaurs), ABC books, counting books, how-to books, rhyming books, all-about books, or riddle books. They can learn how to conduct surveys and write the results or predict what will happen during science experiences and then record their observations. They can write silly menus, compare versions of stories, and compose want ads. During minilessons teachers read aloud examples of the genre and point out some of the salient aspects of the genre. One kindergarten teacher has children write a letter home to parents each week (LeVine, 2002). She demonstrates writing "Dear _____" and "Love, _____." She shows children how to write one sentence about what they have been learning and then ask one question. Parents are expected to write back answering the questions.

Figure 4.5 presents Quintavious's recipe for Yuck Soup written during kid writing after the teacher read the book *Yuck Soup* (Cowley, 1989) during shared reading. After reading the book, the teacher taught a minilesson during writing workshop where she modeled how to write a Yuck Soup recipe. Figure 4.6 presents a riddle composed later in the year during writing workshop. During a minilesson the teacher modeled how to write two ideas related to an object and then write the riddle question "What am I?." Madeline's riddle ("I am stinky. I go in the locker. What am I?") was accompanied by an illustration of a tennis shoe!

FIGURE 4.5. Quintavious's recipe for Yuck Soup. (*Yuck Soup: a hand, shoes, socks, toothbrushes*).

SUMMARY

Effective kindergarten teachers use interactive read-alouds daily to introduce new vocabulary words and engage children in using comprehension strategies by asking thoughtful questions. They guide children in explaining events from books after reading. They reread these books and guide children's retellings and extended discussions by connecting

FIGURE 4.6. A riddle (*I am stinky. I go in the locker. What am I?*).

events in books to their lives. Teachers also use shared reading daily to teach alphabet letter names and letter–sound associations, develop phonemic awareness of rhyme and beginning phonemes, and foster concepts about print. These books are read and reread so frequently that children memorize their texts and use them in their own independent reading. Table 4.2 summarizes the different purposes, techniques, and materials used in interactive and shared reading.

Teachers use shared and interactive writing to demonstrate concepts about print, to teach alphabet recognition, and to promote knowledge of letter–sound relationships. Through shared and interactive writing, children learn the different functions and features of various forms of printed text including invitations, thank-you notes, and grocery lists. In kid writing children learn to compose messages and spell words by using invented spelling. Their knowledge of phonics is extended. Each of these four instruction routines provides opportunities for children to acquire foundational concepts in reading and writing.

The instructional routines introduced in this chapter provide the "whole" of reading and writing. It is important for children to have opportunities to see how the "parts" of reading and writing (letters, phonemes, and words) fit within the larger whole of reading and writing stories, poems, riddles, lists, menus, and information books. Through interactive read-alouds, shared reading, shared and interactive writing, and kid writing children learn that reading and writing are about communicating ideas. Children who have a larger understanding of literacy as an act of communication seem to learn to read and write with more success than children who have little grasp of the real purpose for reading and writing (Purcell-Gates & Dahl, 1991). The activities presented in this chapter are specifically designed to allow children to grasp the all-important larger picture of what reading and writing are all about.

TABLE 4.2. Reading Aloud: Using Different Techniques for Different Purposes

Purpose/focus	Technique	Materials
Interactive Read-Alouds		
Develop vocabulary	Teachers select vocabulary; highlight meanings of words while reading.	Complex picture books, fantasy, realistic fiction, informational books, traditional literature (may be in big-book format)
Develop comprehension	Teachers introduce book. Teachers select places to comment. Teachers ask a few questions. Teachers guide discussion after reading (infer and explain questions). Teachers guide recall in second and third rereadings.	
Shared Reading		
Alphabet recognition	Children chant text. Teachers may read with pointer (if big book). Teachers pause at end of page to connect letter and sound.	Alphabet book in regular or big-book format
Identify rhyming words or words with same beginning phoneme	Children chant text. Teachers may read using a pointer. Teachers stop at end of page and call attention to rhyming words or words with same beginning phoneme. Teachers may ask questions. Children may predict.	Language play books in regular or big-book format
Develop concepts about print and books	Children chant text. Teachers point out concepts/print. Teachers read with a pointer. Teachers may ask questions. Children may predict.	Predictable books in big-book format or charts of songs or poems.
Fingerpoint read	Children memorize text on pocket chart and fingerpoint read (see Figure 4.1 for activities).	Pocket chart text

CHAPTER 5

SMALL-GROUP LITERACY INSTRUCTION

One of the most critical components of a kindergarten reading and writing program is small-group instruction. In this chapter we describe a model of instruction for small groups. We discuss how teachers can deliver lessons that help children learn the foundations of reading and writing: alphabet recognition, phonemic awareness, letter–sound relationships (i.e., phonics), spelling, decoding (i.e., figuring out how to read an unfamiliar word), writing compositions, and comprehension. We also describe how teachers help children use these skills in the context of guided reading: first during guided shared reading, then in guided fingerpoint reading, and finally in guided reading. We discuss the kinds of texts that children need for each of these kinds of reading. We end the chapter with a discussion of core-reading programs that teachers may be expected to use in their reading instruction in kindergarten.

TEACHING THE CONVENTIONS IN SMALL-GROUP INSTRUCTION

Chapter 3 described the kinds of knowledge that children are expected to develop in kindergarten. Table 5.1 presents a list of 15 end-of-the-year accomplishments that research suggests kindergartners are expected to master. These end-of-the-year accomplishments are a critical tool for kindergarten teachers. Teachers will use this list to select assessments (we will explain how to do this in greater detail in Chapter 7) and to determine the objectives of their instruction. Helping each child reach these high levels of knowledge assures that all children will begin conventional reading successfully.

In order to reach these end-of-the-year goals, most kindergartners will need guided reading instruction delivered in small groups. A few kindergarten chil-

TABLE 5.1. End-of-the-Year Kindergarten Literacy Accomplishments

Alphabet knowledge

  Recognize and write most upper- and lower-case alphabet letters fluently.

Phonemic awareness and phonics

  Isolate initial and final phonemes from spoken words.

  Associate phonemes/sounds with consonant letters (and consonant digraphs).

  Read words by blending new consonant letters to familiar word families.

  Segment and blend two- and three-phoneme words.

  Invent spellings with boundary phonemes (initial and last phonemes) and sometimes middle phonemes.

Concepts about print

  Locate and copy known words posted in the classroom (e.g., locate the words *the* or *Happy Birthday* for use during journal writing).

  Fingerpoint read short text so that spoken words are matched with written words of the text with one-to-one accuracy.

  Use tracking during fingerpoint reading to locate and identify words.

Oral comprehension and vocabulary

  Predict and infer during interactive read-alouds.

  Acquire new vocabulary from reading and other classroom activities.

  Willingly engage in dramatic play activities pretending to read and write for a variety of purposes (e.g., pretend to read newspapers or coupons, and write grocery lists or checks).

  Willingly retell or dramatize familiar stories (e.g., choose to retell stories with retelling props in the book center).

  Recount familiar stories with accurate details regarding the characters, settings, problem, and events using past tense.

  Recount familiar information books with accurate details including information about the topic and either characteristics, sequences, or comparisons related to the topic using timeless present tense.

dren may be able to develop these skills by participating in the whole-group routines we described in Chapter 4. However, most children will need small-group instruction where the teacher carefully prepares lessons that match children's individual needs and maximize all children's opportunities to participate. Some school districts may expect kindergartners to go even further in accomplishment than those we list. Therefore, it is critical for teachers to examine state and district curriculum guides and standards to determine what is expected in their state and district.

Selecting Children for Small Groups

Selecting children for small-group instruction in reading usually means that teachers group children together who have similar levels of knowledge. To do this, teachers will need to gather a great deal of information from assessments to determine children's accomplishments and needs. Different types of assessments will provide teachers with a composite picture of the child to help determine group placement. Chapter 7 describes the types of assessments that kindergarten teachers will use. Especially useful early during kindergarten are assessments of children's letter recognition, phonemic awareness, phonics, and concepts about print including fingerpoint reading. Later, teachers will add assessments of high-frequency word recognition, comprehension, and running records.

Alternate rank ordering is one way to assign children to groups before teachers have an opportunity to conduct thorough assessments. This method, based mainly on teacher judgment, allows teachers to form small groups during the early weeks of school. In order to use this technique, teachers list all the children in the class, placing the child judged as having the highest level of literacy knowledge at the top of the list, the child judged to have the lowest level of knowledge at the bottom of the list, and the other children in order of skill levels in between. To assign groups, teachers first determine the number of groups they intend to create—usually four or five groups allows for manageable group sizes. Then teachers select the children ranked first and last to start two different groups. They place the five or six children ranking highest together. Similarly, they place the lowest ranking five or six children together. Teachers continue working from the top of the ranking to the bottom to form four or five groups. Each time teachers select children for a group, they consider whether these children have skills similar enough to be in the same group. When the answer to that question is no, then teachers start a new group. After meeting with the groups created by alternative rank ordering several times, teachers make adjustments in group membership where needed. As children are assessed on a regular basis, their grouping placement may change.

Guidelines for Small-Group Instruction

Teachers are careful to place children in groups for instruction purposefully. Teachers group children by level of reading for small-group reading instruction, but also use other types of groups throughout the day so that students never associate themselves only with their small group for reading skills. Guidelines for small-group instruction in reading include:

1. Children are assessed regularly so that their group placement changes when their needs change.
2. The number of groups formed is not set. Instead, it is determined by the number of different levels of reading abilities represented in a given classroom. Typically there are four to six groups.

3. Materials selected for instruction should meet the needs of the students.

4. Activities provided for children who are not in small groups are often in centers. Children are actively engaged in interesting, productive work while they practice skills they learned in other lessons.

5. The teacher often writes notes to parents to take home. Each note suggests homework for the child and how parents can help.

What Does a Small-Group Reading Lesson Look Like in Kindergarten?

Teachers will keep in mind the needs of the children in each group in alphabet knowledge, phonemic awareness, phonics, and comprehension and vocabulary. Objectives for small-group lessons follow from what children need to learn. Teachers identify objectives based on what children need to know, provide direct instruction on those skills, and assess children's learning of those skills on a regular basis as a part of *systematic direct instruction*. Each lesson provides experiences directed at a variety of skills. A model of small-group instruction includes word study, contextualized text reading, and writing (Morris & Slavin, 2003; Reutzel & Cooter, 2004).

Word study involves systematic instruction in alphabet recognition, phonemic awareness, phonics, and word reading and decoding. Children learn to recognize alphabet letters, associate phonemes with letters, segment spoken words into phonemes, build new words by substituting new letters onto familiar word families, and decode and spell two- and three-phoneme words. Children may also learn some high-frequency sight words (i.e., words that are found frequently in all texts, including *the, is, for, and, he,* and *she*) and how to add suffixes to words (e.g., *-s* and *-ed*).

Text reading involves reading little books in which children use concepts about print, phonics, and decoding in the context of memorized reading or actual conventional reading. During text reading children participate in guided shared- and fingerpoint-reading activities, reread those texts many times, find and match words in the texts, and track print to locate words. *Writing* includes having children compose a sentence or two about what they have been reading, spell words using familiar patterns in word families, write a sentence dictated by the teacher, or participate in shared or interactive writing.

Small-Group Instruction in Action

To help understand the use of small-group lessons, we offer the following vignette from Mrs. Keefe's kindergarten classroom. Mrs. Keefe believes that small-group reading instruction is the only way she can learn what individual children know and what they need to learn in order to design her instruction. She has organized the class into four groups of five to six children each. Within each group the children have similar needs and are capable of achieving similar skills. Children frequently move from group to group based on Mrs. Keefe's ongoing assessment of their progress. She meets with each group three times a week for about 15 minutes.

A lesson could include word work such as working on a skill involving letter recognition, phonemic awareness, phonics, or word reading and decoding. The lesson also includes text reading such as reading a familiar text used in previous shared or guided reading, introducing a new text for shared or guided reading, and conducting word study activities for that text or developing comprehension skills associated with it. Lessons frequently include a writing activity. Mrs. Keefe tries to do some type of assessment with at least one child during each group meeting by listening to children's fingerpoint reading or oral retellings of stories to check on their comprehension. Later, when some children have begun conventional reading, she may do a running record of oral reading and recording errors to determine the skill needs of those children (see Chapter 7 for a description of running records). When the children are not working in small group with Mrs. Keefe, they are working independently in centers.

Before small-group instruction begins, Mrs. Keefe facilitates the beginning of independent center work. When students are working well on their own, she calls on her first group for small-group reading instruction. This is a group of children who are not yet reading conventionally; however, they do display considerable knowledge about the alphabet, phonemic awareness, and letter–sound relationships. In this lesson she works on helping children understand the text and fingerpoint read by tracking print. She begins her small-group lesson with a familiar little book that each child has in his or her baggie. She calls this "a book in a bag," and every day the children bring it to reading group. Each child points to the words as he or she chants the words of the text together.

Next, Mrs. Keefe teaches a minilesson to help the children use the strategy of first-letter clues to confirm whether a word fits the text. She writes one of the sentences from a new book that the children will read later in the lesson on a chart and leaves a blank for a word on which children can practice this strategy. She reads the sentence to the children and asks them to predict what word might make sense in the blank. She writes the words the children say, and they try each one in the sentence to be sure it makes sense. Next, Mrs. Keefe writes the first letter of the word in the blank. She asks the children which of the words that they previously predicted could be the actual word in the sentence, and they discuss both looking at the first letter of a word and thinking about what would make sense as a strategy for reading. They do this activity again with three more sentences. Mrs. Keefe reminds the children that good readers figure out words by looking at the first letter in the word, predicting what the word could be, and making sure that word makes sense in a sentence.

At this time, Mrs. Keefe introduces a new book about animals. She has written a few names of animals that are in the story on 3" × 5" cards with illustrations representing the different animals. As the children say the names of the animals, she places the word cards in a pocket chart. Mrs. Keefe also has prepared sentence strips that come from the text of the new book with the new animal words left out. She places the sentence strips in the pocket chart, and reads each sentence. The children fill in the blanks with the correct word.

The teacher introduces the book by providing a *guided book introduction*. The children look through the book and describe what they see in each illustration. The teacher points out some of the vocabulary words they will encounter on that page. During this guided book introduction, children locate words using clues such as beginning sounds, beginning letters, or meanings. For the first reading of this new book, Mrs. Keefe reads a sentence, pointing to each word as she reads, and then has the entire group reread the same sentence using *echo reading* (Brown, 2003). The teacher reads a sentence, then the children reread the same sentence while also pointing at the words. The teacher continues through the entire book reading each sentence while children echo her.

For the second reading Mrs. Keefe has children echo-read page by page rather than sentence by sentence. The children are able to echo-read page by page because the text has a predictable pattern that is easy for the children to remember. Each day Mrs. Keefe selects a focus child in each of her groups and takes careful notes on his or her literacy behaviors as he or she attempts to fingerpoint read the text. Tomorrow when she meets with this group again, another child will sit by her side to be assessed.

After the second reading, the children and the teacher discuss the story. Mrs. Keefe asks questions that relate to details in the text and questions that require students to connect the story to circumstances in their own lives. Mrs. Keefe takes a few moments to teach a phonemic awareness and phonics skill using small wipe-off boards. She introduces the phoneme /ch/ by having children decide whether the phoneme is in a word or not (she orally says the words *chicken, lion, cheetah, church, elephant,* and *Chinese* while the children put thumbs up or down). She tells children that this sound is spelled with the letters *ch* and challenges children to find two words in their story with the *ch* spelling and write them on small white wipe-off boards. She ends the lesson by helping children read new words (*chat, chap, chest, chin, chip,* and *chop*) by substituting the letters *ch* for the beginning letters on the familiar words *hat, rap, best, fin, rip,* and *hop.*

As the lesson ends, Mrs. Keefe writes a short note to all the children's parents about their progress, what they were learning, what they needed help with, and what their homework is. Homework asks the parents to read the book with their child and to sign the note and return it. Parents are challenged to brainstorm words with *ch* spellings and write the list for their children. When the group finishes its work for the day, all members put their books in their plastic bags with their homework note. They place their materials in their own box, which sits on the windowsill, until it is time to go home. Mrs. Keefe then meets with another small group, working on a skill that meets their instructional needs and reading a text that is appropriate for their level of development. She meets with two other groups until lunchtime.

Teaching Skills in Small Group during Word Study and Writing

Word study can occur before or after text reading or can comprise the entire small-group lesson, depending on the needs of children. Children will need instruction on alphabet letter recognition, phonemic awareness, and phonics.

Alphabet Recognition Instruction

Kindergarten children need to develop strong and fluent alphabet recognition; therefore, many small-group lessons focus on this objective, especially early in the year. Many children entering kindergarten already know the names of most alphabet letters, although they still might confuse *W* and *M* . However, there are children who come to kindergarten not even knowing any of the 26 names associated with letters; this is especially true for English language learners. Therefore, *alphabet name-learning activities* are critical for children who have had little previous experience with the alphabet, books, or other print before attending school. They will need to learn the alphabet's 26 names as new vocabulary words. Because it is a great deal easier to learn to recognize alphabet letters and to correctly identify them when children already know the names of the letters, the purpose of alphabet name-learning activities is to make the 26 names of the alphabet familiar to children. Activities such as singing the "Alphabet Letter Song" while pointing to individual alphabet strips or listening to the teacher read many different alphabet letter books are examples of alphabet name-learning activities.

The second kind of alphabet-learning activity helps children distinguish one letter from another. *Alphabet-distinguishing activities* help children pay attention to the unique and distinguishing features of the shapes of each alphabet letter. They draw children's attention to letters that are very similar except in orientation (such as *b, d*, and *p*, or between *W* and *M*) or features (such as *E* and *F* which differ by only one feature: two vs. three horizontal lines). Research has shown that children frequently ignore orientation and small feature differences so that they easily confuse letters such as *W* and *M* or *H* and *A* (Gibson, Gibson, Pick, & Osser, 1962). Sorting games can help children learn to pay attention to differences in orientation and letter features (Schickedanz, 2003). Teachers provide children with sets of letter tiles, plastic letters, or wooden letters. Each child has several examples of four to six easily confused letters (e.g., *M* and *W; E, F, T,* and *L*). Letters included in sorting games are carefully selected so that children learn to compare and contrast easily confusable letter features and orientations. For example, *E, F, T,* and *L* differ only in the number of horizontal lines and their location on a vertical line.

Learning to write letters in letter-writing guessing games is another activity that helps children distinguish among confusable letters. In a letter-guessing game teachers begin writing the first line of a letter, and children guess which letter the teacher is intending to write (Schickedanz, 1998). When children guess the wrong letter, teachers provide feedback on how the letter the child guessed is like the letter that will be written, but also how the letter is different. Write On after shared writing can also be used to provide demonstrations of writing a letter.

There are many activities that help children learn to recognize or identify a letter by name, a process called "letter recognition or identification." *Letter identification activities* include playing alphabet concentration or bingo games. Children also enjoy playing with letter puzzles, cutting letters out of magazines, writing letters on a computer, and playing alphabet-matching games. Using Step Up and Write On after shared writing is another way children learn to recognize letters. As with all letter identification activities, it is most effective to include a small set of letters in a game or instructional activity rather than all 26 letters.

Another skill taught during kindergarten is how to write all 26 upper- and lower-case letters. Teachers demonstrate the appropriate method of writing each letter, often by using a standard way of talking about each stroke. We recommend that teachers demonstrate the strokes of the letters following sorting or other activities aimed at teaching letter identification. Again, rather than teaching one letter each day or week, we recommend demonstrating how to write three or four letters (letters that can be confused) over several days. Appendix B provides a model for teaching the alphabet letters with standard language to describe the letter strokes in each letter.

To extend alphabet-learning opportunities, teachers can construct many kinds of alphabet puzzles and games. For example, teachers can cut pictures from extra copies of alphabet books to match to plastic or wooden letters. Teachers can write eight to 10 alphabet letters on a laminated sheet along with pictures of words found in alphabet books that begin with that letter; children match letter tiles or plastic letters to each of the letters. Games can include laminated sheets for practicing writing letters. After use in small-group lessons, these materials can be placed in the letter and word area of the literacy center for children's independent exploration.

Phonemic Awareness Instruction

Children in kindergarten need to acquire phonemic awareness: to distinguish rhyming words and words that have the same beginning sound (called "alliteration"), to isolate the beginning phoneme from a word, and to blend words that have been segmented into syllables, onset and rimes, and individual phonemes. Phonemic awareness activities are only conducted orally (alphabet letters are not part of phonemic awareness).

It is critical that teachers plan a sequence of small-group word study lessons that systematically teaches children phonemic awareness and phonics skills (Morris & Slavin, 2003). If teachers are using a core-reading program, the scope and sequence of that program will provide a sequence for teaching phonemic awareness and phonics. In the discussion that follows we suggest a possible sequence for teaching phonemic awareness and phonics skills.

In general, instruction in phonemic awareness focuses on onsets and rimes before reaching phonemes (Yopp & Yopp, 2000). Instruction usually is designed to ask children to judge whether a phoneme is included in a word before they are asked to match pictures of or objects with that phoneme. Next, children are taught to say the beginning phoneme of a word in isolation followed by isolating the ending phoneme of a word. Blending phonemes into words, and segmenting all the phonemes in a word, are usually not taught until after children have demonstrated some skills in judging, matching, and isolating phonemes (Murray, 1998; Stahl & Murray, 1994).

To teach the most simple levels of phonemic awareness, teachers model, invite children to imitate them, and then repeat the model. For example, teachers model how to listen to a phoneme and judge whether it is in a word or not. They say: "I am going to listen to the sound /m/. You say that sound /m/. Let's say that sound again, /m/. I am going to say some words. When I say a word that has the /m/ sound in it, you put your thumb up [demonstrating action of turning thumb up]. If you don't hear /m/ in the word, you put your thumb down [demonstrating turning the thumb down]. The first word is *mud, mmmmud* [slightly emphasizing and elongating the /m/ phoneme and then demonstrating thumbs up]. Yes. I hear /m/ in *mud.* The next word is *rub, rrrub* [slightly emphasizing and elongating the first phoneme and then demonstrating thumbs down]. No, I don't hear /m/ in *rub.*" This activity continues with more words, some words having the /m/ at the beginning of the word and some at the ending of the word, while other words do not have the /m/ phoneme at all.

The easiest phonemes to introduce in phonemic awareness lessons are called *continuants* because their sounds can be elongated or stretched out (Yopp & Yopp, 2000). Continuants include /f/, /j/, /l/, /m/, /n/, /s/, /v/, /w/, /z/, /sh/, and /th/. Once two continuants are introduced in judging activities, teachers can introduce sorting activities. They gather pictures or objects of words having the two continuant phonemes, and children sort the objects or pictures into groups by beginning phoneme. Teachers continue to introduce new phonemes in judging and sorting activities, while gradually introducing the more difficult noncontinuant phonemes.

Once children can sort objects or pictures with the same beginning phoneme, teachers introduce children to saying "the first little bit of sound" they hear in a word (i.e., isolating phonemes). Teachers demonstrate listening to a word (*lion*) and saying its first sound (*llll*). Then children are invited to try. At first many children will not be able to segment on their own, so teachers continue to demonstrate and invite imitation. Later, teachers pause before presenting a model to assess which children are beginning to acquire the skill independently.

Finally, teachers introduce blending and segmenting activities. First, teachers can segment a word into its onset consonant phoneme and then the remainder of the word (called a "rime"). For example, the word *lake* can be segmented into its onset beginning consonant (*llll*) and the remainder of the word, its rime (*ake*). Teachers segment the word by saying the onset, pausing 3 seconds, and then saying the rime. Children are invited to guess the mystery word. Later in the year teachers segment every phoneme in a word, and children guess the whole word.

Phonics Instruction

Phonics instruction focuses on knowing the phonemes associated with alphabet letters and vice versa. Sometimes this ability is called *letter–sound matching* or relationships because letters must be matched or related with their sounds (phonemes). Spelling requires just the opposite, hearing a sound (phoneme) in a word and relating or matching it with a letter. Some kindergarten teachers teach letter identification, phonemic awareness, and phonics together during letter-of-the-week activities. However, research suggests that this may not the most efficient method of teaching letter names or letter–sound relationships. Children usually know a few alphabet letters before they acquire the ability to hear phonemes or learn letter–sound relationships (Stahl & Murray, 1994). In addition, children learn to distinguish among confusable letters only when they engage in activities with multiple alphabet letters rather than with one letter at a time. Therefore, we advise that teachers should introduce children to multiple letters at a time including some confusable letters.

When children demonstrate the ability to judge whether some words have a target phoneme, then teachers will include the alphabet letter in sorting activities with pictures and objects. When alphabet letters are included as a part of phonemic awareness games, these games are more appropriately called "phonics activities." Phonics activities begin with a few minutes of phonemic awareness warm-up (judging, matching, isolating, blending, and segmenting phonemes without alphabet letters), followed by several minutes of letter–sound practice. For example, teachers may begin by having children sort a set of pictures by their beginning sounds and then have children match the pictures with letters. Or they might play "Concentration," a game in which children pair sets of pictures by their beginning phoneme, and then add letter cards to the game so that children match the same pictures with letters. In kindergarten, children learn the sounds related to all the consonants letters (beginning with the continuants). They also learn to blend consonants to familiar word families to read and spell new words. Then they may learn consonant digraphs, short vowels, and perhaps long vowels depending on the child's level or on expected levels of achievement in core programs.

To teach children to read new words by blending consonant letters to familiar rhyming-word families, we recommend beginning with short-vowel high-frequency families. High-frequency word families can be found in a great number of words (Wylie & Durrell, 1970, pp. 787–788), so that once children know them, they can read hundreds of words. The short-vowel high-frequency word families include the *ack, an, ap, ask, at, ell, est, ill, in, ip, it ,ock, op, ot, uck, ug, ump* and *unk* families. To teach children how to blend new words, teachers write a word in one of the word families, such as the word *back*, on a wipe-off board and then read the word. They point out that the letter *b* says /b/ and that the rest of the word says /ack/. They demonstrate saying the word segmented at the onset and rime, /b/ + /ack/ and blended together as /back/. Then they remove the *b* and replace it with another letter, for example, the letter *p*. They say: "This is a new word that I can read. I know that the letter *p* says [pausing for children to say /p/] and the rest of the word says [pausing for children to say /ack/]. "Then teachers say the onset and rime in isolation—/p/ + /ack/—and then demonstrate blending the two parts together to say the word. Teachers continue the lesson, adding several more consonant letters and modeling how to say the beginning phoneme and blend the rime to pronounce the new word.

After children are familiar with blending consonants to familiar word families, teachers may introduce children to the short-vowel sounds in isolation. They help children blend new words using consonant and short-vowel sounds in CVC (consonant–vowel–consonant) words such as *mat, lap, win, wit, mop, not,* and *jug.* During these lessons teachers demonstrate how to "keep your motor running" and "bulldoze it fast."

Teachers demonstrate *keeping your motor running* by running a pencil under the letters of a word and sustaining the sound of each letter until the next sound is pronounced (Brown, 2003). This is easier to demonstrate when the word begins with a continuant consonant (all vowels are continuants). Teachers point to the first letter, elongate the consonant sound, and then slide to the next letter before saying that sound (/mmmmm/aaaaaa/t/). *Bulldoze it fast* means that children should try to say each of the sounds as quickly as they can—for example, saying /mm/aa/t rather than /mmmmm/aaaaaaa/t (Brown, 2003). They also should look for larger chunks of words they say as a chunk rather than saying each phoneme included in the chunk—for example, by saying the /at/ as a chunk (/mmm/at/) rather than saying all three phonemes. Once children can bulldoze and use several short-vowel family chunks, teachers might want to introduce the long-vowel high-frequency families including *ail, ain, ake, ale, ame, ate, eat, ice, id , ight, ine, oke,* and *ore.* Decoding short- and long-vowel words may not be expected in some states and districts.

Putting Skills into Action: Text Reading in Small Groups

During small-group instruction through word study and writing, teachers provide instruction in the "parts" of reading: alphabet recognition, letter–sound relationships, phonemic awareness, and blending to decode new words. In order to see the "whole" of reading, children need to practice using these skills in the actual context of reading a book. During text reading, teachers provide books that allow children to use their skills as they read along with their teachers. In order to meet the varied needs of children at different points in their reading development, teachers use three kinds of books and text-reading activities: guided shared reading with short, highly predictable little books, guided fingerpoint reading with predictable little books, and guided reading with decodable or other easy-to-read text. While shared and fingerpoint reading also occur in whole-group instruction using big books and pocket charts, guided shared reading and fingerpoint reading in small group use little books and take a slightly different form.

Guided Shared Reading in Small Groups

Guided shared reading is appropriate for children with few print skills; they are still learning many alphabet letters, are only able to segment beginning phonemes with much teacher support, and know few—if any—letter–sound relationships. The short, very predictable *little books* used in guided shared reading allow children to use their meager print skills to follow along as the teacher reads. These books have from one to seven words per page and use a highly predictable word pattern, changing only one word on each page of text. During guided shared reading in small group, all children have a copy of the same text in little books.

Teachers first present a *guided book introduction* that helps children learn the predictable pattern of the text, locate some words in the printed text, and understand the illustrations. Teachers begin the guided book introduction by having children discuss the front cover and each illustration. For example, when introducing the book *Playing* (Prince, 1999), teachers can read the title and say: "This book is going to be about playing. Where do you like to play?" Once children have talked about some locations for playing, then teachers say, "Let's turn to the title page and see where this girl is playing." Next, teachers draw attention to the print on the title page by saying, "Point to the word *playing* on the title page." As children look at the first double spread (a girl running and the girl peeking from behind a tree), teachers say: "What is she doing? Yes, she is running. This is a story about what this girl likes to do. She likes to . . . [pause for children to say *run*]. The text says *I like to run*. Point to the word *I*."

The next page in the illustration does not match the text as well as it does on all the other pages of this text, so teachers make explicit the words of the text without asking children to predict the words. Teachers say: "The text says, *I like to hide*. So what is she doing in this picture?" Teachers continue to restate the pattern of the language used in the text. Teachers say, "Can you find the word *like*?" Teachers continue to go through each page of the book, reinforcing the sentence pattern ("I like to _____") and familiarizing children with the new word added to the phrase.

After the guided book introduction, teachers begin the guided shared-reading technique. Teachers read aloud portions of the text, and children *echo-read* those same portions. Teachers make decisions about how much text they will read aloud, making sure that children can memorize the predictable pattern of the text. Teachers return to the title of the book and begin reading the book one sentence or one page at a time, pointing to each word as they read. After the teacher reads, children echo-read and attempt to fingerpoint read by pointing to each word as they echo the text. Children at this stage of reading will make mistakes as they attempt to point to each word, especially with multisyllabic words. Teachers model a critical prompting strategy for these children by holding their finger on these words longer and talking about two- and three-beat words—children need to notice long words and think about holding their finger still through two or three beats when a long word is spoken (Brown, 2003). Children read and reread their shared reading texts many, many times, bringing each text to memory. Teachers follow up guided shared reading by having children locate alphabet letters in these texts or using words from these texts to teach phonics lessons. Copies of these texts are placed in special tubs in the library corner, and children are frequently assigned to the library corner for reading to a partner during center time.

Word study lessons for shared-reading groups present skills that these children lack: teachers help children learn to distinguish among and identify alphabet letters, and to judge, sort, and isolate beginning phonemes. They will also begin to learn letter–sound associations. After children learn to match words with the same beginning sounds, teachers will demonstrate saying "just a little bit" to teach isolating beginning phoneme. Teachers are likely to spend as much or more time in word study as in text reading to build children's foundational skills. Teachers will demonstrate writing alphabet letters. Children will practice writing letters and locating words they want to write from their shared-reading texts. Teachers can also present many skills through shared- and interactive-writing activities as a follow-up to text reading.

Guided Fingerpoint Reading in Small Groups

Guided fingerpoint reading in small groups is very similar to guided shared reading; however, it is intended for children who have acquired more literacy knowledge. Children who benefit from guided fingerpoint reading know several alphabet letters, can segment beginning phonemes without support, and know some to many consonant–letter relationships. They may be able to invent spellings with at least one letter–sound relationship with teacher support. Guided fingerpoint reading requires text that is predictable, but slighter longer and more complex. Texts used for fingerpoint reading need to have at least two lines of text per page to develop children's ability to track print using the return sweep required for reading the second line of print.

Teachers present a guided book introduction similar to the guided book introduction used for shared-reading texts. However, children in guided fingerpoint reading need more emphasis on using first-letter cues to identify some words. Teachers encourage children to discuss the text, but point out some words that might be unexpected. For example, teachers might introduce the book *My Bike* (Buxton, 1997) by saying: "What do you notice on the cover of this book? How many words are in the title? The first word in the title is *My*. What letter does the second word begin with [pausing for children to say *b*]? What sound does that letter make [pausing for children to say /b/]? Do you see anything in the picture that might begin with that sound [pausing for children to say *bike*]? Yes, the title says [pointing to each word and pausing for children to say *my bike*]. Now let's turn to the title page and read the title [pointing to each word in the title and pausing for children to read my bike]. I'm wondering where she is riding her bike. Where do you think?" The teacher has children turn to the first double spread and talk about the illustrations. Then teachers say: "This girl rode her bike over the grass and over the stones. Point to the picture where she rode her bike over the grass, point to the picture where she rode her bike over the stones. The first word on this page is [pause for some children to say "I"]. Yes, it is the word I. This page says "I rode my bike over the" [pause for children to say "grass"]. Point to the word grass. How can we be sure it is the word grass [pausing for children to discuss the first letter and sound]? Now point to the word bike. Before you do, what letter do you expect bike to start with [pause for children to say b]?" Teachers continue to introduce each page of the text having children use beginning letter–sound clues to locate one or two words per page

Guided fingerpoint reading includes less echo reading. The teacher may read several pages of the book before inviting children to echo-read on their own. Children are expected to reread the predictable text from their memory of the pattern established during the book introduction and the teacher's reading. They are also expected to point to the words in the text and check on first-letter clues. All of the children fingerpoint read the text in soft voices as the teacher listens to one child. Teachers point out good behaviors they notice, such as pointing to each word, checking the first letter to make sure the word said matches that letter, and fixing errors by starting again and using the first-letter clues. Then teachers read another portion of the text, and children echo-read those pages. After the first read, children pair up and read the entire text again to their partners while one child reads it to the teacher alone.

As children read, they will encounter difficulty remembering a word. In fact, teachers intentionally select text that presents children with a few challenging words. When children encounter a difficulty, teachers prompt children to try and use what they know to figure out the word. Teachers usually prompt fingerpoint readers to use first-letter clues to check if a word that is spoken matches the written word. This prompt is called a "word recognition prompt." Word recognition prompts are assistance teachers provide when children have made a mistake or miscue as they are reading. During fingerpoint reading, children are relying on their memories of the text, but they are also pointing to each word and can look to make sure the word they are saying begins with the same letter as the word to which they are pointing. When they make a mistake, teachers prompt for that kind of thinking by first pointing to the word the child misread using a pencil to point at the first letter, then saying, "Look at this word again, first sound?" (Brown, 2003, p. 726). After children say the sound of the first letter, teachers help children remember the word they read and determine if that would could be correct using both meaning and first-letter clue. Then teachers help children brainstorm words that match the first-letter clue and make sense in the sentence.

On the second day of guided fingerpoint reading, children practice reading the text several times as a group and then with partners. Then, some of the text of the story is written on sentence strips and placed in a pocket chart (perhaps the first two or three pages). Now the text is more challenging to read because there are no picture clues. Teachers invite individual children to step up to the pocket chart and fingerpoint read the text. Teachers guide children so that they accurately point to each word as they speak that word, and help children remember the pattern. They support children as they use beginning letter–sound clues to read the final unpredictable word in each pattern of the text. All the children reread the pocket chart several times and individual children point to each word using a pointer. Then each child gets a printed booklet with the story text, and they read this book to partners or to the teacher. These *print-only little books* are sent home for homework practice. Later, children will illustrate them as an assigned center activity.

Word work for children in fingerpoint reading includes learning the remainder of the consonant letter–sound relations, learning to build and read new words in familiar short-vowel families, and learning to blend CVC words that their teacher has segmented into phonemes orally. They learn to isolate ending phonemes and practice locating and writing high-frequency sight words on the word wall and from their fingerpoint reading books. Word work activities lead into writing as children practice writing new words, writing their own sentences using a combination of invented spelling and locating words from their fingerpoint reading texts, and copying words from the classroom word wall. They also write sentences from teacher dictation to practice phonics skills and stretch invented spelling. These activities move children to the next level of reading, guided reading.

Guided Reading in Small Groups

Children who benefit from guided reading know most alphabet letters, can segment beginning and ending phonemes often without support, know most consonant sound–letter relationships, and can blend new words by adding consonants to familiar word families. They can fingerpoint read with one-to-one accuracy and can invent spellings with boundary phonemes and sometimes vowels. They are now ready to learn short-vowel sounds and how to decode CVC words on their own. They have acquired some sight words and have accomplished nearly all of the 15 end-of-the-year kindergarten skills. These children have the foundational knowledge needed in order to begin conventional reading. The most appropriate books for children at this stage of reading are books with some high-frequency words including words children have already learned and many words that children can decode independently. These books are often called "decodable books" (Brown, 2000).

Decodable books that are appropriate for kindergartners include phonics readers available from many commercial companies, such as *Phonics Ready Readers* (Scholastic, 2000), *Phonics Readers* (Educational Insights), *Bob Books* (Maslen, 1994; Scholastic) and *Dr. Maggie's Phonics Readers* (Allen, 1999; Creative Teaching

Press). All decodable books begin with stories that include many words with /short a/ word families and a few high-frequency words. Knowing the consonant letter–sound relationships for the letters *m, t, s, c, d, n, p*, and *b*, along with the /short a/ phoneme in word families such as *ap, ad*, and *an*, allows kindergarten children to read several books in these sets of readers. Many core-reading programs also have decodable books intended for the beginning of conventional reading (although these books might be included in the first grade program rather than in the kindergarten program).

During guided reading of a new decodable book, teachers provide shorter introductions to the text, usually talking briefly about the content of the book and providing practice decoding a few words. Children do not look through the book and talk about what they observe in each illustration as they did in guided shared and fingerpoint reading. Instead, during guided-reading book introduction, teachers provide some information about the content of the book. They also help children practice decoding some of the words that will be encountered in the text. For example, to introduce the book *A Cat Nap* (Phonics Readers, 1990) teachers have children count the number of words in the title. They point to the first word and invite a child to read it. Then they point to the second word and model reading it using "keeping your motor running," a new strategy the teacher taught during word work. Children help read the third word in the title using the same strategy. Then they discuss what a "cat nap" is. Then teachers remark that many of the words in this book will be from familiar word families and write the words *nap, fat*, and *bag* on a wipe-off board. Children identify the word chunks *ap, at*, and *an* and form new words by adding other consonants to those word chunks. The teacher demonstrates bulldozing it fast as she reads a sentence from the book. Then the children read two sentences applying the strategy as the teacher provides feedback and support.

Then children are paired up and each child reads to his or her partner. One child (a different child each day) reads to the teacher. The teacher helps that child use the strategies of keeping your motor running and bulldozing it fast. Children reread the story to their partners at least three times (and the teacher listens to three more children), each time trying to read more words without using keep your motor running. Children discuss the illustrations, favorite parts, and funny words. The lesson ends with another word study lesson focusing on spelling and reading additional short-a word family words encountered in the story.

When children first begin guided reading, teachers may read a page and have children echo-read that page. This builds confidence in this new kind of text which is not predictable. However, teachers should expect that the fluency children developed during echo reading of predictable texts in fingerpoint reading is likely to disappear as children slow down to actually read each new word in their texts. Teachers need to be especially supportive of halting attempts to sound out words. The number of words teachers introduce before children read the text should help children be able to read the text with at least 90% accuracy during the first read. If children cannot read the text with this level of accuracy, the text is too difficult. Teachers can either echo-read this text to give children a foundation for their own reading, or find simpler text that includes sight words children can recognize and a few words children can decode. All instructional text should present children with a few tricky words (up to 10% of the words) so that children can practice decoding.

Word recognition prompts for children in guided reading become more complex. Now children are ready to be prompted to look all the way through a word rather than merely to look at the first letter. Keep your motor running and bulldoze it fast are critical strategies to prompt during guided reading. Children's initial attempts are often not very successful without teacher modeling. However, blending rapidly enough to trigger the word in memory is a watershed event in learning to read (Brown, 2003), and children need to practice this skill frequently until it is fluent. Teachers can prompt blending rapidly through a word by inserting a pencil in the text and pointing out the tricky part or a part the child does know. Or teachers might cover the tricky part and have children sound out the other parts of the word and then uncover the tricky part. Teachers might also have children isolate and say the vowel sound first. *Vowel-first decoding* occurs when teachers point out the vowel and prompt children to identify its sound, then go back to the beginning of the word to bulldoze quickly.

During text reading children are only helped by a few (up to three) word recognition prompts on each challenging word. Teachers might begin with a general prompt for self-correction. At the end of a sentence containing a miscue, teachers say: "Something tripped you up. Start here and try it again." Teachers start children at the beginning of a meaningful phrase or the sentence in order to give children a running start (Brown, 2003). When children do not self-correct with this prompt, teachers put their pencil on the problem word and ask the child either to pronounce the vowel (if the child has received instruction that would suggest he or she could do this) or invite the child to identify either the tricky part or parts he or she knows. The final prompt is to point to the beginning of the word and then tell children to bulldoze it quickly. Often the word is beyond the ability of an early reader to decode, and teachers give them the word. Word recognition prompts are intended to help children use what teachers have taught in the context of actual reading. It is not a time to teach an extended phonics lesson that interrupts actual reading.

Word study for guided reading groups includes learning short vowels and practicing blending, segmenting, and decoding CVC words. Increasing emphasis is placed on spelling sight words. Teachers may continue to dictate sentences for children to write. Eventually, children may learn long-vowel families and blending new words by adding consonants and consonant digraphs. Children continue to add to their store of high-frequency words. Spelling practice is an important part of word study. Much of the word study activities for guided reading is considered first-grade-level phonemic awareness and phonics skills. Nonetheless, some children in kindergarten reach this level of skill. However, teachers should not expect that all kindergarten children will do so.

Leveled Texts

It is critical that teachers consider the level of text read during guided reading. Guided reading is usually intended for children who can actually read conventionally. They do know some words by sight and can decode regular CVC short-vowel words. In order to use this beginning level of conventional reading skills, children should be given texts to read during guided reading that are at their *instructional reading level*. This means that the child can read the text with 90–95% accuracy (Clay, 1993b)—they will read 90–95 out of 100 words correctly on their own without teacher support. If the text is too easy (children can read 98 out of 100 words without support), there is not an opportunity to teach new strategies. Teachers teach new strategies by using word recognition prompts when children encounter difficulty reading a word; thus each text must present children with a few tricky words. If the book is too difficult, children will not understand what they are reading, and the activity becomes an exercise in decoding rather than in trying to understand what the words mean in the larger context of a story.

Because teachers need many books that meet the instructional levels of children to use in guided reading, many commercial companies have developed leveled books. *Leveled books* are a series of books for children to read that follow a gradient of difficulty. The first level of books has text that is considered the easiest for children to read, and successive levels of books have texts considered more difficult. Having a large set of leveled reading books makes it easy for teachers to select particular books needed for particular groups.

Guided reading lessons usually begin by having children reread a familiar book recently read. These books are usually on children's *independent reading level*. Children can read these book on their own with 98–100% accuracy. Rereading these books moves words that children earlier had to decode using the bulldozing it quickly strategy into sight words (children no longer have to "sound out" a word, but merely look at it and know it). When most words are sight words, then texts are read with more *fluency*. Fluent reading is smooth, sounds more like spoken language, and captures the phrasing and pauses that indicate comprehension. Table 5.2 summarizes the three forms of guided reading used in kindergarten small-group reading instruction.

MANAGING SMALL-GROUP INSTRUCTION

The purpose of small-group work is for children to learn skills that will systematically lead them to conventional reading and writing. In order to be able to do this, other children not in the group must learn to work independently of the teacher

TABLE 5.2. Small-Group Instruction in Kindergarten

Guided shared reading: for children who know few alphabet letters, may not identify rhyming words or words with the same beginning sounds, and do not fingerpoint read

Materials

- Short, highly predictable books with one to seven words per page

Book introduction/reading

- Page-by-page guided introduction
- Establish predictable pattern in introduction
- Child locates one word per page
- Echo-read line by line
- Echo-read page by page

Focus of word work and writing

- Alphabet recognition and writing
- Rhyme, beginning phoneme sorts
- Consonant letter–sound relationships
- Isolate beginning phoneme

Word recognition prompts

- Fingerpoint reading with support
- Notice word with two or three beats during fingerpoint reading

Guided fingerpoint reading: for children who know several alphabet letters, can rhyme and match words with the same beginning sounds, can isolate beginning phoneme with support, know some letter–sound relationships, are beginning to fingerpoint read with support, can invent a spelling with at least one letter–sound match

Materials

- Predictable books with at least two lines of text per page
- Pocket charts
- Print-only little books

Book introduction/reading

- Page-by-page guided introduction
- Establish predictable pattern in introduction
- Child locates two or more words per page by beginning letter/sound
- Echo-read several pages of text
- Echo-read entire book
- Read text in pocket chart
- Read text in print-only little books

Focus of word work and writing

- Consonant letter–sound relationships
- Isolate ending phoneme
- Blend consonants to familiar rhyme family
- High-frequency sight words
- Write sentences dictated by teacher
- Blend CVC words orally segmented by teacher

Word recognition prompts

- First letter?
- Monitor fingerpoint reading with first letter and sense

cont.

TABLE 5.1. *cont.*

Guided reading: for children who know most alphabet letters, know many consonant letter relationships, can isolate beginning and ending phonemes, can invent spellings with boundary phonemes and sometimes vowel, can fingerpoint read with one-to-one accuracy, can identify new words by blending consonants with familiar rhyming word families, and can read some sight words

Materials	Focus of word work and writing
• Decodable books	• Short vowels
• Easy-to-read books with high-frequency words	• Blending, segmenting, decoding CVC words
• Books of increasing level of difficulty	• Sight words
	• Write sentences dictated by teacher
	• May learn long vowels in high-frequency families
Book introduction/reading	**Word recognition prompts**
• Introduce some word patterns	• Decoding all the way through
• Introduce topic and read title	• Keep your motor running
• May use echo reading in early levels of books	• Bulldozing it fast
• Daily rereading to build fluency	• Vowel-first decoding
	• Something tripped you up, start again
	• Cover the tricky part
	• Point to what you know

and in cooperative social settings with peers. This occurs as children work in centers. Center time is an occasion for children to practice skills they have already learned. During center time children engage in assigned and self-selected reading and writing activities that they work on independent of the teacher. During small-group instruction, the teacher cannot be disturbed; therefore, the children who are not a part of the group need to know exactly what to do. The following is a description of Ms. Rosen's kindergarten. Here we see how she organizes her independent work to keep her students productively engaged.

At the beginning of the school year, Ms. Rosen spends time introducing children to the centers in the room and the types of activities they include. She has her class practice working at the different activities. During this time, Ms. Rosen does not take small groups for instruction; she helps the children so that they eventually will be able to work alone.

The children are assigned some tasks and can select others to do. The tasks engage the children in activities that promote skill development. Ms. Rosen assigns activities 1, 2, 3, and 4 (listed below) to all children. They can select to do activities 5 or 6 (also listed below) after they finish the required tasks.

1. For *partner reading*, children pair off and read the same book together. Children are partnered with another child in their reading group. They read from

a special collection of books previously read in shared, fingerpoint, or guided-reading instruction. All children know where to locate these books in tubs that are clearly labeled. After they read one or two books from this tub, they may read other books in the library corner. Because the class is studying animals, children may select books from the open-faced bookshelves that include stories and expository texts about animals. Children are expected to talk with their partner about what is read or interesting in the pictures. Each child must fill out an index card with the title of the book read, draw a picture, or write one sentence about a book he or she read during partner reading.

2. The *writing activity* requires the children to write a story or draw a picture about the book *Ask Mr. Bear* (Flack, 1932) that Ms. Rosen read that morning during whole group. In their drawings they are to include two things that happened in the book and the ending of the story. If they are writing, they can copy words or a sentence. They may consult copies of the book to locate words or use the class word wall. Each day there is a different writing activity related to the story read.

3. For the *working with words* activity, the teacher has placed animal words and pictures for matching in the letter and word center. There are additional activities in this area including games for reinforcing rhyme, beginning phoneme, letter–sound associations, and blending rhyming words from previous small-group instruction.

4. The *listening center* has taped stories about animals. For each story, there is a sheet of paper to draw a picture about the story or to answer a question about the story. Two titles included are *Is Your Mama a Llama?* (Guarino, 1989) and *Arthur's Pet Business* (Brown, 1990).

5. The *art center* has magazines with many photos of animals that children can use to create animal collages.

6. The *computer center* has literacy software and writing activities.

Ms. Rosen has an organizational chart that she uses for assigning children to centers. The rotations occur in coordination with the groups that she meets with for small-group instruction. If children finish before group rotations, they can start one of the optional activities or go on to the next task if there is space at the center. There is a basket for completed work, and every center has sign-in sheets and requires a finished product to be handed in.

At the beginning of the school year, some teachers start center time in a structured fashion. They assign the groups and tasks. As children learn to function independently, they are given opportunities for making decisions on their own and to select groups to work with or tasks to accomplish.

The management of center time is crucial for its success. Students must know their choices, the activities in which to participate, the rules that guide participation concerning the selection of materials, and what is to happen in groups or when working alone. Children can help generate the guidelines and rules for working independently. Figure 5.1 presents rules for center time.

Ms. Rosen's kindergartners sit in groups of four or five at tables. These children are heterogeneously grouped and move together from one center activity to another. From time to time, Ms. Rosen will change these groups so children have the opportunity to work with others. When Ms. Rosen meets with her first small group, the other children have designated center assignments. When the first reading lesson ends, all children move to the next center area with their group to work on a new project. Later in the school year, the children are allowed to select their activities and to do them in whatever order they wish. As they complete one activity, they immediately move to the next.

CORE READING PROGRAMS

Because of recent federal laws (No Child Left Behind), many schools must select a *core reading program*. A core reading program is usually a commercially purchased program. It is an instructional tool that provides a scope and a sequence of skills children are expected to learn, materials for children to read, alphabet and sound cards, instructional manuals for teachers, and assessment tools. The core program ensures that children are provided with instruction to meet all the skills in the scope and sequence so that they will meet or exceed national grade-level expectations and standards. This program is expected to serve the needs of the majority of children in the classroom, and to provide suggestions for intervention when children are not achieving to standards. Historically, core programs were referred to as "basal reading programs." Core reading programs cannot provide every piece of the instructional materials that teachers will need, nor will they meet the needs of every student. Nonetheless, they are intended to serve as the primary means by which all children are taught.

Core reading programs differ in the materials they provide for kinder-

Do all "have-to" jobs before you do free-choice activities.

Speak in soft voices.

Put materials back in their place.

Take care of the materials so they are in good condition for others.

Put your completed work in a "finished" basket.

Record completed work in your log.

If you have questions, use the "Ask Three and Then Me" rule (seek help from other students before asking the teacher when she is involved in small-group reading instruction).

FIGURE 5.1. Rules for using materials and completing work.

garten teachers and children; however, in general, most programs include a teachers' manual, reproducible materials for children, books for reading aloud, and sometimes small reproducible books for children to take home. Many programs provide large alphabet cards to display on the classroom wall, tapes or CDs of poems and songs, photographs to use in phonics and phonemic awareness activities or for vocabulary development, and assessments.

Teachers' manuals provide the scope and sequence of skills that will be taught during the program. Most core programs are organized around units or themes and most programs have six to eight themes. During each theme lessons are organized in a daily routine so that children learn alphabet letters, letter–sound associations, and phonemic awareness skills, and listen to stories read aloud in regular-sized or big books. The teachers' manual provides teachers with suggestions on how to conduct lessons to teach these skills, and how to use the materials provided in the program. Reproducible materials are worksheets that teachers can copy for each child. These worksheets are intended to provide children with practice in matching or writing letters or words that have been taught. Alphabet cards and CDs or tapes or poems and songs are used to support children's learning of phonemic awareness skills or letter–sound associations. Small reproducible books that children can take home reinforce alphabet, phonemic awareness, and letter–sound skills, as well as providing practice reading familiar predictable or decodable text.

SUMMARY

Teachers provide small-group instruction in kindergarten using guided shared reading, guided fingerpoint reading, and guided reading. During these small groups, teachers provide instruction in literacy skills during the word study and writing portions of the lesson. Children put those skills into practice during text reading in little books selected to support their level of reading development. These lessons help children progress from knowing very little about actual reading to beginning to read conventionally. Guided shared reading, guided fingerpoint reading, and guided reading meet the needs of children at different levels of literacy development and use different kinds of texts. Teachers provide instruction in skills tailored to meet the needs of children in each small group. Teachers use centers to manage children who are not involved in small-group reading instruction. Many kindergarten teachers will be expected to use core-reading programs that lay out a sequence of skills to be taught and provide plans for daily lessons. Teachers will supplement their core program with activities like those we described in this chapter.

CHAPTER 6

DIFFERENTIATING INSTRUCTION TO MEET THE NEEDS OF ALL LEARNERS

The purpose of this chapter is to provide insights into how to plan and provide differentiated instruction that accelerates the learning of children at different levels of accomplishment and for children who are English language learners. We begin by discussing differentiated instruction and scaffolding. We describe how to differentiate instruction to meet the needs of children at different phases of literacy development. Then we describe scaffolding and show how scaffolding provides more support for children who struggle and less support for children who have advanced levels of knowledge. We discuss how scaffolding in combination with adjusting tasks supports children with special needs. We also describe the unique challenges that English language learners (ELLs) face and methods of teaching that support these learners. Finally, we describe the critical role that families can play in providing differentiated instruction tailored to meet children's needs.

DIFFERENTIATED INSTRUCTION FOR DIFFERENT DEVELOPMENTAL LEVELS

Differentiated instruction is instruction that meets the specific and different needs of individual children in a classroom. While it is obvious that teachers cannot plan 22 different lessons for their 22 different children in reading and language, they also cannot expect that whole-group instruction alone will meet the needs of 22 children. However, teachers can provide differentiated instruction for small groups of children based on their needs (as we described in Chapter 5). Teachers can also respond in different ways to different children during whole- or small-group lessons and purposely add activities to centers that meet the variety of different needs of the children in the classroom. One way to begin thinking about differentiating instruction is to consider the developmental level of children's reading and writing. Children go through predictable developmental changes as they move toward conventional reading and writing (International Reading Association and National Association for the Education of Young Children [hereafter IRA/NAEYC], 1998). Knowing these predictable phases of development and what children can do and need to learn in order to progress to the next phase is an important tool for differentiating instruction.

Developmental Phases in Learning to Read and Write

All children from preschool through the early elementary grades go through broad phases of literacy development (IRA/NAEYC, 1998). Children begin learning about reading and writing in the phase of *awareness and exploration*. In this phase, children notice the print around them and observe how it is used; they learn to write their names and to recognize some alphabet letters; they enjoy saying nursery rhymes and singing songs with alliteration. This is a long phase, one that begins for most children when they are 2 or 3 years old. It is frequently signaled when children start to notice environmental print (such as the word *McDonald's*). This phase continues until children have learned most of the alphabet. Therefore, many children are in this phase of development when they enter kindergarten. Some researchers call this phase of literacy developing *learning about print* (Brown, 2003).

Some children begin kindergarten well along in the phase of print learning. Through instruction, they gain a greater awareness of concepts about print, learn most of the alphabet letters, and can match words that rhyme or that have the same beginning phoneme. These activities prepare children to enter into the next phase of literacy development: *experimenting with reading and writing*. Here children learn letter–sound correspondences and begin to invent spellings, track print with nearly one-to-one correspondence (fingerpoint read), and reread short, familiar, predictable texts. They learn to build and read new words using familiar rhyming-word families and their knowledge of consonant-letter sounds. Children in this phase of literacy development are *fingerpoint readers and early invented spellers*. It is expected that most children will reach this phase of development before the end of kindergarten.

The experiences that children have as fingerpoint readers and early invented spellers pave the way for the next phase of reading: *early reading and writing*. Here children begin to read print conventionally as they acquire high-frequency sight words, learn short vowels and how to blend CVC words, and practice reading short, decodable, easy texts. Not all kindergarten children reach this phase of literacy development, but some do. It is expected that in first grade all children will quickly reach this phase of development.

Matching Instruction with Phases of Literacy Development

Based on our experiences, we believe it is useful to think about kindergarten children in these three phases of literacy development. However, the first phase of learning about print is broad, and most children have experiences in preschool or in their homes that have already started their learning. Unfortunately, some kindergartners may not have acquired many early literacy concepts because their preschools or homes did not offer these experiences or their family members did not speak or read English. Therefore, in kindergarten, we have found that some children may be in earlier phases of learning about print. At the early print-learning level, children will exhibit very few, if any, of the foundational concepts of alphabet recognition, phonological awareness, or concepts about print, and their level of language and vocabulary development may be delayed. This level of knowledge is expected in preschool, but may signal a need for more intensive instruction and careful assessment in kindergarten. Without rapid and accelerated learning, these children may not end kindergarten with the levels of knowledge that they will need to be successful in first grade. We recommend that teachers provide early-print learners with daily instruction in small groups aimed at accelerated learning of these foundational concepts. Teachers may also provide additional interactive read-alouds and shared reading during small-group instruction so that these children will have additional opportunities to participate in discussions that will build language and concepts. As children acquire some foundational literacy skills, teachers may engage them in guided shared reading with very simple books with one to four words of text. Teachers will monitor the progress of these children to make sure they are learning the alphabet letters that have been taught, beginning to match rhyming words, and mastering writing their names.

Other children enter kindergarten at the later print-learning phase; they will know more of the foundational literacy concepts. They will recognize some alphabet letters, may write their names in a recognizable form, may be able to recognize rhyming words or to judge whether words begin with the same phoneme with teacher support, and will willingly answer questions about books. We recommend that children who exhibit these characteristics be taught in guided shared-reading groups (described in Chapter 5) as they continue to learn alphabet letters, develop phonemic awareness, and learn some letter–sound correspondences. The goal for these learners is to learn nearly all the alphabet letters, be able to isolate a beginning phoneme from a word, match words with the same beginning phoneme, learn some consonant letter–sound relationships, and begin to fingerpoint read.

Some children enter kindergarten as fingerpoint readers and emergent writers (the phase IRA/NAEYC identifies as "experimenting"), they know most alphabet letters, can write their first and last names, can sort rhyming words and words with the same beginning phonemes, and can segment beginning phonemes with support. They know several letter–sound relationships, and can be guided to invent spelling. In kindergarten, the ability to fingerpoint read and invent spellings marks a transition in which children will transform from emergent, nonconventional readers into real, conventional early readers. We recommend that children who exhibit these characteristics be taught in guided fingerpoint-reading groups (described in Chapter 5). The goal of instruction is to teach all the consonant letter–sound relationships, isolate the ending phoneme on words, use consonant blending to read new rhyming-word families, use consonant letter relationships to invent spellings, monitor fingerpoint reading with first-letter clues, and establish a few high-frequency sight words.

Some children in kindergarten will become early readers and writers. These children know most or all of the alphabet letters, have advanced levels of phonemic awareness including being able to segment the beginning and ending phonemes of words, and know many letter–sound correspondences. They can read new words built from combining consonants with familiar rhyming-word families. They can invent spellings with boundary phonemes and sometimes with vowels. They are ready to acquire a basic core of sight words and to learn short-vowel sounds and to decode CVC words. We recommend that children who exhibit these characteristics be taught in guided reading groups (described in Chapter 5).

Figure 6.1 summarizes the phases of reading and writing development that we have just described. It includes a summary of what children know and can do in each phase of development, and what children will need to learn in order to move them to the next phase of development. This figure will help teachers differentiate instruction for children in different phases of literacy development and identify target skills for instruction.

Providing different instruction for children in different phases of development is a good start at providing differentiated instruction. However, within any small group, children will still have differing needs and learn in different ways. Children come from different backgrounds, have cultural experiences that differ, and have different orientations toward learning. Teachers will be expected to meet the needs of children with identified disabilities, children who speak a different home language than English, and children who enter kindergarten with advanced levels of reading and writing. Teachers will need to develop a repertoire of teaching strategies that meet the needs of the various children in their classrooms. We recommend that teachers support individual children's learning through scaffolding.

MEETING THE NEEDS OF DIVERSE LEARNERS THROUGH SCAFFOLDING

Scaffolding is a term coined by Wood, Brunner, and Ross (1976) to describe the different kinds of help teachers provide children as they engage in a learning activity. The kind of *scaffold* used in building construction is a platform erected around the building as it is constructed to provide support for workers as they build concrete

Early print learners (small-group instruction on foundations and some guided shared reading)

Know	May not	Will learn to
• Few if any alphabet letters • Few concepts about print • How to comprehend read-alouds (comprehension may be advanced or suppressed depending on book experiences)	• Know how to write a recognizable signature • Attempt to read and write during dramatic play • Demonstrate phonological or phonemic awareness	• Recognize alphabet letters • Sort rhyming words • Sort words with the same beginning phoneme • Demonstrate early concepts about print

Later print learners (small-group instruction in guided shared reading)

Know	May	Will learn to
• Some alphabet letters • Some concepts about print	• Write a recognizable signature • Pretend to read and write during dramatic play • Know some rhyming words • Know some words with the same beginning phoneme	• Recognize and write most alphabet letters • Associate consonant letter–sound relationships • Demonstrate advanced concepts about print • Sort and isolate beginning phonemes • Fingerpoint read with support

Fingerpoint readers and invented spellers (small-group instruction in guided fingerpoint reading)

Know	Can	Will learn to
• Many alphabet letters • Some letter–sound relationships • Rhyme • Many concepts about print including fingerpoint reading (although they may not consistently use one-to-one voice-to-print matching)	• Invent spellings using at least one letter–sound relationship • Match words with the same beginning phoneme • Segment beginning phonemes • Self-correct fingerpoint reading with first-letter clues with prompting	• Associate all consonant letter–sound relationships • Read a few sight words • Isolate ending phonemes • Read words by blending consonants to familiar rhyming-word families • Monitor fingerpoint reading with first-letter clues

cont.

FIGURE 6.1. Phases of reading and writing in kindergarten.

Early readers and writers (small-group instruction in guided reading)

Know	Can	Will learn to
• Nearly all the alphabet letters • Many consonant letter–sound relationships	• Read simple decodable books or books with predictable sequences and sight words • Invent spellings with beginning and ending letters and increasingly with vowels • Isolate ending phonemes • Identify new words by blending consonants to familiar rhyming words • Identify some words by sight	• Associate short-vowel letter–sound relationships • Decode short-vowel words by segmenting and blending beginning, middle, and endings of CVC words • Recognize a larger store of sight vocabulary • Read text with increasing difficulty

FIGURE 6.1. *cont.*

walls, lay bricks, or nail boards. Without the scaffold, the workers would not be able to complete their jobs. The scaffold is temporary and movable; as the building is constructed, workers can raise the platform higher. After it is not needed, workers remove it to a new construction site.

Teachers provide scaffolding when they help young children complete tasks that they could not otherwise do on their own. When children have not yet developed the concept of rhyme, they cannot sort rhyming words without help. When children have not yet learned the names of all the alphabet letters, they cannot participate in an alphabet concentration game without help. Helping during these activities does not mean that teachers tell children the answers. Instead, teachers provide helpful information through reminding children of strategies they can use so that they will be successful in finding a rhyme match or saying the name of the letter. Doing these tasks successfully with help is the bridge children need between not knowing a strategy or skill and learning it. Theories of learning and development suggest that young children learn through a process whereby they first practice a new strategy or skill with the help of a teacher, peer, or adult before they are able to complete the strategy on their own (Vygotsky, 1978). The support provided by the teacher or adult is called "scaffolding," and it can take various forms. Sometimes children need a great deal of help in order to complete a task successfully and sometimes children need only a little help.

Because most teachers will have a range of children in their classrooms including children with special needs and English language learners, their ability to adjust the level of scaffolding from high to medium to low allows all children to participate in an instructional activity with success. We next describe several kinds of scaffolds and show how they provide a range of support for children (Notari-Syverson, O'Connor, & Vadasy, 1998).

Scaffolds That Provide Only Low Support for Children

Children who have had previous practice engaging in a particular activity are likely to need only a little help to be successful in using a new strategy or skill. Teachers will need to provide only low levels of support in order to intensify children's participation and learning. *Asking open-ended questions* provides children with very little information or help in doing a task. These kinds of questions merely invite children to elaborate on their own ideas by communicating them to others. Or they help children to tell what they are doing or what they plan to do next. Open-ended questions are questions that do not have only one correct answer—rather, several responses may be considered as appropriate. They can be used to help children describe how they are performing a task, what is puzzling them, or what further steps or difficulties they anticipate. For example, when children are fingerpoint reading and notice that they have run out of words to say but there is still a word left in the text, teachers might say: "What happened?" or "What is something you might do to solve this problem?" Asking open-ended questions helps children to consolidate their learning. As children respond to open-ended questions, they say for themselves what they know and what steps they plan to take to solve a problem. Being able to explicitly state for others how to solve a problem or the steps to take in a process indicates the children are ready to complete the task independently. As children match pictures of words with the same beginning sounds, teachers can help the process of knowledge consolidation by asking, "How are you finding those matches so easily?" If children cannot answer open-ended questions, teachers follow up with medium- or high-level support strategies that provide more direction ("What did you do first? Then what did you do?").

Another kind of low-support strategy is to provide praise for work that is accomplished. Teachers can *make encouraging remarks* to increase children's confidence in using a strategy or skill. Teachers say: "That's a good idea. I see that those two words rhyme" or "You used the strategy of keeping your motor running to say each of those sounds." Receiving encouraging remarks is critical for children who are unsure of their responses. It helps them gain confidence about their own knowledge and sustain their efforts. Early learning of new concepts and strategies takes concentration and effort. Encouraging remarks reward the effort and sustain concentration.

One kindergarten teacher regularly uses a combination of open-ended questions and making encouraging remarks during an instructional activity called *What Can You Show Me?* (Richgels, Poremba, & McGee, 1996) to provide support for children on a variety of different development levels. Before reading a big book, a song recorded on a chart, or an enlarged copy of a letter sent to the class from a special friend, the teacher invites children to look at the print and illustrations. She says: "I am looking at this print and thinking about what it might say. I am also noticing some things I know. When you see something you know, or you have ideas about what this might say, raise your hand." Children step up to the chart or big book and point to the print and tell their peers what they know. Sometimes children identify an alphabet letter they know, sometimes they point to letters that repeat, sometimes they point to a word and say it is on the word wall, sometimes they can read a word, sometimes they guess that it might say "Dear Kindergartners," and sometimes they merely point. To every response, the teacher praises the child for such good looking and thinking and makes a comment about the print element the child noticed. Then the teacher reads the text using shared-reading techniques. On the next day before reading the same text, the teacher uses the What Can You Show Me? activity again. Now, the teacher expects every child to notice something about the text. This combination of open-endedness and praise is highly effective in motivating every child to make a contribution. Even the simple act of being willing to step up and point is accepted and praised.

Another low-level scaffold that teachers can use is to *make clarifying comments* that restate what a child has said in a more comprehensive manner. For example, when children are trying to answer a why question during interactive read-alouds, teachers might restate something one child said to make it more obvious to all the children. For instance, when reading *Me and Neesie* (Greenfield, 1975), the teacher asked why Neesie was no longer around, and the children offered various explanations (see Figure 3.7). The teacher clarified by saying: "Oh, did you hear what C'ansarita said? Maybe Neesie thought that Janelle wouldn't be her friend anymore." Clarifications emphasize children's successful and effective thinking and make the information available to everyone in the group. When teachers make clarifying restatements, they help groups of children reach higher levels of understanding than would be possible without a clarification.

Scaffolds That Provide Medium Support for Children

Children with less experience with an activity, who have less awareness or knowledge of a skill or strategy, or who have failed to respond to an open-ended question may need more support. Medium-support strategies reduce the memory load (teachers help children remember ideas) or remind children of the goals, rules, definitions, or sequences involved in the activity. When *stating goals, rules definitions, or sequences*, teachers may remind children of the purpose of the activity. For example, when playing a phoneme-matching activity, teachers might say: "You are trying to find a match for that picture. Say the name of the picture and feel your mouth. Can you find another picture where your mouth is the same?," or during dramatic play teachers might prompt a child to take an action by saying: "Your baby is sick, you might want to call the doctor and make an appointment." When children are playing a concentration game, teachers might say: "Now you see that Micah has turned up the letter B. You will want to remember where that B is. I am going to put my eyes on that place and then remember *B*." Children need to learn to be strategic rather than random; restating a sequence or a strategy is very helpful. These medium-level scaffolds help orient children to the task and its relevant rules or strategies. They are used when the teacher is fairly sure children can accomplish the strategy or skill, but need reminders of how to be more strategic during activities.

Other medium-level support strategies *provide summaries or restatements* of what has already been accomplished. These strategies reduce the memory load of accomplishing complex tasks. These strategies are most frequently used during writing. For example, during kid writing, teachers help children remember the whole sentence they will attempt to write by repeating the sentence with the child several times. As children write, teachers say: "Remember we are writing *I like to go to the beach*. Let's reread what you have written so far. *I like*. What is the next word you need to write?" Or, when helping a child invent a spelling for a word, teachers might help the child hear additional sounds by saying: "*Bike, bike,* do you hear any sounds at the end of that word?" In each of these examples, teachers repeat words and sentences that later children will remember on their own.

Scaffolds That Provide High Support for Children

Children who have had little experience with an activity and who are just learning a new strategy, skill, or concept need high levels of support. Two ways of making a task easier to complete are by making it memorable and by reducing alternatives. *Making a skill or strategy memorable* means that teachers provide short witty comments and physical movements that embed information critical for the strategy or skill. For example, the Open Court core reading program uses short sayings such as "Dinah, the dancing dinosaur, had huge and clumsy feet that went /d/ /d/ /d/ /d/ as Dinah kept the beat" (Adams et al., 2000, p. T302). Children easily learn this short verse and repeat it often when they see the letter *D*. This verse contains information about the phoneme associated with the letter.

Asking questions is a form of scaffolding. Teachers ask "What letter is this?" or "What word rhymes with house?" or "What sound does the letter *T* make?" However, questions can be overused and frequently are not helpful to children. Children who can answer questions like "What rhymes with *house*?" already know the skill; children who can not answer the question need another kind of scaffold than a question to learn the skill. A more effective method of asking questions is to ask questions that *reduce the alternatives*. This occurs when teachers reduce the number of different items being sorted, matched, or learned. For example, instead of having 16 rhyming-word cards with eight different rhyming pairs, teachers may use only use six cards with only three pairs. When a child is having difficulty identifying a letter, teachers might say, "Is it an *S* or a *T*?," reducing the alternatives from 26 to only two.

Scaffolds that provide the highest level of support for children include teacher modeling and eliciting imitation. In *modeling* teachers demonstrate how to complete the skill themselves as they talk aloud about what they are doing: *"Cat, hat. Those two pictures rhyme."* Then they *elicit imitation from children*: "Now you say them. *Cat, hat. Yes, cat, hat* rhyme." Teachers may add physical movement to make children's participation even more active. Teachers might say: "*Cat, hat.* Let's bump those cards together gently and say the rhyme, *cat hat.*" Teachers can also *coparticipate* with children. After modeling three sets of rhyming words and eliciting children's participation in gently bumping the rhyming-word cards together, teachers say: "Let's bump them all together. Let's start with *cat hat. Cat hat, moon spoon, car star.*" Teachers say the rhyming-word pairs and bump the cards along with the children. Notice that these strategies ensure that children who have not yet developed the concept of rhyme are successful in engaging in the rhyme-matching activity.

When teachers use high levels of support during an activity, they plan that same activity the next day or soon after and use lower levels of support. Children are accelerated in their learning when the task itself is familiar (e.g., children are familiar with the sets of rhyming pictures, know how to arrange pictures for sorting, and know how to make decisions about correct matches) and when they are provided with scaffolds that ensure their success.

Scaffolding Special-Needs Children

Many kindergarten children with special needs are included in regular kindergarten classrooms. Kindergarten teachers may have children with developmental delays or with language, hearing, visual, or physical special needs. Children who later will be identified as having learning disabilities or attention deficits have not yet been identified; they will also be included in the kindergarten classroom. For children identified as having special needs, teachers will need to examine children's *Individualized Education Plans* (IEPs) in order to understand the instructional goals and *accommodations* that individual children require. Teachers will consult with special education teachers for information about specific techniques for working with individual children. Most of all, special-needs children require supportive teachers and caring environments. They also require teachers who scaffold instruction that is targeted to their level of reading and writing development. Thus, the developmental continuum we presented in Figure 6.1 will be useful when planning instruction for all children.

Recommendations for meeting the needs of children with special needs include helping children learn how to learn, making instruction explicit, and repeating instruction until mastery is achieved (Gunning, 2003). *Learning how to learn* means learning to pay attention, stay on task, and listen for specific information. These behaviors are not usually explicitly taught or mentioned during small- or whole-group instruction in literacy. However, with special-needs children teachers may need to use an explicit signal for when children should pay attention (perhaps by raising a finger in the air and looking the child in the eye). Children should be taught to look directly at the teacher when they see the signal. Then teachers can direct children's eyes to the materials that will be used in instruction by pointing. Teachers may use another signal to indicate children should listen for directions or information (perhaps by pulling on the teacher's ears). Many children do come to kindergarten without these necessary behaviors of looking directly at the teacher and the materials and actively listening. Using concrete materials, simple directions, modeling, and calling for imitation are recommended for many special-needs children. Scaffolds such as modeling, eliciting responses, and coparticipating are elements of direct instruction that may be effective with special-needs children. Repeating an activity several times so children are familiar with the routine and experience success is also recommended.

Many special-needs children in kindergarten need physical accommodations. They may not be able to hold books or pencils in their hands (they may be learning to write by holding a pencil in their mouths or by using assistive technology such as a writing/spelling program). These children will have aides who will provide many of the accommodations. Teachers will need to consult with special education teachers to determine what children's needs are and discuss how these can be met in the classroom.

In general, children with special needs will advance through the same phases of learning as do other children (given appropriate accommodations) with the support of teachers. Many of the activities we have described in this book are appropriate for special-needs children. The kind of instruction they need is related to their level of reading and writing development just as it is for all children. However, teachers can best meet their needs by careful observation of children's behaviors and responses during instruction. Teachers may need to provide higher levels of support through scaffolding or different kinds of scaffolds to meet individual children's needs.

THE SPECIAL CASE OF ENGLISH LANGUAGE LEARNERS

Entering kindergarten can be challenging for all young children. However, *English language learners* (ELLs) face unique challenges. They may experience for the first time a setting with language that is different from their familiar home language. Many children grow up in homes and communities in which only the home language is spoken; business transactions, conversations, television, and radio are all conducted in the home language. Even adults find it daunting to be in an environment where their language is not spoken and where street signs, environmental print, and other supports for daily living are entirely unfamiliar.

The support provided for ELLs differs from school system to school system, and different states have different expectations about the outcomes of education.

Some school systems provide bilingual programs where both English and home languages are taught to children. Some school systems provide English as a Second Language (ESL) instruction, in which ELLs are taught English by specially trained ESL teachers. In these situations, children are usually expected to develop English at school while it is assumed that their home language will be supported at home. However, it is often the case that English instruction for ELLs will be the responsibility of the regular classroom teacher (Au, 2000).

ELLs are doubly at risk when they are in school situations in which they are expected to learn to speak English (Tabors, 1997, p. 35). In order to be socially accepted into play with other children, they need to be able to communicate. However, the way they *learn* to communicate in English is by interacting with their English-speaking peers. They can *only* gain competence as English speakers by communicating with other English speakers (Barone, Mallette, & Xu, 2004). However, English-speaking children often reject attempts of ELLs at friendship because of their lack of language skill. Therefore, careful and sensitive teacher intervention may be needed to support ELLs' interactions with other children, and eliminate the double-risk factor.

Second Language Development and Language Instruction

Figure 6.2 presents a chart outlining the phases of oral language development for ELLs that can be expected in kindergarten. These phases broadly parallel the stages of first-language acquisition (Hadaway, Vardell, & Young, 2002). The first stage is the *stage of preproduction*. Children in this phase of learning either speak no English or very little, and therefore they are silent during most of the school day. They are listening to the noises around them and trying to make sense of the actions and sounds they hear. They intuitively learn variations in intonation, speed, pausing, loudness, and pitch in English. They can respond to limited English commands such as "Line up" or "Come sit in the circle" (after teachers physically guide children to perform the actions as they slowly speak the command).

However, children must move beyond merely being able to silently respond to simple commands: they must learn to comprehend some words and phrases. Therefore, teachers should work hard to build children's listening comprehension of familiar words and phrases. Teachers can help children learn vocabulary related to basic survival topics such as school objects (e.g., *scissors, marker, glue, paper, chair, table, rug, calendar, book center, blocks, book, reading, coloring, painting, building*), colors, days of the week, shapes, body parts, food, clothing, family concepts, parts of houses or items in the home, and animals using *total physical response* (TPR; Asher, 1982; Hadaway et al., 2002). TPR encourages children to respond physically rather than verbally to indicate their understanding. Teachers can use sets of photographs from speech–language specialists, digital photographs of objects around the classroom, or pictures from magazines, catalogues, or children's books. Teachers can teach children to stand up if the teacher says the name of the

Speech characteristics	Learn	Materials and instruction
Children in preproduction		
• Speak very little or no English • Silent • Understand only gestures, pictures, objects • Listen to make sense of sounds and actions	• Intonation, pausing, loudness • To respond to simple commands ("Come to the carpet") • Classroom routines (when to go to centers, line up)	• Digital photographs and other pictures • Objects and physical movements • Concept books on survival topics with few words per page, strong match between text and illustrations • Very simple ABC books • Total physical response
Children in early production		
• Imitate words/actions of teacher and peers • Use formulaic phrases ("Wanna play?") • Use pointing, gestures, and facial expressions to communicate • Understand routine commands or phrases used in play ("It's time to clean up," "Gimme that block") • Produce telegraphic speech • Still rely heavily on visual and action clues to understand	• Survival vocabulary • Vocabulary frequently used in the classroom • Vocabulary that allows children to play with non-ELL children • Very simple sentence patterns	• ABC books, concept books on survival topics with slightly more text per page • Highly predictable text with short, repeated sentence patterns; text on each page is limited • Total physical and verbal response
Children in speech emergence		
• Speak in simple sentences • Overgeneralize syntactic patterns and grammatical rules • Rely on visual clues to understand, but are acquiring ability to understand more spoken English	• Wider range of vocabulary • Variety of simple sentence patterns • Grammatical rules	• Predictable and cumulative texts with slightly more text and complexity with simple but varied sentence are patterns • Poems with rhythm and rhyme • Books grouped by theme • Simple stories and information books with strong visual support in illustrations and ELL interactive read-alouds • More complex stories and information books with ELL interactive read-alouds

FIGURE 6.2. Phases of language acquisition.

picture. For example, the teacher could introduce digital photographs of the class calendar, a pile of blocks, a book, a marker, and a pair of scissors. She would name the item. Then she would use the TPR activity. Children are to stand up if she shows a picture and names it correctly. Alternatives are for children to clap, tap their feet, or touch their noses.

Like all children, ELLs need to become familiar with the classroom routine. However, learning the language that signals transitions in the classroom routine presents a challenge for ELLs. Teachers should use visuals, demonstrations, and gestures to make explicit each transition during the first few weeks of school. We recommend that teachers display the daily schedule on a pocket chart, accompany the schedule with photographs of children engaging in the activity, include a printed word identifying the activity, and employ a picture of a clock indicating the beginning time of the routine (Barone et al., 2004). For example, to call children's attention to the transition from whole-group time to center time, teachers point to the picture of the classroom in which children are playing in centers and say: "It is time for centers [holding up the *centers* word card]. It is 9:00 [pointing to the picture of the clock on the pocket chart]. We will go to centers."

The second phase of second language development is the *stage of early production* (Hadaway et al., 2002). During this stage children try to speak. They use very limited language, drawing upon their stored knowledge of words and gestures gained during the silent period. They frequently imitate the teacher or peers by repeating what was just said or by using formulaic phrases (e.g., "Hello," "I'm good," "Wanna play?"). Children also use pointing, gestures, and facial expressions to communicate meaning. Children can comprehend more commands including ones children frequently use during play, such as "Gimme that block," "You be the mama," or "It's time to clean up." When children do generate speech rather than imitate or use formulaic language, it is telegraphic, using only one or two words to convey the meaning of an entire sentence, such as saying "cookie" when meaning "I want a cookie." They may learn the phrase "I want" and use it with their limited knowledge of English vocabulary. Children at this stage of second language learning focus on words related to who, what, and where rather than how and why (Hadaway et al., 2002).

Alphabet and concept books make excellent read-aloud materials for ELLs at the stage of early production. These and other concept books can focus on basic survival topics and extend the vocabulary children learned earlier from simple pictures and TPR activities. Figure 6.3 presents a list of books related to some basic survival topics. As teachers read these books, they should slow down their rate of speaking so that children have a better chance of picking out vocabulary words from the rapid flow of speech (Echevarria, Vogt, & Short, 2000). Teachers can point to relevant details in illustrations and follow up reading with TPR-response activities. TPR continues to be an appropriate teaching activity; however, teachers can ask children in this stage of language aquisition to participate verbally as well as physically. For example, as they read *Freight Train* (Crews,

Numbers and Counting
- Berenstain, S., & Berenstain, J. (1969). *Bears on wheels.* New York: Random House.
- Dann, P. (1999). *Five little ducks.* Hauppauge, NY: Little Barron's.
- McGrath, B. B. (1998). *The Cheerios counting book.* New York: Scholastic.
- Baker, A. (1998). *Little rabbit's first number book.* New York: Kingfisher Books.

Colors
- Baker, A. (1994). *White rabbit's color book.* New York: Kingfisher Books.
- Crews, D. (1978). *Freight train.* New York: Greenwillow Books.
- Walsh, E. S. (1989). *Mouse paint.* San Diego, CA: Harcourt Brace Jovanovich.

Shapes
- Baker, A. (1994). *Brown rabbit's shape book.* New York: Kingfisher Books.
- Ehlert, L. (1989). *Color zoo.* New York: Lippincott.

Seasonal Changes
- Fleming, M. (2000). *Autumn leaves are falling.* New York: Scholastic.
- Hall, Z. (2000). *Fall leaves fall!* New York: Scholastic.
- Muldrow, D. (1997). *We love fall!* New York: Scholastic.

Food and Eating
- Cowley, J. (1996). *The birthday cake.* Bothell, WA: Wright Group.
- Ehlert, L. (1989). *Eating the alphabet: Fruits and vegetables from A to Z.* San Diego, CA: Harcourt Brace Jovanovich.
- Smith, M. K. (1997). *A smiling salad.* Austin, TX: Steck-Vaughn.
- Westcott, N. B. (1987). *Peanut butter and jelly: A play rhyme.* New York: Dutton.

Daily Activities
- Canizares, S., & Chessen, B. (1999). *In the kitchen.* New York: Scholastic.
- Chessen, B., & Chanko, P. (1999). *Thank you!* New York: Scholastic.
- Dalton, A. (1992). *This is the way.* New York: Scholastic.

Animal Names
- Beattie, K. (1997). *Feet.* Bothell, WA: Wright Group.
- Canizares, S., & Moreton, D. (1998). *Who lives in a tree?* New York: Scholastic.
- Canizares, S., & Waugh, B. (2000). *On a farm.* New York: Scholastic.
- Koch, M. (1991). *Hoot howl hiss.* New York: Greenwillow Books.
- Porter-Gaylord, L. (1991). *I love my daddy because . . .* New York: Dutton.

Feelings
- Canizares, S. (1999). *Feelings.* New York: Scholastic.
- Carlson, N. (1988). *I like me!* New York: Viking.
- Hood, S. (1999). *I am mad!* Brookfield, CT: Millbrook Press.

Clothes and Body Parts
- Intrater, R. G. (1995). *Two eyes, a nose, and a mouth.* New York: Scholastic.
- Morris, A. (1989). *Hats, hats, hats.* New York: Lothrop, Lee & Shepard Books.
- Neitzel, S. (1992). *The dress I'll wear to the party.* New York: Greenwillow Books.

Houses and Homes
- Canizares, S., & Moreton, D. (1999). *Shelter.* New York: Scholastic.
- DuQuette, K. (1999). *The house book.* New York: Putnam.
- Morris, A. (1992). *Houses and homes.* New York: Lothrop, Lee & Shepard Books.

Spatial Relationships
- Berenstain, S., & Berenstain, J. (1971). *Bears in the night.* New York: Random House.
- Hill, E. (1980). *Where's Spot?* New York: Putnam.
- Reid, M. (1998). *Homes in the ground.* New York: Scholastic.

FIGURE 6.3. Books related to basic survival topics.

1985), teachers can have children stand up and say the color words when they hear them in the story.

Additional appropriate literature to read aloud with ELLs in the phase of early production are highly predictable books with repeated words and phrases and strong picture clues to meaning. The best books are ones with short, repeated, and very predictable phrases. Children can learn to use sentence stems such as "I am _____," "I like _____," "I can _____," and "I have _____." Teachers can extend the sentence stems that children understand and use by reading very predictable texts like those found in commercial early readers. For example, *Well Done, Worm!* (Caple, 2000) includes four little books using four repeated sentence stems: "Worm paints a _____," "Worm sees a _____," "Worm is a _____," and "Worm gets a _____."

The next phase of second language development is the *stage of speech emergence* (Hadaway et al., 2002). Here children develop a wider range of simple sentence structures as well as continue to learn vocabulary. Children often overgeneralize the syntactic rules they are acquiring, so their sentences are not likely to be grammatically correct. Children's competence still continues to be dependent upon face-to-face interactions accompanied by visual clues. Predictable books continue to be important for helping children gain experience with more syntactical structures and vocabulary. Teachers can select predictable and cumulative books that include more complex sentences such as *There Was an Old Lady Who Swallowed a Fly* (Taback, 1997). Books that ask and answer questions, such as *Where Is My Baby?* (Ziefert, 1996), also are useful at this stage of language acquisition. Children at this stage of language production are ready for simple stories and information books; however, they will continue to need additional support when vocabulary, concepts, and sentence structures are unfamiliar.

English-speaking children usually enter kindergarten in the stage of intermediate fluency. They have acquired sufficient vocabulary and fluency with a variety of sentence structures, and they are ready to acquire academic concepts such as science concepts, concepts about print, phonemic awareness and phonics, and math concepts. ELLs spend up to 9 months in preproduction, as many as 6 months in early production, and up to 1 year in speech emergence before reaching the beginning of intermediate fluency (Hadaway et al., 2002). Therefore, ELLs who have begun learning English at home or in preschool will have a head start on their peers who do not begin learning English until the day they enter kindergarten.

Making Adjustment in Literacy Instruction for ELLs

ELLs face many obstacles in learning to read and write in English that are caused by cultural incongruities, linguistic incongruities, and print incongruities. Cultural incongruities arise when teachers are unfamiliar with the cultures or languages of their ELLs or when books present concepts that are different from children's cultural expectations. For example, Barone and colleagues (2004) point out that breakfast food in the United States includes both hot and cold foods that may be either cooked or uncooked. Yet in China breakfast foods are always cooked. Therefore, the concept that a mouse, as in *Mouse Mess* (Riley, 1997), would eat cornflakes, crackers, and even peanut butter for breakfast would be unfamiliar to these children.

Cultural Adjustments

Teachers who have little or no experience with minority cultures in the United States or other cultures abroad and do not speak another language must seek ways to become more knowledgeable. Thus, teachers need to find out more about the children's home language and experiences and about languages in general in order to bridge the gap between school cultures and children's home cultures. One resource for learning more about different languages is to read children's books that present familiar phrases in different languages such as *Hello World!* (Stojic, 2002), which offers greetings in 42 languages; *Baby Einstein* (Aigner-Clark, 2001), which teaches phrases in four languages; and *Can You Count Ten Toes?: Count to 10 in 10 Different Languages* (Roche, 1999), which offers number words in 10 languages. Teachers should make sure that a welcome or hello greeting is posted near the classroom door in every language spoken by children in the classroom.

Another way to find out more about the language and culture of ELLs is to take a walk through the school's intake neighborhood (Orellana & Hernadez, 1999) with children (if parents give their permission) or with someone familiar with the community. Teachers can take photographs of the environmental print and signs found in busy markets, video stores, and restaurants frequented by the members of the neighborhoods. Teachers can post the photographs in the classroom and invite children to tell about their experiences in these locations. Children can be invited to bring in print from their homes that can be used in show-and-tell and for small-group skill instruction in alphabet recognition and letter–sound associations (Xu & Rutledge, 2003). These materials can be included in classroom displays. Children can also use these materials to make books by pasting familiar environmental print into pages stapled together. These books can be placed in the book center.

Another way teachers can become more familiar with the cultures of their children is to conduct family interviews. Teachers may use school or district parent liaisons to translate during parent interviews. Teachers will want to find out the child's name in English and in the home language, the language and dialect spoken by the family, preschool experiences (either in the United States or in the home country), and grade level or ages of siblings. Teachers will want to learn the parents' assessment of the child's fluency in their home language and experiences they have had with everyday print items such as newspapers, magazines, catalogs, or children's books in both English and the home language. They will want to find out if adults or others sing with children, read to children, help children write their names, or provide markers and crayons for writing and drawing (Barone et al., 2004). It would be helpful to learn what kinds of games children play in their home, what kind of behaviors are most valued, and what parents expect from teachers and the school (Ashworth & Wakefield, 1993). During family interviews, teachers may ask parents to write their child's name in the home language. This label can be displayed along with the child's picture and name written in English in a classroom display.

Cultural incongruities also arise from differences in children's previous experiences with playing and using classroom materials. Many children come from cultures where they have never played with water or sand (such as at the water and sand table), may never have had experiences in which they are free to choose among materials (such as at the art center), and cannot recognize many of the materials widely available in most kindergarten classrooms. Teachers may want to limit the amount of materials in centers during the first few weeks of school as well as the number of choices available to children. As they do with all children, teachers will demonstrate for ELLs how to use each material included in a center and make clear expectations for cleanup. Teachers can label each classroom center in English as well as in all the home languages spoken by children in the classroom (parent liaisons may be able to help or may suggest community resources).

ELLs may need addition support in learning how to select a center, select materials, and sustain interaction with those materials. When children are confused, they may wander from center to center and never find an activity in which to engage. Teachers can invite ELLs to a particular center and then coplay with them, demonstrating different ways to use materials and engaging them in conversation. As teachers sit with children, they can invite other children to join in, encouraging friendships among ELLs and non-ELLs. This provides opportunities for teachers to facilitate conversations among children who speak different home languages. During these conversations teachers demonstrate using *comprehensible input* (Krashen, 1985), which means reducing the amount of language used, slowing down the rate of speech, and limiting the number of words used. Simplified language is used in conjunction with gestures, pointing, repetition, pictures, and dramatic movements. The purpose of using comprehensible input is for ELLs to understand and participate in the conversation as much as possible even if it is only through gestures, pointing, facial expressions, or dramatic movements. ELLs rely on dramatic gestures and other visual clues to understand what is being said because of their limited vocabulary. For example, the teacher may comment, "You are building high," emphasizing the word *high* with a dramatic gesture and repeating that word. The ELL shakes his head and smiles.

Print and Linguistic Incongruities

Children's home language and English are likely to have some properties that are the same and some that are different. When the linguistic and print properties are the same in the two languages, learning about them in English is easier (Cummins, 1989). For example, English is an alphabetic language, meaning that letters represent speech sounds. Children who speak other alphabetic languages such as Spanish are likely to grasp the alphabetic principle more easily than children who speak nonalphabetic languages such as Japanese. Directionality differs across languages; not all written languages proceed from left to right and from top to bottom. In some languages, such as Chinese and Korean, word characters are all the same size; in English, words are many different sizes. Even names can be problematic for some children. In some languages a family surname is written before the first name rather than after it, as in English. Therefore, a list of first and last names in English will likely confuse Korean or Chinese children who would not expect this order. Not all languages have the same phonemes; some phonemes in English are not found in all home languages. Therefore, children who speak these languages will have more difficulty acquiring these phonemes. The concept of rhyming words does not exist in all languages. Even the order of letters, and thus phonemes, may be unusual. We consider words to move from left to right across letters, but in Korean sounds are represented in the upper-left, upper-right, and bottom portion of a single symbol (Barone et al., 2004). Teachers who are aware of these incongruities understand the necessity of providing explicit demonstrations of these print concepts as they are teaching ELLs foundational reading and writing skills.

Adjust Instruction in Foundational Skills of Reading and Writing

ELLs need four adjustments in instruction: different kinds of books are more appropriate at different levels of English proficiency; children need different kinds of read-aloud techniques in order to maximize vocabulary and comprehension development; children need more experiences with language prior to and following print experiences, with greater use of visual aides, concrete items, and movement: and children may need explicit instruction in using a variety of English syntactic patterns during writing.

Selecting Books for ELLs and Adjusting Read-Aloud Techniques

Figure 6.1 included characteristics of appropriate books to read aloud to ELLs at three levels of English proficiency. During early-stage preproduction teachers will use concept books with little text that are focused on survival topics, and alphabet books that have little text and a high degree of congruence between text and illustrations. Sets of alphabet books that include a book for each letter of the alphabet and only a few pages of text are appropriate at this stage (e.g., the *Cambridge Alphabet Books* published by Cambridge University Press). Children at this stage of language production rely on gestures, objects, pointing, dramatic movement, and illustrations in order to understand.

At the second stage of early production, teachers may select easy predictable books with simple language patterns for read-alouds. Teachers can continue to read slightly more complex concept books on survival topics. Text and illustrations should continue to be highly related, and text on each page should be limited. Children may be introduced to very simple short stories and informational books. As children enter speech emergence they need books that have simple but varied language patterns, and include an increasing amount of text on each page. Children enjoy shared reading of short poems that have strong rhythm and rhyme and browsing through information books with high levels of visual support in the illustrations. They benefit from books read in thematic groupings, from more complex predictable books, and from longer, more complex books read aloud using the ELL interactive read-aloud procedure.

The *ELL interactive read-aloud procedure* (Hickman, Pollard-Durodola, & Vaughn, 2004) is designed to build vocabulary and comprehension and is intended to introduce longer, more complex picture story and information books to ELLs (Figure 6.4 presents a list of appropriate books to use with the ELL interactive read-aloud procedure). These are the books that English-speaking kindergarten children hear in interactive read-alouds. However, without modification these books would prove overwhelming to ELLs. The ELL interactive read-aloud procedure is similar to that used in the interactive read-aloud we described in Chapter 4, but there are four differences. First, teachers divide these longer, more complex texts into three or four segments that are read on successive days. Thus, ELLs hear shorter segments of text each day. Second, only three or four vocabulary words are targeted for instruction each day. Therefore, ELLs have more opportunity to repeat and use these words as they discuss the text. Each day teachers introduce new vocabulary and continue to review previously introduced vocabulary. Third, the segment of the book is read and reread at least twice each day, it is reviewed and retold the next day, and the entire text is reviewed and reread the final day. Therefore, ELLs have repeated exposure to the same text. Fourth, teachers ask *who* and *what* questions only. They do not ask *why* questions because children's language at this level of acquisition makes these kinds of questions very difficult to answer.

The steps in the first day of the ELL interactive read-aloud procedure are

➤ Introduce the text and three new vocabulary words in a book introduction.

➤ Read a segment of the text and offer contextualized information (by providing a short definition, pointing to an illustration, and using dramatic gestures or facial expression) about the three vocabulary words.

➤ While reading, ask three questions (two questions that can be answered by direct recall of text information and one question that requires an inference).

➤ Reread the text, drawing attention to the three vocabulary words.

➤ Guide children in responding to the text by recalling the events, connecting to their experiences, or using vocabulary in their own words.

Fall Changes
- Maass, R. (1996). *When autumn comes.* New York: Scholastic.
- Maestro, B. (1994). *Why do leaves change color?* New York: Scholastic.
- Robbins, K. (1998). *Autumn leaves.* New York: Scholastic.

Plant Growth
- Cole, H. (1995). *Jack's garden.* New York: Greenwillow Books.
- Gibbons, G. (1991). *From seed to plant.* New York: Holiday House.
- Hickman, P. (1996). *A seed grows: My first look at a plant's life cycle.* Tonowanda, NY: Kids Can Press.
- Kottke, J. (2000). *From acorn to oak tree.* New York: Scholastic.
- Rockwell, A. (1998). *One bean.* New York: Walker.

Tricky Animals
- Cronin, D. (2000). *Click, clack, moo cows that type.* New York: Scholastic.
- Mollel, T. M. (1993). *The king and the tortoise.* New York: Clarion Books.
- Soto, G. (1995). *Chato's kitchen.* New York: Putnam.
- Stevens, J. (1995). *Tops and bottoms.* San Diego, CA: Harcourt Brace.

Special Relationships with Mothers and Fathers
- Say, A. (1989). *The lost lake.* Boston: Houghton Mifflin.
- Wells, R. (1985). *Hazel's amazing mother.* New York: Scholastic.
- Williams, V. B. (1982). *A chair for my mother.* New York: Scholastic.

Books by Kevin Henkes
- Henkes, K. (1990). *Julius: The baby of the world.* New York: Trumpet.
- Henkes, K. (1991). *Chrysanthemum.* New York: Mulberry Books.
- Henkes, K. (1996). *Lilly's purple plastic purse.* New York: Greenwillow Books.

Imagining You Are a Pirate
- Burningham, J. (1977). *Come away from the water, Shirley.* New York: Crowell.
- Fox, M. (1994). *Tough Boris.* San Diego, CA: Harcourt Brace.
- Long, M. (2003). *How I became a pirate.* Orlando, FL: Harcourt.
- McPhail, D. (1997). *Edward and the pirates.* New York: Scholastic.

Books about Going to School
- Bloom, B. (1999). *Wolf!* New York: Orchard Books.
- Brown, T. (1986). *Hello, amigos!* New York: Holt.
- Herman, G. (2000). *The puppy who went to school.* New York: Scholastic.
- Tomioka, C. (1992). *Rise and shine, Mariko-chan!* New York: Scholastic.
- Wells, R. (1981). *Timothy goes to school.* New York: Dial Books for Young Readers.

Books about U.S. Historical Events
- Waters, K. (1996). *On the Mayflower: Voyage of the ship's apprentice and a passage girl.* New York: Scholastic.
- Winter, J. (1988). *Follow the drinking gourd.* New York: Dragonfly Books.

Books about Plants Important in the United States
- Aliki. (1976). *Corn is maize: The gift of the Indians.* New York: HarperCollins.
- Fowler, A. (1994). *Corn—on and off the cob.* Danbury, CT: Children's Press.
- Gibbons, G. (1999). *The pumpkin book.* New York: Scholastic.

Books about the Neighborhood
- Flanagan, A. K. (1998). *Mr. Yee fixes cars.* New York: Children's Press.
- Flanagan, A. K. (1998). *Buying a pet from Ms. Chavez.* New York: Children's Press.
- Flanagan, A. K. (1998). *Choosing eyeglasses with Mrs. Koutris.* New York: Children's Press.
- Flanagan, A. K. (1998). *Learning is fun with Mrs. Perez.* New York: Children's Press.
- Flanagan, A. K. (1998). *Mr. Santizo's tasty treats!* New York: Children's Press.

FIGURE 6.4. Books for ELL interactive read-alouds.

➢ Summarize the main events or ideas of the text using the three vocabulary words.

The words selected for focus in ELL interactive read-alouds continue to be sophisticated words not found in children's current vocabulary, but words that children are likely to encounter again in real life or books (see Chapter 4 for a discussion of selecting vocabulary). ELLs will need to continue to develop awareness of more common words as well. Figure 6.5 presents examples of two books appropri-

---

A Chair for My Mother (Williams, 1982)

Section 1—Introduction
- Tips—money given to a waiter or waitress at a restaurant to thank them for serving the food.
- Bargain—a really good price on something you want to buy.
- Savings—extra money put aside to buy something special.
- Armchair—a chair with places to rest your arms.

Section 2—The Fire
- Tulips—a flower that has many different-colored blooms.
- Flames—flickering lights from a fire.
- Spoiled—damaged, ruined.
- Charcoal—the black ashes left after the fire burned out.

Section 3—Their New Home and Chair
- Comfortable—soft.
- Exchanged—traded.
- Furniture store—places where they sell chairs, tables, beds, and couches.
- Delivered—some stores use a big truck to bring furniture to your house.

Tops and Bottoms (Stevens, 1995)

Section 1—Introduction
- Lazy—someone who does not want to work.
- Hare—another word for rabbit.
- Clever—smart.
- Debt—something that you owe because you borrowed money that wasn't yours

Section 2—The Clever Plan
- Business partners—a team that works together.
- Harvesting—picking all of the plants when they are ready.
- Profit—the extra stuff you get for hard work—money or food.
- Crops—plants like vegetables such as corn or carrots

Section 3—Bear and Hare Become Neighbors, Not Business Partners
- Cornstalk—the stem of a corn plant.
- Roots—the part of a plant that is underground.
- Tassels –the strings on the top of the corn.
- Vegetable stand—a place where you sell vegetables from a garden.

FIGURE 6.5. Vocabulary for ELL interactive read-alouds.

ate for ELL interactive read-alouds, and three vocabulary words and short definitions selected for three or four segments of those books.

The second day of ELL interactive read-alouds is very similar, except another step is added. Before giving an introduction to the next segment of text, teachers guide children in summarizing the text they have already read. The final day of ELL interactive read-alouds includes guided recall of the entire text, focusing on all vocabulary words; rereading the entire text; and asking new questions for each segment of the text (two questions for each segment that call for recall of information from text and one question for each segment that calls for an inference). Children may follow up these readings with drama, shared writing, or art explorations. To make the ELL interactive read-alouds even more powerful, we recommend that teachers read two or three related books to build even stronger understandings about concepts and vocabulary.

Using Visual Aids, Objects, and Pictures

Merely displaying print around the classroom will not be enough for ELLs. ELLs need picture support to make sense of words printed on word walls, calendars, job charts, and center assignment posters. Teachers can make simple line drawings, locate computer graphics, or cut illustrations from magazines or coloring books to accompany each printed word displayed in the classroom. Teachers will want to collect a picture file, and ELLs will enjoy sorting these pictures and talking about them. The picture file becomes a real resource as teachers introduce new concepts in science and social studies or when reading books aloud. When reading books aloud, teachers can also plan ahead and gather simple props—real objects or replicas make huge differences for ELLs' understandings. Placing these props and related books in the book center will entice ELLs to revisit the book.

Environmental print items are great for ELLs because they are meaningful in children's everyday experiences (Xu & Rutledge, 2003). They can be used to teach vocabulary and letter identification or letter–sound associations at the same time. Teachers have children talk about their print items and locate words and alphabet letters. Teachers can place some of these items on the classroom word wall. Teachers can draw attention to environmental print when it is pictured in illustrations. For example, there are many kinds of environmental print shown in the illustrations of *The Day of the Rainbow* (Craft, 1991). Teachers can help children spot the print, talk about its meaning, and explain how it is used in everyday life.

Wordless picture books provide excellent visual support for ELLs. Illustrations in these books clearly depict actions, provide hints of characters' thoughts and emotion, and show cause and effect. They make excellent books to share with small groups of ELLs. Children can be invited to tell stories in their home language using a parent or community volunteer when the teacher does not speak the home language (Hadaway et al., 2002). Children at the stage of speech emergence can be coaxed into telling the story in English with support.

Books with tie-ins to television shows or movies make great use of visual information (Barone et al., 2004). Children may watch these shows in their home language, and therefore bring stronger background knowledge as teachers read these books aloud. Examples of books with television tie-ins are *Snowbound* (*The Wild Thornberrys*) (Thorpe, 2000) and *My Favorite Letters (Blue's Clues)* (Reber, 2001).

Explicit Attention to Syntactic Patterns during Writing

All children in kindergarten eventually use simple sentence patterns to generate a lot of writing from a little knowledge of words. Many kindergarten children use sentence patterns such as "I like _____," "I can _____," I am _____," and "I want _____" during kid writing in journals. English-speaking children naturally select these simple starters, and eventually discard them as they gain confidence in spelling and in finding other words they need on the classroom word wall or in familiar books. ELLs need explicit help in noticing and using English sentence patterns. Teachers can demonstrate using sentence patterns as a writing strategy during minilessons prior to writing or during shared writing. For example, teachers can use the sentence stem "Leaves are _____" to write a poem about leaves as a shared writing activity after reading *Autumn Leaves Are Falling* (Fleming, 2000). The book *Fall Leaves Fall!* (Hall, 2000) provides two additional sentence patterns: "We like to _____" and "Some leaves are _____." Again, teachers can use these sentence patterns to guide children in creating another poem about fall as a shared writing activity.

CAPITALIZING ON FAMILY INVOLVEMENT TO DIFFERENTIATE INSTRUCTION

No one cares more for a child than loving family members. All family members have cherished memories of their children. They remember that sometimes the baby was serious, sometimes she smiled, sometimes she reached out to tap the book. Occasionally she made talking sounds as if reading along. Because the experience was daily and positive, the baby became familiar with story readings and welcomed that time. Family members remember putting books all around the home. The baby had accessible bookshelves in her room. There was a crate of books with her toys for her to use at all times. There were books in the kitchen, in the bathroom, and in play areas. In addition family members had their own books, both professional literature and recreational materials such as novels, magazines, and newspapers. Family members remember times when the child crept near as they were reading, to silently join in reading one of her books.

There are children who come to school with family members who have fond memories of reading to their young children, and there are children who come to school with family members who have cherished remembrances of birthday parties and family celebrations rather than of sharing books. There are children who come to school never having had a book read to them. Yet families need to learn to be supportive of their children's reading and writing; this means telling them stories or reading to them daily. Dealing with family literacy as a part of the literacy curriculum is critical. Every teacher should include families in her or his reading program.

What is Family Literacy?

Family literacy encompasses the ways that family members use literacy at home and in their community. Family literacy occurs naturally during the routines of daily living and helps adults and children "get things done." Examples of family literacy might include using writing or drawing to share ideas, composing notes or letters to communicate messages, keeping records, making lists, following written directions, or sharing stories and ideas through conversation, reading, and writing. Family literacy may be initiated purposefully or may occur spontaneously as family members go about the business of their daily lives. Family literacy activities also may reflect the ethnic, racial, or cultural heritage of those involved. One of the goals of a family literacy program is to make family members aware of what they are doing already that promotes literacy and what more they can do.

Multicultural Perspectives Concerning Family Literacy

In the United States, many families do not speak English and therefore are not able to help their children in the ways that schools may suggest. In addition, there are many family members who have limited literacy ability and, although they are eager to help, they cannot do so in the mainstream approach. In some cases the family member is a teenager who has dropped out of school. Therefore, when we speak of "family literacy," in many situations we need to recognize that it must be an intergenerational matter in which environments are created to enable adult learners to enhance their own literacy, and at the same time to promote the literacy of their children. Many low-income, minority, and immigrant families cultivate rich contexts for literacy development. Their efforts are different from the school model we are accustomed to. We must learn from and respect families and children from cultures in which books are not readily available, although evidence of literacy activity, such as storytelling, exists. The types and forms of literacy practiced in some homes are different from those that children encounter in school. Although literacy activity is present in one form or another in most families, the particular kinds of events that some families share with children may have a great deal of influence on school success. Conversely, the kinds of literacy practiced in classrooms may not be meaningful for some children outside school. Family literacy must be approached to avoid cultural bias, and activities must be supportive rather than intrusive.

How Teachers Can Provide Family Involvement

Teachers need to view families as partners in the development of literacy. Every teacher has the responsibility to inform families about what is happening in school on a regular basis and how they can help their child. Teachers need to involve families in school activities during the day, and provide activities for families to do at home. Families need to feel that they are welcome in school. Families should be partners with the school in the education of their child. Because no two communities are the same, family literacy programs need to be tailored to the needs of the individuals they serve. However, here are some tested guidelines to follow that will help programs be successful:

➤ Hold meetings at varied times of the day and on different days of the week to accommodate all schedules.

➤ Hold meetings in accessible locations that are friendly and nonthreatening.

➤ Provide transportation if no public transportation is available, or if parents do not have a way of getting to meetings.

➤ Provide childcare at meetings.

➤ Provide food and refreshments at meetings.

➤ Work with parents alone and with family members and children together. There should be sharing times when family members and children work together.

➤ Provide support groups for families to talk about helping their children and to find out what they want to know.

➤ Provide families with ideas and materials to use at home.

➤ Provide easy-to-carry-out functional literacy activities that family members consider useful such as talking and reading about childrearing concerns, community life problems, and the like.

➤ Include the opportunity for parental participation in school activities during school hours.

Following are some suggestions about ways to make parents an integral part of the school:

➤ At the beginning of the school year, send home the goals to be achieved in kindergarten, in a format that can be understood by all.

➤ With each new unit of instruction or new concept being taught in literacy, send a newsletter to notify families about themes and what they can do to help.

➤ Invite families to school for informational workshops, parent meetings about curriculum decisions, parent conferences, and school programs.

➢ Invite families to help with literacy activities in the classroom such as reading to children, helping with bookbinding, taking written dictation of stories, and supervising independent activities while teachers work with small groups and individual children.

➢ Send home activities for families and children to do together. Require some feedback from the parents or child about working together. Include activities such as writing in journals together, reading together, visiting the library, recording print in the environment that they see, writing notes to each other, cooking together and following recipes, putting toys or household items together that require following directions, and watching and talking about specific programs on television. Participating in homework assignments is extremely important.

➢ Invite families to school to share special skills they may have, to talk about their cultural heritage, and the like.

➢ Send home notes when a child is doing well. Do not send notes only for problems.

➢ Provide lists of literature for families to share with their children.

➢ Families should be invited to school to participate with their children in literacy activities. During center time, for example, family members can help to supervise independent activities, see what the literacy environment is like at school, and become a more integral part of the child's literacy development.

➢ Have family members and child meetings about progress and projects.

Figure 6.6 presents a form that can be sent to parents every month so they can plan ahead and continuously sign up to come to school and participate. This list can be modified depending on the families being served. It can be translated into home languages or shortened. Parent liaisons in schools or districts make excellent resources for providing feedback on the form and content of messages sent home to families.

What Families Can Do at Home

Elements that affect the quality of the literacy environment in the home are the interpersonal interactions or the literacy experiences shared by children, parents, siblings, and other individuals in the home; literacy materials in the home; and the aspirations parents have for the literacy achievement of their children. A list such as the one below can help families learn about things to do with their children and to check what they are already doing. Figure 6.7 presents a set of guidelines that can be shared with parents. These guidelines should be available in the child's home language. These guidelines may be shortened, or presented orally in parent meetings.

Family Members Wanted: Visit Your Child's Classroom

Dear Family Members,

Please come to school and be a part of our reading and writing time. On the form below list the types of things you can do when you visit. There is a space for you to let us know the time of day and dates that you can attend. We are flexible and will arrange our time when it is convenient for you. All family members are welcome—brothers and sisters, babies, grandparents, and of course parents. Please come and get involved in your child's education, and help us form a true home and school partnership.

Sincerely,

_____

Please fill out the following form and send it back to school with your child:

Your name: _____

Your child's name: _____

The days I can come during the week are: _____

The time of day I can come to school is: _____

When I come to school I would like to:

1. Watch what the children are doing.

2. Participate with the children.

3. Read to a small group of children.

4. Read to the whole class.

5. I am from another country and I would like to tell the children about my country and show them clothing, pictures, and books from there.

6. I have a hobby and would like to share   My hobby is: _____
   it with the class.

7. I have a talent and would like to share   My talent is: _____
   it with the class.

8. I'd like to tell the children about my job.   My job is: _____

9. I'd like to give children who need it some extra help.

10. I'd like to help supervise during center time.

11. I'd like some help in deciding what to do.

12. I would like to come on a regular basis to help.

FIGURE 6.6. Family letter.

Your child's ability to read and write depends a lot on the things you do at home. The following list suggests materials, activities, and attitudes that are important in helping your child learn to read and write. Check off the things you already do. Try to do something on the list that you have not done before.

Materials

1. Have a place at home to store books and magazines for your child.
2. Subscribe to a magazine for your child, if you can.
3. Place some of your child's and some of your own books, magazines, and newspapers in different places in your home.
4. Provide materials for your child to use in telling stories, such as puppets or small people toys.
5. Provide materials for writing, such as crayons, markers, pencils, and paper in different sizes.

Activities

1. Read or look at books, magazines, or the newspaper with your child. Talk about what you looked at or read.
2. Visit the library and take out books and magazines to read at home.
3. Tell stories together about books, about your family, and about things that you do.
4. Talk about pictures in catalogs, advertisements, and other mail.
5. Provide a model for your child by reading and writing at a time when your child can see you.
6. Point to print outside, such as road signs and names of stores.
7. Write your child's name and talk about it as you write.
8. Point out print in your home such as words on food boxes or recipes, directions on medicine, or instructions on things that require assembly.
9. Visit the post office, supermarket, and zoo. Talk about what you saw. When you get home, draw and write about it.
10. Leave a note for your child. Write lists together such as food lists, lists of errands, and lists for holiday shopping.

Foster Positive Attitudes toward Reading and Writing

1. Reward your child's attempts at reading and writing, even if they are not perfect, by offering praise. Say kind words like, "What nice work you do"; "I'm happy to see you are reading"; "I'm happy to see you are writing. Can I help you?"
2. Answer your child's questions about reading and writing.
3. Be sure that reading and writing are enjoyable experiences.
4. Display your child's work in your home.
5. Visit school when your child asks. Volunteer to help at school, attend programs in which your child is participating, attend parent conferences, and attend parent meetings. This lets your child know you care about him or her and school.

Visit School and Speak to Your Child's Teacher

1. If you want to volunteer to help in any way.
2. If you want to visit your child's class during school hours.
3. If you have concerns about your child's reading and writing.
4. If you feel your child has problems with vision, hearing, or other things.   *cont.*

FIGURE 6.7. Guidelines for promoting early literacy at home.

5. If you need help because the language you speak at home is not English.
6. If you need help with reading and writing yourself.
7. If you would like to know more about how you can help your child at home.
8. If you want to know more about what your child is learning at school.

FIGURE 6.7. *cont.*

A Favorite Home–School Activity: Thematic Backpacks

Sending home a special backpack with books, activities, and materials is an especially motivating family literacy activity. Teachers assemble a theme-based backpack with the following materials: a class journal; five to seven books that represent a variety of genres and reading levels; a folder with materials and directions; games, poems, songs, and/or experiments related to the theme under study; and other related items such as videos, cassettes, or stuffed animals. The children take the backpack home weekly on a rotating basis. Teachers instruct the children to share the activities and books with their family members. It may be helpful to show a backpack and model some of the activities for the parents at back-to-school night. They may also be put on display at parent–teacher conferences so parents may become acquainted with the materials and procedures.

Under parental guidance, the children respond to what is asked of them in the class journal that is in the backpack—for example, "Which was your favorite book and why was it your favorite?" Or, to go along with a food theme, for example, the children may be asked to share a family recipe. A music theme may include a tape recorder and blank tape to record a favorite song. When the backpack is returned to school, the child shares the journal response with the class. The children and parents can hardly wait until it is their turn for the next backpack! (We thank Shannon Corcoran, a kindergarten teacher, for this useful idea.)

Highlighting Family Involvement at School

Family activities may be planned monthly. These activities provide opportunities for children to bond with their own families and other families, and to share their diverse cultural backgrounds with their classmates. The activities can take place during school hours, immediately after school, on weekends, or in the early evening. To emphasize the importance of these activities and others, teachers keep cameras in school so when parents participate they can take their pictures for display in a school showcase. The following are the activities at school that help fill the showcase and bring parents to the building:

> *Weekend themes.* These are weekend days devoted to different topics, such as other countries, where children and parents can learn together. Families share artifacts and then read, write, and do art projects about the theme.

➢ *Cooking evenings.* Families bring easy favorite recipes to share and make together. The best part is eating the goodies when the cooking is done.

➢ *Book sharing after school.* Everyone brings a favorite book and reads or tells about their favorite part. The book can be in another language; if necessary, a translator is used so everyone can participate.

➢ *Sharing family photos.* On this day we ask everyone to bring family pictures they want to share. We talk and write about them. Each family makes an album with the photos, and we encourage them to continue to fill the album they started at school. (We thank Margaret Youssef, a kindergarten teacher, for these helpful ideas.)

SUMMARY

It is essential that teachers provide differentiated instruction to meet the varied needs of their children. An important way teachers differentiate instruction is to group children and then to provide different groups of children with small-group instruction directly related to their instructional needs. Knowing the phase of literacy development of each child in the classroom supports this kind of differentiated instruction. Teachers also scaffold instruction by offering children different levels of support. They present open-ended activities or ask open-ended questions and provide praise. This helps children communicate what they are learning and promotes confidence. Teachers can remind children of strategies to use, help them remember information, and ask questions that reduce the alternatives. Teachers can also model, elicit children's imitation, and coparticipate with children. This range of scaffolding allows teachers to meet the instructional needs of all children including children with special needs.

English language learners present special challenges; children need additional emotional and social support as they acquire a new language and adjust to new routines that may be very different from home experiences. Teachers who are aware of phases of language development and activities matched to these levels will provide more effective instruction for these children. Teachers can make adjustments in their instruction to meet the needs of English language learners by learning more about children's cultural backgrounds and home experiences. They can select appropriate books for read-alouds and use modified procedures to make sure ELL children understand books and acquire vocabulary. Teachers will make extensive use of visual cues or pictures, and teach children some syntactic patterns during writing.

Finally, teachers reach out to families and help family members support literacy instruction at home. Children learn best with the school and family work together toward achieving common goals.

CHAPTER 7

ASSESSMENT

The purpose of this chapter is to describe a systematic approach to assessing literacy development in kindergarten. First, we present a possible list of standards for reading and writing that identify the kinds of literacy strategies and skills that kindergartners should learn. Effective teachers select assessments that allow them to monitor whether their children are making progress toward reaching these standards. We offer a variety of assessment tasks that teachers may administer to individual children in order to focus instruction and monitor progress. Second, we describe how teachers can collect data during instructional activities—for example, by having children dictate or compose stories as a part of writing workshop. Third, we discuss how teachers gather information from observations of children's self-initiated reading and writing by taking anecdotal notes as children reread favorite books in the library corner or write a grocery list in the dramatic play center. We describe why these many different kinds of assessments are needed in order to track children's growth over time and to determine whether children are mastering required benchmarks and standards. Throughout the chapter we discuss how to make instructional decisions based on the outcomes of assessments. We describe a systematic approach to assessment that includes determining standards and benchmarks, developing a timeline for administering assessments at particular times during the year, selecting and administering assessments, and interpreting the results. Together, information from assessment tasks, from children's work samples, and from observations of children during reading and writing activities provide the best evidence of what children can do.

WHAT LITERACY SKILLS AND STRATEGIES SHOULD BE ASSESSED IN KINDERGARTEN?

Kindergarten is a time of great growth in literacy development. Some children enter kindergarten not knowing how to write their names or unable to recognize any alphabet letters. Other children have learned to write both their first and last names and know nearly all their alphabet letters. All children are expected to end kindergarten having acquired many concepts about print, recognizing nearly all the alphabet letters quickly and easily, knowing how to write alphabet letters, being able to isolate beginning phonemes of words, knowing the relationships between nearly all consonant letter–sounds, and inventing spellings with at least one or two letters. Children are also expected to develop larger vocabularies and to be able to retell complex picture books with many details. They are expected to participate in book-reading activities by predicting, making comments, and answering questions that require them to infer and analyze. They are expected to fingerpoint read in familiar books introduced during shared reading. In some districts children are also expected to have learned some sight words and to have begun reading simple books independently.

Literacy Standards Guide Instruction and Assessment

All states have standards regarding the level of literacy that all kindergartners in that state are expected to achieve, and many school districts within states have their own set of standards. Many state standards provide only a minimum; they identify what most children can and do achieve by the end of the kindergarten year. We recommend that kindergarten teachers use rigorous standards that are based on research showing what kindergartners can do with effective instruction. Figure 7.1 presents a possible list of standards that identifies children's expected achievements in alphabet recognition and writing, concepts about print, phonemic awareness, phonics, text reading, writing, and comprehension and vocabulary. This list also includes *benchmarks*, intermediate steps along the way toward reaching the final goals expected at the end of the year. End-of-the-year accomplishments are indicated in Figure 7.1, and some standards or benchmarks go beyond what is expected of all children.

These standards guide teachers in making decisions about what they will teach throughout the kindergarten year and the nature of assessments that they need to use to document children's achievement. It is not expected that teachers will give kindergartners tests that will assess their achievement of all the skills and strategies identified on any list of standards and benchmarks. Instead, effective teachers use three strategies for monitoring children's progress in achieving standards. First, they will choose a few assessment tasks to administer to individual children at selected times throughout the school year. Second, they will systematically collect samples of children's reading and writing, write an analysis of what these samples tell them about children's learning, and place the sample and written analysis in a portfolio for each child. *Portfolios* are folders or expandable files in which teachers keep one child's assessment records. Third, they will observe children as they are engaged in reading and writing during center work or other free-play times. Teachers will take notes about what they observe, write an analysis of

1. Develops alphabet recognition and writing.
    1.1. Writes name.
        1.1.a. Writes first name with a few recognizable letters.
        1.1.b. Writes first name with nearly all recognizable letters.
        1.1.c. Writes consistently recognizable first name.*
        1.1.d. Writes first and last name with conventional upper- and lower-case letters.
    1.2. Recognizes upper- and lower-case alphabet letters fluently.
        1.2.a. Recognizes 0–13 alphabet letters.
        1.2.b. Recognizes 13–26 alphabet letters including some lower-case letters.
        1.2.c. Recognizes 26–48 upper- and lower-case letters.
        1.2.d. Recognizes 48–52 upper- and lower-case letters.*
        1.2.e. Fluently recognizes 52 upper- and lower-case letters.
    1.3. Writes alphabet letters and words.
        1.3.a. Writes 1–5 recognizable letters (mostly in own name).
        1.3.b. Writes 5–13 recognizable alphabet letters including letters not in name.
        1.3.c. Writes 13–26 alphabet letters mostly upper-case but with some lower-case.
        1.3.d. Writes 26–52 upper- and lower-case letters.*
        1.3.e. Locates known words and asks for spellings of words.*
    1.4 Pretends to write during dramatic play.
        1.4.a. Pretends to write for a variety of functional purposes (messages, grocery lists, restaurant orders, and traffic tickets).
        1.4.b. Uses letters to pretend to write in play.*
        1.4.c. Uses invented spelling to write in play.*
2. Develops Concepts about Print.
    2.1. Develops directionality concepts.
        2.1.a. Uses linear pointing for tracking.
        2.1.b. Attempts to pretend read using memory and pointing at words for tracking.
        2.1.c. Attempts to match one spoken word or syllable with one written word during tracking.
        2.1.d. Fingerpoint reads, matching spoken and written words with one-to-one correspondence.*
        2.1.e. Monitors fingerpoint-reading accuracy using beginning letter–sound associations with support.*
    2.2. Develops letter and word concepts.
        2.2.a Matches letters and words in shared writing or fingerpoint texts.
        2.2.b. Counts words in text.*
        2.2.c. Locates and identifies words by beginning letter.
        2.2.d. Counts the number of letters in words.*
        2.2.e. Identifies the letter at the beginnings and ends of words.*
        2.2.g. Identifies long and short words.*

*Expected end-of-the-year kindergarten achievement.

cont.

FIGURE 7.1. Kindergarten literacy standards *with benchmarks.*

2.2.h. Reads new rhyming words in word-building activities. *

2.2.i. Writes new rhyming words in word-building activities.

3. Develops phonemic awareness.
   3.1. Recognizes rhyming words.*
   3.2. Recognizes words with the same beginning phoneme.
       3.2.a. Recognizes if phoneme is in a word.
       3.2.b. Matches words with same phoneme.
       3.2.c. Sorts words by beginning phoneme. *
   3.3. Produces rhyming words.*
   3.4. Produces a word with the same beginning phoneme.*
   3.5. Isolates beginning phonemes in words.*
   3.6. Isolates ending phonemes in words.
   3.7. Blends segmented syllables, onset/rimes, and phonemes into words.

4. Uses phonics to spell and decode.
   4.1. Learns letter–sound associations.
       4.1.a. Learns consonant letter–sound associations. *
       4.1.b. Learns letter–sound associations for consonant digraphs. *
       4.1.c. Learns short-vowel letter–sound associations in familiar word patterns.
   4.2 Invents spellings.
       4.2.a. Spells with initial or other salient consonants. *
       4.2.b. Spells with boundary phonemes (first and last phoneme). *
       4.2.c. Spells with beginning, middle, and ending phonemes.
       4.2.d. Spells with conventional consonant and short-vowel letter–sound associations.
   4.3. Decodes words.
       4.3.a. Blends phonemes with familiar rhyming words to read new words. *
       4.3.b. Begins to decode short-vowel CVC words.
   4.4. Identifies words by sight.
       4.4.a. Identifies up to 10 words by sight. *
       4.4.b. Identifies 25–50 words by sight.
       4.4.c. Identifies 50–200 words by sight.

5. Reads text.
   5.1 Rereads familiar shared- and fingerpoint-reading texts.
       5.1.a. Reads familiar guided shared- and fingerpoint-reading text using tracking, memory, and beginning letter–sound monitoring. *
   5.2. Reads unfamiliar decodable text in guided reading using sight words, word families, and decoding.

6. Writes.
   6.1. Composes stories, informational text, and other texts as a part of shared writing.
   6. 2. Composes stories, informational text, and other texts.
       6.2.a. Composes by dictating to the teacher or other adult.
       6.2.b. Composes by pretending to write.   cont.

FIGURE 7.1. *cont.*

> *6.2.c. Composes by inventing spellings.* *
>
> *6.2.d. Composes texts with some genre elements.* *
>
> 7. Develops oral comprehension, language, and vocabulary.
>
>   7.l. Retells, reenacts, or dramatizes stories without support.*
>
>   7.2. Makes predictions based on illustrations or story information.*
>
>   7.3. Retells stories with some sophisticated vocabulary (uses past tense consistently).*
>
>   7.4. Retells information books with some details (frequently uses timeless present and generic nouns).*
>
>   7.5. Learns sophisticated new vocabulary words from listening to books.*
>
>   7.6. Answers why questions about stories (inference and explanation).*
>
>   7.7. Makes comments about story illustrations that connect to other books.*
>
>   7.8. Memorizes predictable patterns in stories with advanced syntax and produces new content to fit the patterns.
>
>   7.9. Applies comprehension strategies to books read in shared, fingerpoint, and guided reading.*

FIGURE 7.1. *cont.*

what these observations tell them about children's learning, and place them in the children's portfolios. Teachers will frequently reflect on the results of assessment tasks, on their analysis of children's work samples, and on their analysis of observations to plan instruction, change placement in small groups, and alert parents and other school personnel of potential difficulties.

Selecting Assessments Based on Standards

Teachers can use a variety of quick, easy-to-administer assessment tasks to measure children's knowledge in alphabet recognition and writing, concepts about print, phonemic awareness, phonics, text reading, writing, and comprehension and vocabulary. Later in this chapter we describe several assessment tasks that teachers can construct (these assessments can be found in Appendices C through H). Children who are making adequate or fast progress will need fewer assessments. Children who enter kindergarten with very little knowledge about literacy or who seem to be making little progress even when provided with focused instruction in both whole and small groups will need careful watching. For these children teachers may want to administer several of the same assessment tasks over a few weeks to document how levels of knowledge change over time so that they can make targeted instructional decisions that will accelerate learning.

Some states have mandated assessments that kindergarten teachers are required to administer. These assessments are standardized literacy measures given during the first 4–8 weeks of school, and their scores provide useful information for grouping children for instruction. For example, some states use the *Dynamic*

Indicators of Basic Early Literacy (DIBELS; information about DIBELS can be found at dibels.uoregon.edu) or the *Phonological Awareness Literacy Screening* (pals; information about pals can be found at pals.virginia.edu). When teachers work in states or districts that require the use of assessments such as DIBELS or pals, they will not need to use all, or even any, of the assessment tasks that we discuss in this chapter. However, teachers may want to administer some additional assessment tasks to complement the standardized assessment (e.g., DIBELS does not assess comprehension and vocabulary, concepts about print, text reading, or writing). All children need additional assessment information gathered through observation and systematic collection of work samples.

USING ASSESSMENT TASKS TO IDENTIFY WHAT CHILDREN KNOW AND TO MONITOR PROGRESS

Figure 7.2 presents a list of several assessment tasks (*early literacy knowledge assessment tasks* [ELKA]) that can be used in kindergarten. The assessment tasks included in this list are comprehensive; these tasks cover all areas of literacy development from early print learning, to fingerpoint reading and invented spelling, through early reading and writing. Kindergarten teachers are never expected to administer *all* of the ELKA assessment tasks for *every* child in their classroom. Some of the assessments capture children's literacy knowledge at the very beginnings when children are learning early print concepts. Some assessments capture children's literacy knowledge at more advanced levels as children discover the alphabetic principle. Still other assessments capture children's literacy knowledge beyond what is expected in kindergarten. In general, the tasks included in Figure 7.2 are listed within each category by level of difficulty. The earlier tasks assess knowledge that is expected to develop earlier in the continuum of literacy development. Teachers will select ELKA assessments to match children's developmental levels as they enter and move through kindergarten. Therefore, different ELKA assessment tasks are more applicable at the beginning, middle, and end of the school year.

Alphabet Recognition and Writing

Four ELKA assessments can be used to assess children's alphabet knowledge: name writing and letters-in-name recognition, upper-case recognition, lower-case recognition, and alphabet letter writing. We recommend beginning with upper-case letter recognition. If children identify five or fewer letters, then teachers will want to administer the easier name-writing and letters-in-name recognition assessment tasks and skip the more difficult lower-case letters recognition and writing assessments. When children know more than five upper-case letters, we recommend that teachers administer the lower-case letter recognition and

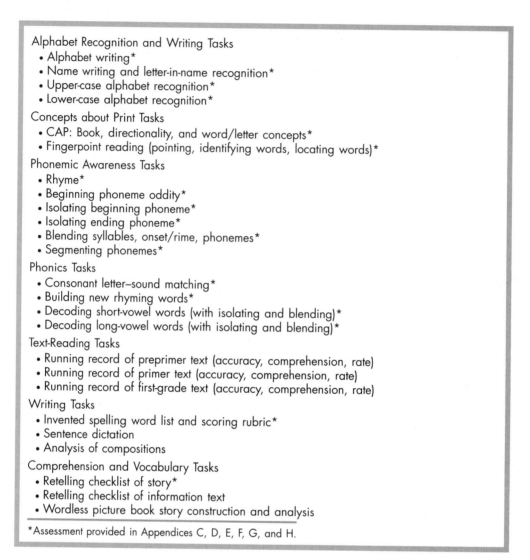

Alphabet Recognition and Writing Tasks
- Alphabet writing*
- Name writing and letter-in-name recognition*
- Upper-case alphabet recognition*
- Lower-case alphabet recognition*

Concepts about Print Tasks
- CAP: Book, directionality, and word/letter concepts*
- Fingerpoint reading (pointing, identifying words, locating words)*

Phonemic Awareness Tasks
- Rhyme*
- Beginning phoneme oddity*
- Isolating beginning phoneme*
- Isolating ending phoneme*
- Blending syllables, onset/rime, phonemes*
- Segmenting phonemes*

Phonics Tasks
- Consonant letter–sound matching*
- Building new rhyming words*
- Decoding short-vowel words (with isolating and blending)*
- Decoding long-vowel words (with isolating and blending)*

Text-Reading Tasks
- Running record of preprimer text (accuracy, comprehension, rate)
- Running record of primer text (accuracy, comprehension, rate)
- Running record of first-grade text (accuracy, comprehension, rate)

Writing Tasks
- Invented spelling word list and scoring rubric*
- Sentence dictation
- Analysis of compositions

Comprehension and Vocabulary Tasks
- Retelling checklist of story*
- Retelling checklist of information text
- Wordless picture book story construction and analysis

*Assessment provided in Appendices C, D, E, F, G, and H.

FIGURE 7.2. Early Literacy Knowledge Assessments (ELKA).

alphabet-writing tasks and skip the name-writing and letters-in-name recognition task.

The *name-writing and letters-in-name recognition assessment* (Bloodgood, 1999; Hildreth, 1936; Villaume & Wilson, 1989) includes five subtasks: name writing, name recognition, spelling letters in the name, identifying each letter in the name, and matching the letters to a printed signature. Appendix C presents an overview of this task, directions for making materials used in the task, and guidelines for analyzing children's responses to the tasks. In the first task children are invited to write their name. If children respond that they cannot write their names, teachers say: "Some children write like this [demonstrate making a scribble]. Some children write like this [demonstrate writing a linear mock cursive scribble], and some children write like this [demonstrate writing individual circles and lines that do not resemble letters]. Some children write like this [demonstrate writing in upper- and lower-case letters a name—but not the child's first name]. You can write any way you want." If children still refuse, then teachers move to the second subtask: name recognition. Teachers prepare four name cards for this activity. One card has the child's printed name; two other cards have names of other children in the classroom—names that do not begin with the same letter as the target child's name. The fourth card includes the printed name of a child in the classroom whose name begins with the same letter as the target child's (if there are none in the classroom, teachers write a name that does begin with that letter). Children are shown all four cards and asked to find their name and read the other children's names.

For the third subtask, spelling the name, teachers say: "Tell me the letters that spell your name." The fourth subtask requires that teachers type and cut out the letters in the child's name using upper- and lower-case letters. The letters are scrambled and the target child is asked to identify the letters and then use the letters to spell his or her name. The last subtask, letter matching, requires that teachers prepare a card on which the child's name has been typed. The child matches the set of typed letters used in the fourth task to the name typed on the card. Appendix C presents the directions and examples of materials used in the name-writing and letters-in-name recognition task

Teachers analyze children's responses to the five tasks to determine children's knowledge of alphabet letters, name recognition, and name writing. Children's signatures generally fall into seven categories (Bloodgood, 1999; Hildreth, 1936). Figure 7.3 presents an example of children's signatures that fall into each of these seven categories.

Teachers analyze whether children recognize their own name (or are confused by the name with the same beginning letter) and whether children can recognize the other names. They determine whether children can spell their names (say the letters), whether they can identify the letters in their names when they are presented in isolation on cards, whether they can arrange the letters correctly to spell their name, and whether they can match the letters correctly to their signature. Teachers may consider whether children are aware of letter orientation (children may match letters correctly but put some letters upside-down or turned sideways). They can determine whether children are beginning to notice print (they can recognize one or two other children's names). Teachers may consider whether children can write their names, but cannot spell their names or even recognize the letters in their names. This assessment provides teachers with a starting point for instruction (most children learn the first letter in their names as one of the first letters they can identify). Learning to write a recognizable signature provides children with opportunities to learn about letter features, words, and other concepts about print.

1	Scribble	Mack
2	Linear mock cursive	Mack
3	Separate symbols (not mock letters)	Ashanti
3.5	Separate symbols with one/two recognizable or mock letters	Ashanti
4	All mock letters and recognizable letters may have orientation difficulties	Grace
5	Recognizable letters with few orientation difficulties	Chance
6	First name with conventional letters	LaRicky
7	First and last name with small conventional letters and with consistent sizing	

FIGURE 7.3. Signatures at seven levels of development.

Appendix C presents the *upper-case and lower-case alphabet recognition tasks*. Teachers can copy the entire page to administer the task to children. They point to letters across the lines of the text as they administer the task. A score sheet can be made by simply copying the administration form for each child. Teachers circle letters on the score sheet that children do not know. To administer the task, teachers say: "Some children know the names of alphabet letters. If you know the name of the letter I point to, say it. Sometimes children don't know the name, so just say 'Pass' if you don't know the name." Teachers point to each letter across the line of text. Teachers may want to abandon the assessment if children do not recognize the first eight letters. Children who can identify 22 or more upper-case and 22 or more lower-case letters have reached mastery on this task (Morris & Slavin, 2003) and have achieved end-of-kindergarten goals.

Appendix C also presents the *alphabet-writing task*. Teachers can make copies of the writing score sheet for each child. The administration sheet lists the alphabet letters children should be directed to write. Teachers point to a line on the score sheet, say the letter name indicated on the administration sheet (not showing the letter to the child), and then say: "Write A on this line." Teachers should note which letters children can write, whether they write in upper- or lower-case, and whether they have orientation difficulties. Generally, teachers use a generous scoring method early in the year (where letters are not completely conventional, but still recognizable) and a more strict method later in the year (where letters should be written conventionally). Teachers may abandon this assessment if it is clear that children are not writing any recognizable letters.

Concepts about Print

CAP: Concepts about Book Orientation, Directionality, and Letters and Words (adapted from Clay, 1993a) is presented in Appendix D. This assessment includes 15 questions that assess children's awareness of the parts of a book (front, back, top, bottom) and directionality (left and right pages, page turn, left-to-right reading, and return sweep). It also assesses concepts about letters and words (isolate a word, isolate a letter, find long and short words, and find a word with four letters). In order to administer this assessment, teachers present the child with a book, ask questions about the book following the directions on the CAP task, and score children's responses as correct or incorrect. We recommend that teachers select a commercial-leveled early reading book such as *Too-Tall Paul, Too-Small Paul* (Hood, 1998) to use with this assessment. We selected this particular book because it includes children from diverse backgrounds in the illustrations and has only a few lines of text on each page. We recommend using pages 18, 19, and 20 for the CAP task because these three successive pages have at least two lines of print, there is text on both the left and the right pages, and there are several long and short words in the text—all of these characteristics are required in order to administer the CAP. Appendix D presents the questions and scoring rubric for the CAP task using pages 18, 19, and 20 of the book *Too-Tall Paul, Too-Small Paul*. A score of 13 or more on this assessment indicates that children have acquired knowledge about book orientation and directionality, and have developed early concepts about letters and words. When children answer only a few questions on the CAP assessment, teachers may want to modify the task by using a familiar environmental print item such as a small box of cereal often eaten at school instead of a book.

The *fingerpoint reading* task requires that teachers help children memorize a short text and then attempt to fingerpoint read that text. Appendix D presents a text that is appropriate to use in the fingerpoint reading task (words to the familiar song "Itsy Bitsy Spider"). Teachers introduce the text and talk with the child about his or her experiences with spiders, rain spouts, and what happens when it rains hard. Then they read the text while pointing to each word as they read it. Then teachers reread the text a second time, again pointing to each word as they say it, and invite the child to say the text. The third time teachers read the text, they say: "Now you point to the words while I read the text. You read along with me." During this rereading teachers guide children's pointing so that they do point to each word as that word is spoken. The assessment begins after these three practice readings. Teachers say: "Now you point to the words and say the poem. Start here [teachers point to the first word in the title]." Two additional tasks are administered to analyze children's use of fingerpoint reading to locate and identify words. Teachers point to four words in the text (see the administration sheet in Appendix D for identification of these four words) and say: "What is this word?" Then teachers have children locate four words (the administration sheet in Appendix D lists these words); for example, they say: "Can you find the word *spider*?" Teachers score whether children have identified or located the correct word.

Appendix E provides an analysis sheet for this assessment. Teachers carefully observe children's pointing and write notes. They score whether children were able to locate and identify the words correctly and whether children attempted to use fingerpoint reading to do these tasks. To analyze children's development of fingerpoint reading, teachers consider children's pointing. For each line of text teachers determine whether children

> ➤ Do not point

> ➤ Sweep across the text without attempting to point at words or attempting to match spoken words to text

> ➤ Attempt to point to each word but with inaccuracies

> ➤ Point to each word correctly when no multiple-syllable words are included

> ➤ Point to each word correctly even when multiple-syllable words are included (this is actual fingerpoint reading and the correct response to the task; children receive 1 point for each line of text to which they point to all of its written words while saying the related spoken words)

Children who receive a score of 13 or better on this task (adding together the number of words correctly identified and located and the number of lines of text the child read using fingerpoint reading) indicate mastery of the concept (Morris & Slavin, 2003). Kindergartners are expected to reach this level by the end of the year.

Phonemic Awareness

Appendix E presents five phonemic awareness assessments and a score sheet that teachers can use with all five of these assessments. For the *rhyme task* kindergarten teachers say: "We are going to look for rhyming words. These two words rhyme [show the picture of the star and jar]. *Car* and *star* rhyme. Now you say them. Now we will play a game of finding two pictures that rhyme. Here is how we do it." Teachers will point to the practice line of pictures and say: "*Fish, bug, dish.* Now you say them. I think *fish* and *dish* rhyme. You say them. Now it's your turn. I will say the pictures first, then you will say the pictures and find the two that rhyme." Children are shown 10 sets of three pictures, teachers say the picture names, and children repeat these words. Then children find the two words that rhyme. Teachers count the number of rhyming pairs children correctly identify. Children have mastered rhyme when they correctly match seven or more of the 10 rhyming items (Lonigan, Burgess, Anthony, & Baker, 1998).

In the *beginning phoneme oddity task* (Lonigan et al., 1998; MacLean et al., 1987), children are shown three pictures, and they must select the picture that does not have the same beginning sound as the other pictures. Teachers first demonstrate for children by saying: "We are going to play a game to find the word that does not start with the same sound as the other words. Listen as I say these words: *tent, fork, toe.* Now you say them. Now I am going to pick the word that does *not* sound like the other two. *Tent* and *toe* sound alike, but *fork* sounds different. I pick *fork.*" Teachers say the names of the pictures, children repeat the names of the pictures, and children select the word that does not sound the same as the other two pictures. There are a total of 18 items on this assessment; however, we recommend that teachers only use 10 items to assess this concept at the beginning of the year. Teachers score whether children identified correctly the picture that does not sound the same as the other two. Because this assessment includes an element of guessing, children must score seven out of 10 (or 12 out of 18, if all items are presented) to demonstrate mastery of this concept. A score less than 3 out of 10 (or 7 out of 18) clearly indicates that children are only working at chance level and have not yet developed awareness of beginning phonemes. Teachers may administer all 18 of the items presented in Appendix E after instruction in beginning phonemes to determine which phonemes children have learned and which phonemes can be targeted for instruction.

In the *isolating beginning and ending phonemes task* children listen to the teacher pronounce a word, and then they are asked to say the sound at the beginning or at the ending of the word. Teachers demonstrate the task by saying: "You are going to tell me the beginning sound you hear in words. Let me do this first one. The word is *paint*. I hear /p/ at the beginning of that word [or I hear /t/ at the end of that word]. Now you say /p/ [or /t/]." This is given orally; teachers say the word, and children say either the beginning or ending phoneme. Teachers mark whether children pronounced the correct phoneme.

The isolating beginning phoneme assessment includes a total of 32 items, one item for the phonemes associated with all the consonants; the consonant digraphs *sh, ch,* and *th*; and the long and short vowels. We recommend that teachers deliberately select items that reflect instruction. At the beginning of the year before instruction on phoneme isolation is initiated, teachers might use only 10 items to determine whether children can isolate the beginning phonemes of continuants (e.g., phonemes associated with the letters *f, j, l, m, n, r, s, v, w,* and *sh*) or other consonants (e.g., phonemes associated with the letters *b, d, g, h, k, p, t,* and *ch*). If children do not respond to the first three items correctly, teachers might want to abandon the assessment—these children have obviously not mastered this skill.

Later, in the year teachers will determine whether children can isolate all consonants, consonant digraphs, and the long- and short-vowel phonemes. The ending phoneme assessment includes a total of 16 items, an item for each of the consonant and consonant digraph phonemes most frequently found at the end of words.

In the *blending syllables, onset/rimes, and phoneme task* teachers say words segmented into syllables, onsets and rimes, or phonemes. Teachers say the first segment, pause 2 seconds, and then say the second segment. Teachers introduce the task by saying: "I am going to say a silly word, and you will tell me the real word I am trying to say. *Fire* [pause 2 seconds] *man.* The real word is *fireman.* Let's do another one. *Tooth* [pause 2 seconds] *brush.* That word is *toothbrush.* Now I'll say a silly word and you tell me the real word." Teachers administer the remaining 10 assessment words listed Appendix F. Teachers score children's attempts as correct (i.e., they say the word blended together). Or they score the attempt as incorrect; many young children either repeat just the beginning or ending segment or say the words divided as the teacher did. To be correct, children must say the actual word as a whole. When children cannot correctly blend the first three words, teachers may want to abandon the assessment—these children have not developed this concept. When children can blend, teachers use the score sheet to analyze whether children can blend words at the level of syllable, onset and rime, or phoneme.

For the *segmenting phonemes task* teachers demonstrate by saying: "I am going to say a word and then say each of its little bits of sound. Here is the first word, *tie.* You know, like 'tie your shoes.' *Tie.* Now I'll divide it into its little bits of sounds: /t/ /ie/. Here's another word. The word is *it.* You know, like you are "it." *It.* The little bits of sounds in *it* are /i/ /t/. Now it's your turn. I'll say the word and you tell me the little bits of sounds that you hear."

Appendix E presents 10 words to use in this task; five words with two phonemes and five words with three phonemes. Teachers use the score sheet to circle the phonemes children can isolate. For example, children may be able to isolate the beginning phoneme /t/ in the word *toe,* but not be able to segment the final phoneme. Teachers would circle the /t/. Or children may isolate the little bits of sounds in the word *sheep* into its onset and rime. They would say /sh/ /eep/. Here teachers would circle /sh/, and then circle /ee/ and /p/ together to indicate that the child segmented this portion of the word without isolating the individual phonemes.

Phonics

Appendix F presents four phonics assessments and a score sheet that can be used with all four assessments. These assessment measure children's knowledge of the phonemes associated with consonant alphabet letters, their ability to read new words by blending consonants with familiar rhyming words, and their ability to decode unfamiliar short-vowel and long-vowel words. These last two assessments will be given after teachers have provided instruction, or when children demonstrate this level of achievement. Although a majority of the words included in the phonics assessments are real words, a few nonsense words have also been included. The nonsense words are included to provide a measure of children's ability to blend together phonemes into words when words are not sight words. Again, decoding nonsense words by saying the phonemes and then blending together the phonemes into words is an advanced skill for most kindergartners. However, many school districts and states use assessments (such as DIBELS) that measure this ability during kindergarten.

In the *consonant letter–sound matching task* children are shown a picture and then asked to select the letter (from a set of three letters) that the picture word begins with. Teachers first demonstrate by saying: "You are going to look at the picture, and then the letters. You will say the letter that the picture word begins with. Look, this is a *sock*. I see the letters *L*, *B*, and *S*. The word *sock* begins with the letter *S*. Now it's your turn." Teachers say the name of each picture and then have the children say the letter that the picture word begins with. Teachers score children's attempts as correct or incorrect. There are a total of 18 items on this assessment, one item for each consonant letter. Teachers can use selected items from this assessment to determine whether children have learned letter–sound relationships taught.

In the *blending new rhyming words task* children are shown pictures and written words for five familiar rhyming words (*bat*, *net*, *lip*, *sock*, and *jump*). First, the teacher demonstrates reading a new rhyming word by saying: "Look at the picture of the *bat*. This word is *bat* [pointing to the word *bat*]. Here are some words that rhyme with *bat*. Look—all of these words end like *bat*. Here is the first word that I am going to read. It rhymes with *bat*, but instead of beginning with *b*, it begins with the letter *h*. *H* says /h/, so that word is *hat*. Let's try another one. The next word begins with *s* and *s* says [pause for the child to say /s/ or provide it if the child does not pronounce the phoneme]. So that word is *sat*. Now you try." Teachers point to the next word in the list and have the child read that word. If the child hesitates, teachers can encourage the child to say the name of the first letter and its sound, then say the word. Teachers score the item correct if the child correctly identifies the word.

If children cannot read the first three words of this task, then teachers abandon the assessment. When children meet with some success with the *bat* rhyming words, then teachers move on to the *net* rhyme family. Teachers remind children of the task by saying: "Here is a picture of a net. Here is the word *net*. All these other words rhyme with *net*. Look—*net* ends with the letters *et* and all these other words end with those letters too. Now you read the words that rhyme with *net*." Teachers score children's attempts as correct or incorrect.

When children read many of the rhyming words correctly, teachers may want to administer the *decoding short-vowel words task*. In this assessment children are only shown words and then are asked to read them. The words all have three letters, include only short vowels, and are presented with the vowels mixed (rather than sorted into short-*a* words, etc.). Teachers use the administration sheet as a score sheet and mark words that children read correctly. Teachers may use the sheet to indicate whether children pronounce the word, attempt to decode the sounds and blend the word, or pronounce another word (usually one with the same beginning letter).

Teachers may suggest a strategy for reading the nonsense words included on this assessment by saying: "These words are not real words, but you can use what you know about letters to sound them out. Remember to say the sounds and keep your motor running as you bulldoze through the word quickly." Teachers will note whether children know the phoneme associated with each letter, whether they can sustain the phoneme long enough to blend it with the next phoneme, and whether they can blend the phonemes together quickly enough to pronounce a word.

Appendix F also presents a *decoding long-vowel words task* that is similar in form to the decoding short-vowel words task. This task is very advanced and it is not expected that kindergartners will be able to accomplish this task without appropriate instruction. Again, it includes real and nonsense words. Teachers will have children read the words, noting whether children know the word without decoding, know the correct phonemes, can hold phonemes in memory in order to blend the phonemes together, and can blend quickly enough to pronounce a word.

Appendix F also presents *a consonant phoneme and letter–sound analysis form*. This form helps teachers analyze children's knowledge of consonant phonemes and consonant letter–sound associations. Teachers look across several assessments to check phonemes that children can isolate at the beginning of words, at the end of words, and letter–sounds that children match. They can also check to see if children correctly used those sounds in decoding words in familiar word families, when decoding short-vowel words, or when decoding long-vowel words. In other words, teacher can consider the letter *b* and determine if children can isolate the /b/ phoneme at the beginning of words or at the end of words, whether they match the /b/ picture to the letter *B*, or whether they correctly decoded the familiar word family word *bump*, the short-vowel word *bet*, and the nonsense word *bip*. They would continue to consider each of the consonants across the five assessment tasks. Teachers would determine whether children, for example, isolate the /g/ phoneme at the beginning and ending of words, or whether children matched the letter *G* correctly in the letter–sound matching assessment, whether children correctly blended the familiar word family *get*, and decoded the short-vowel word *got*.

Appendix F presents a *vowel analysis form* as well. This allows teachers to examine whether children correctly read, for example, short-*a* words, in the familiar rhyming-word family (*vat*), in the short-vowel decoding assessment (*ram, rag, had*), or in the short-vowel nonsense words (*fam*). Together the consonant and vowel analysis forms present a complete picture of children's phonemic awareness and phonics knowledge of the phonemes and letter–sound correspondences taught in kindergarten.

Text Reading

The ultimate assessment of conventional reading is whether children can read connected text accurately (with few errors, i.e., 90% or more of the words are read correctly), fluently (the reading has the intonation and phrasing of speech, the rate is fairly fast, and the rate increases as the level of text increases), and with comprehension (can answer 70% of questions correctly including questions that call for recall, inferences, predictions, and explanations). Generally, first-grade benchmarks for text reading are set at the preprimer, primer, and first-grade levels (in many districts kindergartners are not expected to read text independently other than with fingerpoint reading or reading in easy decodable books). Traditionally, texts are graded for difficulty based on the number of unusual words, sentence length and complexity, decodability, kinds of concepts, and use of predictable or repeated language patterns. Easier texts are more predictable because they employ repeated words and phrases, use everyday words, have words that are decodable, present familiar everyday occurrences and concepts, and have short sentences. These texts are considered preprimer; *Go dog, go!* (Eastman, 1961) and *Mrs. Wishy Washy* (Cowley, 1999) are good examples of this level of text. Texts that are longer, with more different words, less repetition, and more complex sentences, are considered primer texts; *More Spaghetti, I Say!* (Gelman, 1993) and *Sheep in a Jeep* (Shaw, 1986) are examples of this level of text. First-grade text includes many more words, no repetition, and longer stretches of text; examples of first-grade texts are *Kiss for Little Bear* (Minarik, 1996) and *Noisy Nora* (Wells, 2000).

When children are reading conventionally, teachers can assess their level of reading by using running records. A *running record* is a recording of the words children read from a text. Teachers use the record to analyze children's miscues or errors. First teachers select a text they believe is on the children's instructional level. To be considered on "instructional level," the text is read with 90–95% accuracy, and children can answer 70–90% questions about the text correctly. When children read with 98% or better accuracy and 90% or better comprehension, the text is considered on their "independent level." When children read text with less than 90% accuracy and less than 70% comprehension, this text is considered on the "frustration level." Running records can be used to determine whether a selected is text is at independent, instruction, or frustration level for a specific child.

In kindergarten, we recommend a slightly modified procedure for running records for children teachers know can read some text conventionally and for children teachers know can fingerpoint read. First, we describe a procedure to be used when teachers know that children are reading independently. Second, we describe using running records when children are fingerpoint reading, but not yet reading conventionally.

Using Running Records with Conventional Kindergarten Readers

To begin, teachers select a text that they have reason to believe that children can read. This may be a text that has been read in guided reading or a new text that teachers suspect is on children's instructional reading level. Teachers can use texts found in standardized assessments such as the *Developmental Reading Assessment* (Beaver, 1997) or texts from commercial companies that have been leveled (such as books from the Wright Group or Sundance). We recommend that teachers find a single text that has 150–200 words. We recommend the following modification of the usual running-record procedure. We recommend that the teacher will read aloud the first 50–100 words of the text, then the child will read the next 100 words for the running record. This procedure helps young kindergartners get a running start on a text before the running record begins. Teachers copy the text of the 100 words that the child will read (copy the pages from the book or type the text using the sentence lining as it appears in the book), and use it to mark errors and self-corrections as the child reads aloud.

Figure 7.4 presents a text used to take a running record of the story of *The Three Bears*. Teachers read aloud the first portion of the text (109 words), and children read the second portion (151 words). The portion read by the teacher introduces the characters, some of the sequence of the story, and some of the vocabulary words. Thus, it provides children with a context for their own reading. We estimate this text is at the primer level.

Figure 7.5 presents the running record, which indicates when the child omitted a word, inserted a word, substituted a word, or made an incomplete attempt at reading the word. It also indicates when the child self-corrected after making a miscue. When the child read the word *tried* as *turned*, she paused and then said: "No, that doesn't make sense. What is that word?" The teacher provided the word (and then marked it as prompted). When the child paused at the word *middle*, the teacher prompted with "Read it the best you can." After a 5-second pause, the teacher supplied the word and counted it as a prompt. The child made 14 miscues (omissions, insertions, substitutions, prompts) and four of these were self-corrected (the child eventually read the correct word, so self-corrections are not counted as miscues) for a total of 10 miscues. Since there were 151 words in the passage, the child read 141 words correctly (151 total words minus 10 miscues). The accuracy rate is determined by finding the percentage of words read correctly (dividing 151 total words by 141 words read correctly). The accuracy rate for this child is 93%. The child answered four questions about this text correctly (she said that the little girl did not sleep on the big bed because she wanted the small bed instead). Her comprehension was 80%; therefore, this text is on her instructional level.

Figure 7.6 presents a *miscue analysis* of this child's reading. It lists the text word, the miscue attempts, and an analysis of whether the miscue retains meaning

(Portion read aloud by the teacher)

The Three Bears

Once upon a time deep in a forest lived a family of three bears, a Papa Bear, a Mama Bear, and a Baby Bear. One day Mama Bear made some porridge, but it was too hot to eat. The Bear Family decided they would take a walk in the woods while their porridge cooled. The three bears left their house. A little girl appeared out of the forest. She had long golden hair. She went inside the house and saw the three bowls of porridge. Goldilocks sat down at the table to try a little bit of the porridge in the three bowls. One bowl was big, one bowl was middle-sized, and one bowl was small.

(Portion read aloud by the child)

She tried the big bowl. It was too hot. She tried the middle bowl. It was too cold. She tried the small bowl. It was just right. She ate it all. She saw three chairs. She sat on the big chair. It was too hard. She sat on the middle chair. It was too soft. She sat on the small chair. It was just right. It broke! The little girl saw three beds. She jumped on the big bed. It was too hard. She jumped on the middle bed. It was too soft. She jumped on the small bed. It was just right. She went to sleep. The bears came home. Baby Bear saw his food was gone. He saw his chair was broken. He saw the little girl still sleeping on his small bed. The little girl woke up. She ran out of the house. The bears never saw her again.

Questions:

What did the little girl break? (chair)

Why did the little girl eat the little bowl? (it was just right, she was hungry)

Why didn't the little girl sleep in the big bed? (it was too hard)

What did the bears look at first when they came home? (they looked at the bowls)

Why did the little girl run away? (she was frightened)

FIGURE 7.4. Text for *The Three Bears*.

of the sentence, retains the structure of the sentence up to the miscue, and whether the miscue has the same letter–sound relationships (at the beginning, middle, and end) as the actual text word. This analysis demonstrates that this reader's miscues frequently maintained meaning, sometimes maintained the sentence structure, sometimes were self-corrected, and very frequently matched the beginning letter–sound of the text word. This child might benefit from instruction in looking for vowel chunks or using vowel-first decoding (see Chapter 6).

The teacher timed the amount of time it took this child to read the text. She read it in 4 minutes and 30 seconds. Thus her reading rate is approximately 33 words a minute. This is an appropriate rate for this level of text. We expect children at the preprimer level to read at a rate of 15–35 words per minute, and to read 30–70 words per minute at the primer and first-grade level (based on Leslie & Caldwell, 2001).

just right. She ate it all ^up^   insertion

the (little) girl   omission

It was too hot ^cold^   substitution

She tried ~~the~~ middle bowl ^P^   prompt

She tried the big bowl ^turned (sc)^ self-correction

She tried the big bowl. ^turned^ ^bowel (sc)^

It was too hot.

She tried ~~the~~ middle bowl ^turned^ ^/m/ P^

It was too cold.

She tried the small bowl. ^little^

It was just right. She ate it all.

She saw three chairs.

She sat on the big chair.

It was too hard.

She sat on the middle chair. ^saw^

It was too soft.

She sat on ~~the~~ small chair. ^in (sc)^

It was just right. It broke!

The little girl saw three beds.

She jumped on the big bed.

It was too hard.

She jumped on the middle bed.

It was too soft.

She jumped on the small bed.

It was just right. She went to sleep. ^/s/ seep (sc)^

The bears came home. ^come^

Baby Bear saw his food was gone.

He saw his chair was broken. ^broke^

He saw the little girl still

sleeping on his small bed.

The little girl woke up. ^wake^

She ran out of the house.

The bears never saw her again. ^were^ ^/a/ (sc)^

FIGURE 7.5. Running record for *The Three Bears*.

Text	Miscue	Meaning	Structure	Letter–sound B	Letter–sound M	Letter–sound E	Self-correct
tried	turned			x		x	
bowl	bowel			x		x	x
tried	turned			x		x	
middle	/m/			x			
small	little	x	x				
sat	saw	x	x	x			x
on	in	x	x				
sleep	/s/ seep			x		x	x
came	come	x		x		x	
broken	broke	x		x	x		
woke	wake	x		x		x	
never	were		x				
again	/a/			x			x
10 miscues		6	4	10	1	6	4 (of 13)
percentage		60%	40%	100%	10%	60%	31%

FIGURE 7.6. Miscue analysis for *The Three Bears*.

Using Running Records with Children Who Fingerpoint Read

Many children in kindergarten are not yet conventionally reading, but they are capable of fingerpoint reading. Running records can be used to determine how well children use their memories, finger pointing, and first letter–sound clues to reread text. Teachers may want to know how well a child can fingerpoint read after only one or two practice readings with the teacher, how well a child can fingerpoint read a text the day following intensive reading and rereading of a text, or how well a child can fingerpoint read a print-only book made from highly familiar text (see Chapter 6).

To make a running record for fingerpoint reading, a teacher copies an entire text used in fingerpoint reading. As the child reads, the teacher marks the miscues on the running record. Teachers can prompt the child when he or she gets stuck on words or when his or her reading really begins to diverge from the text. They mark the prompts on the running record. A miscue analysis of fingerpoint reading usually shows that children liberally substitute meaningful words (e.g., *small* for *little*, *puppy* for *dog*, and *pot* for *kettle*). They should be attempting to self-correct when they notice the word they have read does not start with the same sound as the word they are pointing to. Children may not be able to read the correct word, but they should notice letter–sound discrepancies. Teachers will closely observe a child's fingerpoint reading to see if the child is gaining accuracy. Teachers will also note whether the child is developing sight words.

Writing

Children's spelling can be analyzed using developmental scoring rubrics (based on Bear et al., 2004; Stahl & Murray, 1994). Appendix G presents an invented spelling assessment in which children are asked to spell five words (*man, bug, fit, trade,* and *steep*). Teachers analyze children's spelling using the *spelling scoring rubric* presented in Appendix H (adapted from Morris & Slaven, 2003). When children do not attempt to spell or when they use random letters, teachers give the spelling a 0 score. When children write using at least one reasonable letter–sound match, their spelling is given a score of 1. When children write using two letters with reasonable matches, children are given a score of 2. When children spell with three letter–sound matches, they receive a score of 3. Teachers add the score for each of the five words together for a total. Children area expected to receive a score of 8 or higher before the end of kindergarten (Morris & Slavin, 2003).

Figure 7.7 presents four children's spellings of those five words and the scores each of the spellings was assigned using the invented-spelling scoring rubric. As shown on this figure, these four children are at different points in their spelling development. Charles was willing to spell, but does not yet use letter–sound relationships. He could be called a nonspeller (McGee & Richgels, 2004), and has not likely developed the alphabetic principle. In contrast, all three of the other children have developed the alphabetic principle as evidenced by their use of letters to spell phonemes. Jalexis is an early invented speller. Many of the letters she uses are related to the phonemes she hears in the words, but some are not the conventional letter related to that sound (she spelled the word *trade* with the letter G, indicating she is using manner of articulation rather than conventional letter–sound knowledge to spell this word). She only spells one letter for each word, and consistently spells the beginning of words. Her score of 5 suggests she has not reached the end-of-the-year benchmark for kindergarten. Her teacher will encourage her to hear ending sounds during small-group reading instruction, in interactive writing, and during writing workshop lessons. Ashanti is a more advanced speller. He spells two phonemes in each word and received a score of 10. Keenan is even more advanced; he attempts to use vowels, although only the long vowels are correct. He might be considered a letter–name speller (Bear et al., 2004); he received a score of 15. Ashanti and Keenan have reached end-of-the-year kindergarten expectations. For Ashanti, the teacher will introduce how to blend new words from familiar rhyming-word families, and for Keenan the teacher will teach the short vowels and how to decode short-vowel words.

Another way to assess children's writing and spelling is to give a dictation test (Clay, 1990). Marie Clay recommends using sentences such as "I have a big dog at

Words	Charles Spelling	Score	Jalexis Spelling	Score	Ashanti Spelling	Score	Keenan Spelling	Score
man	XZO	0	M	1	MN	2	MEN	3
bug	OPERZ	0	B	1	BG	2	BEG	3
fit	TOPZ	0	T	1	FT	2	FET	3
trade	OZER	0	G	1	JD	2	TAD	3
steep	ZTPO	0	C	1	CP	2	SEP	3

FIGURE 7.7. Four children's spellings.

home" or "I can see the red boat that we are going to have a ride in" (p. 39). Teachers analyze whether children spell each phoneme in the sentences with unconventional, but acceptable, matches or with conventional spelling patterns. Clay provides a scoring guide for using sentence dictation.

Comprehension and Vocabulary

Teachers can quickly assess children's comprehension by having them retell a story that has been read aloud to them. Appendix H presents a retelling checklist for *Officer Buckle and Gloria* (Rathman, 1995). This is a hilarious story about a boring police officer who gives speeches in schools about safety. When he is paired up with Gloria, a police dog, his speeches become so popular that newscasters video-tape his presentations. Officer Buckle watches himself on the evening news and discovers that Gloria is putting on a funny show behind his back while he is giving his talks. He quits giving speeches, and Gloria turns out to be boring herself with-out Officer Buckle. One day a big accident occurs, and Office Buckle decides that he and Gloria should always stick together and keep on giving important safety talks. The retelling checklist is a list of the important events in the story in the order in which they are presented in the book. Teachers have children retell the story, and teachers mark on the checklist the ideas that children recall. Teachers give credit when children recall the gist of the ideas rather than the exact words in the checklist.

Then teachers analyze whether children recalled some of the imagery in the story or information from the illustrations. *Officer Buckle and Gloria* does not have imagery (similes or metaphors), but it does present much information in the illus-trations that is not stated in the story text (or on the checklist). Teachers will deter-mine whether children's retelling was presented in past tense throughout, some-times in the past tense, or primarily told in the present or some other tense. They will analyze whether children called characters by their names consistently throughout the retelling or only sometimes. They will determine whether children recalled most, some, few, or none of the important main events. They will analyze whether children included information about all the settings in the story, a few of the settings, or did not include details about the settings. Finally, they will analyze whether children included an overall summary (e.g., this story was about a policeman and his dog). Teachers will also note whether children used any of the sophisticated literary words included in this story such as the words *swivel chair, announced, commands, sitting at attention, expression, audience, enormous, thumbtacking,* and *auditorium.*

An alternative method of assessing children's comprehension is to have them tell a story for a wordless picture book (Paris & Paris, 2003). Children tell the story as they look through the book. Teachers can use the narrative composition analysis form (see Figure 7.8) to analyze children's story composition. This will indicate whether children are aware of these elements in stories. Teachers can note the structure of the stories, the use of sophisticated vocabulary, and the amount of detail included in their story compositions.

Teachers can analyze children's retellings of informational text using similar methods. They can construct a retelling checklist for a simple information book, and then have children recount the information provided in the book. Teachers will note whether children use the timeless present tense (e.g., "Fireman put out fires. They ride in big fire trucks"). They will note whether children introduce a topic (e.g., "This book was about firemen") or merely imply the topic throughout their retelling, whether they describe details about the topic, or whether they include descriptions of typical events related to the topic. Some children may compare details about the topic to another situation or topic. Teachers will note children's use of technical vocabulary related to the topic and introduced in the book (e.g., *helmet*).

COLLECTING AND ANALYZING WORK SAMPLES

Work samples are any product that children create as a part of reading and writing activities. One work sample that teachers frequently collect are children's compositions written as an assigned activity during center work or during writing workshop. Compositions can be either children's own writing or dictation given to the teacher or another adult. Teachers collect at least one sample every month or every other month. Children's writing will show tremendous growth over the course of the kindergarten year. When analyzing written compositions, teachers will assess how children communicate their meaning. They will analyze whether children:

➢ Scribble

➢ Write lines of mock cursive

➢ Write lines of mock letters or conventional letters

Elements included:

Characters	[sustained, described by name, have traits]
Setting	[implied, stated, described]
Problem	[implied, stated]
Actions	[related to the problem, short or long sequences of everyday occurrences, creative sequence, complex plot with obstacles]
Solution	[simple and magical, realistic, clever]
Ending	[physical or emotional response to the solution]

Structure (the whole story can be characterized as):

Words, and phrases as labels

Single statement

Nonstructured events without sustained characters or logical sequence

Action sequence without problem

Reactive sequence of causally related events without problem

Simple story (single problem with few attempts)

Complex story (multiple problems, multiple attempts, obstacles)

FIGURE 7.8. Narrative Composition Analysis Form. Based on Donovan (2001).

➢ Write letters in groups to form mock words

➢ Invent spellings.

When children invent spellings, teacher can analyze the level of spelling development using the invented-spelling rubric presented in Appendix G.

For all compositions, dictated or written, teachers will assess the content of compositions by judging whether the compositions are narratives or informational text. For narratives, teachers can analyze whether children:

➢ Sustain the same characters

➢ Include a setting

➢ Indicate a problem

➢ Have a series of events aimed at solving the problem

➢ Include a solution.

Children may only use words or phrases as labels, a single statement, a nonstructured series of events without sustained characters or logical sequence, an action sequence without a problem, or a reactive sequence consisting of a causally related chain of events without a problem. These are intermediate forms of story composing that teachers may expect before children write simple or complex stories with a causally related sequence of events all organized by a problem and its solution (Donovan, 2001).

Figure 7.9 presents two stories. The first story was written at the writing center and later read to the teacher ("We were going on a picnic"). The other composition was constructed by a group of kindergarten children in a small group. The teacher introduced the idea that all stories had a problem and a solution. She had read aloud *Timothy Goes to School* (Wells, 1981) earlier during whole-group time. The children discussed Timothy's problems (he didn't like Claude, Claude didn't play with him, Claude made fun of him) and solutions (he ignored Claude and found another friend). Then the teacher told the children that they would compose a story together that had a problem and a solution. They brainstormed who the character would be and decided on a butterfly. Their story composition is also presented in Figure 7.9.

Teachers can use a narrative analysis form (presented in Figure 7.8) to con-

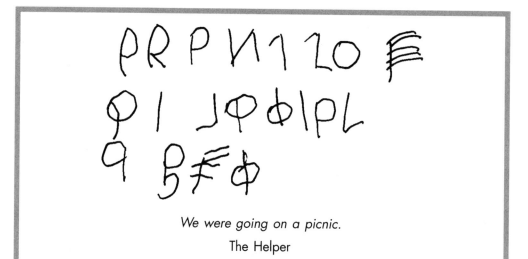

We were going on a picnic.

The Helper

Once upon a time there was a big butterfly. It flew over to a flower and sucked all the nectar. It flew away from the flower. It saw a butterfly that needed help. That butterfly was hurt. The butterfly took the hurt butterfly to a leaf. The butterfly was better. The two butterflies played together and were friends. They played hide and seek around the flowers. The End.

FIGURE 7.9. Two narrative compositions.

sider the level of knowledge demonstrated in these two compositions. The first composition is comprised of three strings of mock and conventional letters. There are no word spaces, and the child is operating as a nonspeller. The composition consists of a single statement that includes characters ("we") and one action ("were going on a picnic"). The statement is presented in the past tense as is expected in narratives. This child needs more practice retelling familiar stories and instruction in consonant letter–sound relationships, along with practice writing alphabet letters and participating in shared writing.

The second narrative is more developed. It includes the formulaic opening ("Once upon a time") and closing ("The End"). It has two characters (big butterfly and a butterfly) that are sustained throughout the story. Big butterfly has an implied trait of helpfulness. The setting is implied (a place where flowers grow). There is a problem (a butterfly was hurt and needed help) and one action required to solve the problem (big butterfly took the hurt butterfly to a leaf). The problem was solved in a simple and magical way (a butterfly was better), and the story had an ending (the butterflies were friends and they played hide-and-seek). Past tense is maintained throughout. This composition has a structure that qualifies as a simple story. The teacher will follow up this lesson by providing many more experiences composing stories and retelling familiar stories. She will observe children as they write during writing workshop to determine whether their story compositions include a problem.

We recommend that teachers collect samples of children's compositions throughout the year and analyze each of the samples much as we did in the preceding paragraphs. Over time teachers should see that children include more elements in their compositions and that their organizational structures will become more sophisticated. As we showed in the second composition, teachers can provide instruction that enhances the quality of children's compositions.

For informational texts, teacher can analyze whether children have introduced a topic, provided details about the attributes of the topic, compared the topic to another topic, or listed a characteristic sequence of events related to the topic. They can note children's use of sentence structure and vocabulary words. Before writing a fully developed information text, children may write with several intermediate forms. They may use words or phrases as labels, present a single statement about a topic, present two related statements, or construct a list of descriptions related to the topic. At more advanced level children may provide a description of two or more attributes of a topic before finally being able to produce a text that includes subtopics in fully developed form (Donovan, 2001).

OBSERVING CHILDREN

The assessment tasks that we have described in this chapter tell teachers what children know. Collecting work samples is one way that teachers determine how children use their knowledge in real reading and writing. Observing children as they engage in self-selected reading and writing activities is another way that teachers can assess how children use their knowledge to solve the puzzles presented in any reading or writing activity. Teachers must observe their children carefully in order to obtain a full picture of what any child is capable of doing, how that child learns, and what instructional strategies seem to be most effective in helping that child learn. Most teachers use anecdotal notes to keep records of what they observe. *Anecdotal notes* are written accounts of what teachers see children doing and what children say as they participate in a reading or writing activity (Rhodes & Nathenson-Mejia, 1992). These are objective accounts, without analysis, that describe the setting, the activity, the children's actions, and their words along with other children's or the teacher's words or actions if they are involved. The accounts need to be brief, but detailed enough so that several months later teachers can re-create in their mind the sequence of events as they occurred. Later (usually the same day as the anecdotal notes were written), teachers analyze what the notes indicate about children's learning and growth. During analysis, teachers refer to standards and benchmarks to determine children's progress toward expected end-of-the-year progress.

For example, a teacher might write in an anecdotal note: "Home center: Quintavious picks up a pencil and the paper beside the telephone. He says, 'Ring, ring. I need a doctor. Tell me what to do for my sick baby.' He writes two lines of mock cursive on his paper and then goes to the baby bed and picks up the doll." Later the teacher analyzed this note: "Quintavious knows that messages can be written. This was his first time to try out this particular purpose for writing in his play: I have demonstrating calling a doctor and writing a message three times over the week. He demonstrated Standard 1.4.a [see Figure 7.1: pretends to write for a variety of purposes]." Anecdotal notes can also be used to analyze more sophisticated behaviors. For another child, the teacher wrote: "Jamika selected the book *Top Job, Mom!* [Allen, 1999] to read during partner reading in the library corner. She got stuck on the word *new*. I told her the word. Later she stopped when she came to the word *blew*. She turned back to the page with the word *new* on it. Then she turned back and said /bl/ /new/ and self-corrected to *blew*." During her analysis of this note the teacher wrote: "Jamika used a strategy of looking back at a familiar word to help decode a new word. Jamika has already mastered Standard 5.2 [see Figure 7.1: reading unfamiliar decodable text using decoding] and exceeds kindergarten expectations. Notes for teaching: teach this strategy to the whole group. Teach the *ew*-word chunk."

In another classroom, a kindergarten teacher planned a center activity in order to assess Standard 1.3 (see Figure 7.1). She wanted to assess whether her children would write recognizable letters in the context of writing a message. Many of her kindergartners could not yet invent spellings. However, this teacher had taught several lessons during kid writing of finding a word in the classroom that you know, and then copying the word for writing. She read aloud the book *I Like Me*

(Carlson, 1988) and said: "I'm going to put this book in the writing center. It has some good words that you might want to use in your writing. It has the words *I like*. I could write lots with those words. I could write 'I like red.' Where would I find the words *I like* and *red?*" The children discussed looking at the front of the book and going to the color chart posted in the classroom to find all the words they would need to write. Later, the teacher observed that two children were using the strategy of finding words around the classroom to write.

Figure 7.10 presents Ashanti's writing. The teacher wrote the following anecdotal note regarding Ashanti's writing (shown in Figure 7.10): "Ashanti copied, 'I like' from the *I Like Me* book, and then said, 'I like you, Steven. Spell your name for me.' Steven spelled it while Ashanti wrote. Ashanti looked around and went to the chart of children's names and photographs. He copied Thomas's name. He came back to the table and said, 'I like Thomas, too.' " Later, the teacher wrote this analysis: "Ashanti knows where to collect words, although he is still not copying words exactly (he left off the *i* in *like*). Letter orientation is still difficult. His *l* is upside-down and he wrote *Steven* from right to left. When he copied *Thomas*, he reversed *h* and *m*. His *S* is still not very recognizable. In this sample he wrote 12 different alphabet letters in recognizable, although not conventional, form. He is approaching Standard 1.3.c" (see Figure 7.1).

It is often difficult to make time in the busy life of kindergarten to write anecdotal notes. Teachers who are most successful keep a clipboard handy on which they have attached four or five sticky notes. As they observe an event worthy of writing an anecdotal note, they quickly write a description on the run, as soon as possible afterward they write more details, and then after school that day they take time to write an analysis. Events worthy of writing anecdotal notes occur when teachers notice that children are using a new strategy or acting differently during reading and writing. Teachers are guided in their observations by their knowledge of the standards and benchmarks children are expected to achieve. Teachers should prepare a notebook in which they keep their anecdotal notes with a copy of the standards and benchmarks for ready reference. Some teachers simply have a three-ring notebook with two or three pages labeled for every child in the classroom. As teachers write sticky notes they attach them (tape securely) on the child's page in

FIGURE 7.10. Ashanti's writing

the notebook, making sure that each note is dated. These notes are transferred to the child's portfolio on a regular basis. The information in the child's portfolio is particularly useful during parent–teacher conferences or when children seem to be making slow progress. Documenting the nature of children's participation in classroom activities provides an important accompaniment to assessments.

Observations and more informal uses of assessment tasks such as those presented in the appendices of this chapter should be used frequently to demonstrate whether individual lessons are successful. If teachers have provided instruction on writing and recognizing the letters L, F, E, T, and I, then teachers need to assess whether children actually can write and identify these letters. They will use a combination of observing children as they complete instructional activities and giving informal assessments: teachers can ask children to tell the names of these letters as the teacher writes them and then ask children to write each of those letters. Teachers will want to know who has learned to write and recognize the letters and who needs more practice.

PLANNING FOR AND SELECTING ASSESSMENTS

Many states now require kindergarten teachers to assess their children at least twice and sometimes three times a year (in the fall, midwinter, and spring). These states specify which assessments teachers will use. Some school districts mandate tests as well. It is rare that teachers are not required to administer some assessment at the beginning and end of kindergarten. The assessments we described earlier in this chapter can be used in conjunction with other mandated assessments to help teachers determine the instructional needs of their children. It is essential that teachers begin the year with knowledge of how many and what alphabet letters their children know and do not know, the level of phonemic awareness they have achieved, and their ability to fingerpoint read. It is essential that teachers have some idea of children's level of comprehension. Therefore, we recommend that teachers administer the upper-case alphabet recognition task first to all children. Children who know five or fewer alphabet letters should be administered the name-writing assessment task and the retelling-checklist assessment. These three assessments will provide teachers with sufficient information to begin instruction. Later, teachers will assess children's performance on other assessments.

SUMMARY

Assessment is a critical part of the instructional cycle. Teachers use assessments to plan instruction for small groups. After instruction, they again assess to determine what children have learned and who may need reteaching or more practice at home. Teachers will use a combination of assessment tasks, collecting and analyzing work samples, and observing children to monitor whether children are making expected progress toward standards. Standards are statements that describe what children are expected to know by the end of kindergarten, and benchmarks are intermediate steps that indicate that children are making progress toward achieving standards. In kindergarten, teachers should administer assessment tasks, collect work samples, and observe children reading and writing to obtain an in-depth understanding of children's development in the areas of alphabet recognition and writing, concepts about print, phonemic awareness, phonics, text reading, writing, and comprehension and vocabulary.

APPENDICES

Appendix A.   Resources for Kindergarten Teachers   179

Appendix B.   Alphabet Letter Formation   193
    B.1. Letter Features, 195
    B.2. Standard Directions for Alphabet Formation, 196

Appendix C.   ELKA Alphabet Recognition Tasks   199
    C.1. Name Writing and Letters-in-Name Recognition, 201
    C.2. Upper-Case Alphabet Recognition, 204
    C.3. Lower-Case Alphabet Recognition, 205
    C.4. Alphabet Writing, 206

Appendix D.   ELKA Concepts about Print Tasks   207
    D.1. CAP: Concepts about Book Orientation, Directionality,
        and Letters and Words, 209
    D.2. Fingerpoint Reading, 211

Appendix E.   ELKA Phonemic Awareness Tasks   215
    E.1. Rhyme, 217
    E.2. Beginning Phoneme Oddity, 219
    E.3. Isolating Beginning Phoneme Task, 222
    E.4. Isolating Ending Phoneme Task, 223
    E.5. Blending Syllables, Onset/Rime, Phonemes Task, 224
    E.6. Segmenting Phonemes Task, 225

Appendix F.   ELKA Phonics Tasks   227
    F.1. Consonant Letter–Sound Matching, 229
    F.2. Blending New Rhyming Words Task, 232
    F.3. Decoding Short-Vowel Words, 233
    F.4. Decoding Long-Vowel Words, 234
    F.5. Consonant Phoneme and Letter–Sound Analysis Form, 235
    F.6. Vowel Analysis Form, 236

Appendix G.   ELKA Writing Task: Invented Spelling List   237
              and Scoring Rubric

Appendix H.   ELKA Comprehension and Vocabulary Task   239

RESOURCES FOR KINDERGARTEN TEACHERS

ALPHABET BOOKS

Agard, J. (1989). *The calypso alphabet.* New York: Holt.

Andreae, G. (2003). *K is for kissing a cool kangaroo.* New York: Orchard Books.

Anno, M. (1987). *Anno's alphabet.* New York: HarperCollins.

Base, G. (1987). *Animalia.* New York: Abrams.

Bayer, J. (1984). *A my name is Alice.* New York: Dial.

Bringhurst, N. J. (2004). *A is for alligator.* Ashland, OR: RiverWood Books.

Browne, P.-A. (2000). *African animals ABC.* San Francisco: Sierra Club.

C is for construction: Big trucks and diggers from A to Z. (2003). San Francisco: Chronicle Books.

Carlson, N. (1997). *ABC I like me!* New York: Viking.

Chin-Lee, C., & de la Peña, T. (1999). *A is for the Americas.* New York: Orchard.

Darling, K. (1996). *Amazon ABC.* New York: Lothrop, Lee & Shepard Books.

Eichenberg, F. (1980). *Ape in a cape.* New York: Harcourt Brace Jovanovich.

Feelings, M. (1981). *Jambo means hello: Swahili alphabet book.* New York: Dial.

Fleming, D. (2002). *Alphabet under construction.* New York: Holt.

Hausman, B. (1999). *A to Z, do you ever feel like me?* New York: Dutton.

Horenstein, H. (1999). *A is for . . .?: A photographer's alphabet of animals.* San Diego, CA: Harcourt Brace.

Johnson, S. T. (1995). *Alphabet City.* New York: Viking.

Kirk, D. (1998). *Miss Spider's ABC.* New York: Scholastic.

Lobel, A. (1981). *On Market Street.* New York: Greenwillow Books.

Martin, B., Jr., & Archambault, J. (1989). *Chicka chicka boom boom.* New York: Simon & Schuster.

Marzollo, J. (2000). *I spy little letters.* New York: Scholastic.

Metropolitan Museum of Art. (2002). *Museum ABC.* New York: Little, Brown.

Milich, Z. (2001). *The city ABC book.* Toronto: Kids Can Press.

Munari, B. (2003). *ABC.* San Francisco: Chronicle Books.

Neumeier, M., & Glaser, B. (1985). *Action alphabet.* New York: Greenwillow Books.

Onyefulu, I. (1997). *A is for Africa.* New York: Puffin.

Pandell, K. (1996). *Animal action ABC.* New York: Dutton.

Schories, P. (1996). *Over under in the garden: An alphabet book.* New York: Farrar, Straus & Giroux.

Seuss, Dr. (1976). *Dr. Seuss's ABC.* New York: Random House.

Wood, A. (2001). *Alphabet adventure.* New York: Blue Sky Press.

LANGUAGE PLAY BOOKS

Ahlberg, J., & Ahlberg, A. (1991). *Each Peach, Pear, Plum*. New York: Penguin.
Allen, S. (1995). *The bug and the slug in the rug*. Bridgeport, CT: Green Bark Press.
Ashman, L. (2002). *Can you make a piggy giggle?* New York: Dutton.
Base, G. (1987). *Animalia*. New York: Abrams.
Bond, F. (2000). *Tumble bumble*. New York: Scholastic.
Clements, A. (1997). *Double trouble in Walla Walla*. Brookfield, CT: Millbrook Press.
Conrad, P. (1995). *Animal lingo*. New York: HarperCollins.
Degen, B. (1983). *Jamberry*. New York: Harper & Row.
Fleming, D. (1991). *In the tall, tall grass*. New York: Holt.
Fleming, D. (2001). *Pumpkin eye*. New York: Holt.
Goldstone, B. (1998). *The beastly feast*. New York: Holt.
Hoberman, M. A. (2001). *Miss Mary Mack*. New York: Scholastic.
Hosta, D. (2003). *I love the night*. Flemington, NJ: Brown Dog Books.
Kuskin, K. (1994). *City noise*. New York: HarperCollins.
Kuskin, K. (1995). *James and the rain*. New York: Simon & Schuster.
Krull, K. (2003). *M is for music*. Orlando, FL: Harcourt.
Langstaff, J. (1991). *Oh, a-hunting we will go*. New York: Aladdin.
McMillan, B. (1995). *Puffins climb, penguins rhyme*. San Diego, CA: Harcourt Brace.
Miranda, A. (2001). *To market, to market*. New York: Harcourt Brace.
Moss, L. (1995). *Zin! Zin! A violin*. New York: Simon & Schuster.
Neitzel, S. (1994). *The jacket I wear in the snow*. New York: Morrow.
Newcome, Z. (2002). *Head, shoulders, knees, and toes: And other action rhymes*. Cambridge, MA: Candlewick Press.
Raffi. (1987). *Down by the bay*. New York: Crown.
Weeks, S. (2002). *Mrs. McNosh hangs up her wash*. New York: Scholastic.
Wilson, K., & Rankin, J. (2003). *A frog in a bog*. New York: McElderly Books.
Wojtowycz, D. (2003). *Can you moo?* New York: Scholastic.

50 BIG BOOKS FOR INTERACTIVE OR SHARED READING

Barton, B. (1989). *Dinosaurs, dinosaurs*. New York: Crowell.
Bellamy, F. (2001). *The Pledge of Allegiance*. New York: Scholastic.
Bick, L. (2001). *Messy moose*. New York: Sadlier-Oxford.
Blakesberg, R. (2001). *Alexander Ant cools off*. New York: Sadlier-Oxford.
Brown, M. W. (1991). *Goodnight moon*. New York: HarperFestival.
Carle, E. (1993). *Today is Monday*. New York: Philomel Books.
Carle, E. (2000). *Does a kangaroo have a mother too?* New York: HarperCollins.
Cauley, L. B. (1997). *Clap your hands*. New York: Scholastic.
Cisco, C. (2001). *Goldilocks and the three bears*. New York: Sadlier-Oxford.
Cowley, J. (1998). *Meanies*. Bothell, WA: Wright Group.
Cowley, J. (1999). *Mrs. Wishy Washy*. Bothell, WA: Wright Group.
Cowley, J. (1998). *The scrubbing machine*. Bothell, WA: Wright Group.
Cowley, J. (2002). *Mud walk*. Bothell, WA: Wright Group.
Crews, D. (1986). *Ten black dots*. New York: Scholastic.
Crews, D. (1993). *The school bus*. New York: Scholastic.
Eaton, D. (2001). *Count with me*. New York: Sadlier-Oxford.
Eaton, D. (2001). *The dinosaur dance*. New York: Sadlier-Oxford.
Eaton, D. (2001). *What bear cubs like to do*. New York: Sadlier-Oxford.

Fleming, D. (1995). *In the tall, tall grass.* New York: Holt.

Freeman, D. (1968). *Corduroy.* New York: Viking Press.

Goldish, M. (2001). *Nice vine, quite fine.* New York: Sadlier-Oxford.

Guarino, D. (1991). *Is your mama a llama?* New York: Scholastic.

Henderson, P. (2001). *Colors at the zoo.* New York: Sadlier-Oxford.

Hillenbrand, W. (2002). *Down by the station.* New York: Scholastic.

Hiltbrand, J. (2001). *Nora plays all day.* New York: Sadlier-Oxford.

Hollander, C. (2001). *Niles likes to smile.* New York: Sadlier-Oxford.

Hutchins, P. (1972). *Rosie's walk.* New York: Simon & Schuster.

Jacobsen, J. (1997). *Getting to know sharks.* New York: Sadlier-Oxford.

Kalan, R. (1989). *Jump frog, jump.* New York: Scholastic.

Keats, E. (1967). *Peter's chair.* New York: Harper Collins.

Kraus, R. (1993). *The carrot seed.* New York: Scholastic.

Lionni, L. (1997). *A color of his own.* New York: Scholastic.

Martin, B. (1983). *Brown bear, brown bear, what do you see?* New York: Holt.

McCloskey, S. (2001). *Patty and Pop's picnic.* New York: Sadlier-Oxford.

Miranda, A. (2001). *The best place.* New York: Sadlier-Oxford.

Neitzel, S. (1994). *The jacket I wear in the snow.* New York: Morrow.

Nicholas, M. (2001). *Stopping by a pond.* New York: Sadlier-Oxford.

Phillips, A. (2001). *A basket full of surprises.* New York: Sadlier-Oxford.

Phillips, A. (2001). *Harry's hat.* New York: Sadlier-Oxford.

Shannon, D. (1998). *No David!* New York: Scholastic.

Stevens, J. (2001). *To market, to market.* New York: Harcourt Brace.

Stuart, M. (2001). *Who can run fast?* New York: Sadlier-Oxford.

Tarfuri, N. (1991) *Have you seen my duckling?* New York: Morrow.

Thryce, M. (2001). *Look at the pictures.* New York: Sadlier-Oxford.

Wadsworth, O. A. (1992). *Over in the meadow.* New York: Scholastic.

Ward, C. (1997). *Cookie's week.* New York: Scholastic.

Wood, A. (1994). *Silly Sally.* New York: Scholastic.

Wood, A. (2000). *Napping house.* New York: Scholastic.

BOOKS FOR INTERACTIVE READ-ALOUDS

Brett, J. (1999). *Gingerbread baby.* New York: Scholastic.

Cameron, A. (1994). *The cat sat on the mat.* Boston: Houghton Mifflin.

Carle, E. (1994). *The very lonely firefly.* New York: Philomel.

Carle, E. (1996). *The grouchy ladybug.* New York: Harper Trophy.

Carpenter, S. (1998). *The three billy goats gruff.* New York: Scholastic.

Chapman, C. (1994). *Snow on snow, on snow.* New York: Dial.

Christelow, E. (1991). *Five little monkeys jumping on the bed.* New York: Scholastic.

Eastman, P. D. (1960). *Are you my mother?* New York: Beginner Books.

Emberly, B. (1967). *Drummer Hoff.* Englewood Cliffs, NJ: Prentice-Hall.

Fox, M. (1992). *Hattie and the fox.* New York: Simon & Schuster.

Fox, M. (1993). *Time for bed.* San Diego, CA: Harcourt Brace.

Fox, M. (2002). *The magic hat.* San Diego, CA: Harcourt Brace.

Galdone, P. (1984). *Henny Penny.* Boston: Houghton Mifflin.

Galdone, P. (1984). *The teeny tiny woman.* New York: Clarion Books.

Hutchins, P. (1971). *Rosie's walk* New York: Macmillan.

Hutchins, P. (1993). *The wind blew.* New York: Aladdin.

Karmes, D. (1993). *The story of the boy named Will, who went sledding down the hill* (J. Gambrell, Trans.). New York: North-South.

Kloes, C. (1995). *At the zoo*. Rocky River, OH: Kaeden.

Kraus, R. (1970). *Whose mouse are you?* New York: Simon & Schuster.

Kraus, R. (1986). *Where are you going, little mouse?* New York: Greenwillow Books.

Lass, B. (2000). *Who took the cookies from the cookie jar?* New York: Scholastic.

McQueen, L. (1985). *Little red hen*. New York: Scholastic.

Numeroff, L. J. (1985) *If you give a mouse a cookie*. New York: Harper & Row.

Numeroff, L. J. (1998). *If you give a pig a pancake*. New York: Harper & Row.

Oxenbury, H. (1989). *We're going on a bear hunt*. New York: McElderry Books.

Piper, W. (1954). *The little engine that could*. New York: Platt & Munk.

Root, P. (1998). *One duck stuck*. New York: Scholastic.

Sendak, M. (1962). *Chicken soup with rice*. New York: Scholastic.

Shaw, C. (1947). *It looked like spilled milk*. New York: HarperCollins.

Slobodkina, E. (1947). *Caps for sale*. Reading, MA: Addison-Wesley.

Tompert, A. (1993). *Just a little bit*. Boston: Houghton Mifflin.

Westcott, N. (1980). *There was an old lady who swallowed a fly*. Minneapolis: Sagebrush Education Resources.

Wildsmith, B. (1983). *Cat on the mat*. Oxford, UK: Oxford University Press.

Williams, S. (1990). *I went walking*. New York: Harcourt.

Wilson, K., & Rankin, J. (2003). *A frog in the bog*. New York: McElderry Books.

Wood, A. (1994). *The napping house wakes up*. New York: Harcourt Brace.

100 NONFICTION BOOKS FOR KINDERGARTEN READ-ALOUDS

Adler, D. (1998). *America's champion swimmer: Gertrude Ederle*. San Diego, CA: Gulliver.

Agassi, M. (2000). *Hands are not for hitting*. Minneapolis: Free Spirit.

Ammon, R. (1999). *An Amish year*. New York: Simon & Schuster.

Ajmera, M., & Ivanko, J. (1999). *To be a kid*. Watertown, MA: Charlesbridge.

Aliki. (1990). *My feet*. New York: HarperCollins.

Ancona, G. (1998). *Let's dance!* New York: Morrow Junior.

Arnosky, J. (1999). *All about owls*. New York: Scholastic.

Arnosky, J. (1999). *All about deer*. New York: Scholastic.

Arnosky, J. (2000). *See animals hiding*. New York: Scholastic.

Bancroft, H., & Van Gelder, R. G. (1997). *Animals in winter*. New York: HarperCollins.

Barton, B. (1989). *Dinosaurs, dinosaurs*. New York: HarperCollins.

Berger, M. (2003). *Spinning spiders*. New York: HarperCollins.

Bradley, K. (2001). *Pop!: A book about bubbles*. New York: HarperCollins.

Branley, F. (1983). *The sky is full of stars*. New York: Harper & Row.

Brenner, B. (1996). *Thinking about ants*. New York: Mondo.

Brenner, B. (1998). *The boy who loved to draw: Benjamin West*. Boston: Houghton Mifflin.

Brown, C. (1995). *Tractor*. New York: Greenwillow Books.

Bunting, E.(2000). *Moonsticks: The seasons of the Sioux*. New York: HarperCollins.

Cardoni, P. (1984). *Leonardo da Vinci*. New York: Scholastic.

Carter, A., & Saller, C. (1999). *George Washington Carver*. Minneapolis, MN: Carolrhoda Books.

Cherry, L. (1992). *A river ran wild*. Orlando, FL: Harcourt, Brace.

Cohen, M. (1998). *Down in the subway*. New York: DK Publishing.

Cole, H. (2003). *On the way to the beach*. New York: Greenwillow Books.

Collard, S. B. (1997). *Animal dads*. New York: Scholastic.

Conrad, H.(2001). *Lights of winter.* San Diego, CA: Lightport.

Cuyler, M. (2001). *Stop, drop, and roll.* New York: Simon & Schuster.

Demuth, P. (1996). *Johnny Appleseed.* New York: Grosset & Dunlap.

DK. (1992). *Look closer series: Desert life.* New York: DK Publishing.

Dunphy, M. (1998). *Here is the coral reef.* New York: Hyperion.

DuQuette, K. (1998). *The house book.* New York: Putnam/Penguin.

Dussling, J. (1996). *Stars.* New York: Grosset & Dunlap.

Ehlert, L. (1991). *Red leaf, yellow leaf.* New York: Harcourt Brace.

Fowler, A. (1998). *Let's visit some islands.* New York: Scholastic.

Gallagher, K. (2001).*Cottontail rabbits.* Minneapolis, MN: Lerner.

Gardeski, C. (2001). *Columbus Day.* New York: Children's Press.

Geisert, B. (1998). *Desert town.* New York: Walter Lorraine Books/Houghton Mifflin.

Gibbons, G. (1967). *The moon book.* New York: Holiday House.

Gibbons, G. (1983). *The planets.* New York: Holiday House.

Gibbons, G. (1995). *Sea turtles.* New York: Scholastic.

Gibbons, G. (2000). *Apples.* New York: Scholastic.

Gibbons, G. (2003). *Chicks and chickens.* New York: Holiday House.

Glaser, L. (1992). *Wonderful worms.* Riverside, NJ: Millbrook Press.

Glaser, L. (1999). *Spectacular spiders.* Riverside, NJ: Millbrook Press.

Guarnieri, P. (1998). *A boy named Giotto.* New York: Farrar, Straus & Giroux.

Haas, J. (1999). *Hurry!* New York: Greenwillow Books.

Hall, Z. (1996). *The apple pie tree.* New York: Scholastic.

Hamanaka, S. (1999). *I look like a girl.* New York: Morrow/HarperCollins.

Hewitt, S. (2000). *Nature for fun projects.* Riverside, NJ: Millbrook Press.

Hoban, T. (1983). *I read signs.* New York: Morrow.

Hoffman, M. (1997). *An angel just like me.* New York: Dial.

Hurd, E. T. (1990). *Starfish.* New York: HarperCollins.

Jenkins, P. (1985). *Nest full of eggs.* New York: HarperCollins.

Jenkins, S. (1997). *Biggest, strongest, fastest.* New York: Houghton Mifflin.

Johnson, S. (1995). *Alphabet city.* New York: Penguin.

King-Smith, D. (2001). *I love guinea pigs!* Cambridge, MA: Candlewick Press.

Klingel, C., & Noyed, R. B. (2001). *Pigs.* Chanhassen, MN: Child's World.

Kroll, S. (1988). *Oh, what a Thanksgiving.* New York: Scholastic.

Krull, K. (1998). *Supermarket.* New York: Holiday House.

Kuklin, S. (1992). *How my family lives in America.* New York: Silver Burdett Ginn.

Lau, A. (1998). *Mama and papa have a store.* New York: Dial.

Lauber, P. (1995). *Who eats what: Food chains and food webs.* New York: Scholastic.

Leedy, L. (1999). *Mapping Penny's world.* New York: Holt.

Lesser, C. (1997). *Storm on the desert.* San Diego, CA: Harcourt Brace.

Lewin, T., & Lewin, B. (2000). *Elephant quest.* New York: HarperCollins.

Locker, T. (1997). *Water dance.* San Diego, CA: Harcourt Brace.

London, J. (1998). *Hurricane!* New York: Morrow.

London, J. (1999). *Baby whale's journey.* San Diego, CA: Chronicle.

Lundell, M. (1995). *A girl named Helen Keller.* New York: Scholastic.

Malam, J. (1998). *Beatrix Potter.* Minneapolis, MN: Carolrhoda Books.

McKissack, P. (1997). *Ma dear's aprons.* New York: Simon & Schuster.

Miller, D. (2000). *River of life.* Boston: Clarion Books.

Miller, M. (1991). *Whose shoe?* New York: Greenwillow Books.

Mitgutsch, A. (1972). *Start to finish books.* Minneapolis, MN: Carolrhoda Books.

Montanari, D. (2001). *Children around the world.* Tonawanda, NY: Kids Can Press.

Morris, A. (1990). *On the go.* New York: Morrow.

Onyefulu, I. (1998). *Grandfather's work: A traditional healer in Nigeria.* Riverside, NJ: Millbrook Press.

Oppenheim, J. (1967). *Have you seen trees?* New York: Scholastic.

Parks, R., & Haskins, J. (1997). *I am Rosa Parks.* New York: Penguin Putnam Books.

Peacock, C. A. (1999). *Mommy far, mommy near: An adoption story.* Morton Grove, IL: Whitman.

Reid, M. (1996). *Let's find out about ice cream.* New York: Scholastic.

Riley, L. C. (1998). *Elephants swim.* New York: Houghton Mifflin.

Rockwell, A. (1998). *Our Earth.* New York: Harcourt Brace/Silver Whistle.

Rockwell, A. (2001). *Bugs are insects.* New York: HarperCollins.

Rogers, F. (1999). *Let's talk about it: Extraordinary friends.* New York: Putnam's.

Rotner, S., & Olivo, R. (1997). *Close, closer and closest.* New York: Simon & Schuster.

Rotner, S. & Kelly, S. (1999). *Lots of grandparents.* Riverside, NJ: Millbrook Press.

Royston, A. (1991). *Diggers and dump trucks.* New York: Simon & Schuster.

Sandeman, A. (1997). *Bones.* Riverside, NJ: Millbrook Press.

Sanders, R. S. (2001). *A place called freedom.* New York: Simon & Schuster.

Selsam, M. E. (1995). *How to be a nature detective.* New York: HarperCollins.

Simon, N. (1998). *All kinds of children.* Morton Grove, IL: Whitman.

Sill, C. (2000). *About mammals: A guide for children.* Atlanta, GA: Peachtree.

Silver, M. (1995). *Who lives here?* San Francisco: Sierra Club.

Smith, C. L. (1999). *Jingle dancer.* New York: HarperCollins.

Tarbescu, E. (1998). *Annushka's voyage.* Boston: Clarion Books.

Taylor, B. (1998). *A day at the farm.* New York: DK Publishing.

Treays, R. (1998). *My town.* London: Usborne.

Walsh, M. (1997). *Do monkeys tweet?* Boston: Houghton Mifflin.

Yolen, J. (1998). *Raising Yoder's barn.* New York: Little, Brown.

Wood, A.(1997). *Birdsong.* New York: Harcourt Brace.

WEBSITES FOR KINDERGARTNERS AND THEIR TEACHERS

Lesson Plans for Teachers

A–Z Teacher's Stuff	www.lessonplanz.com
Children's Literature Web Guide	www.ucalgary.ca/~dkbrown/index.html
Discover School for Teachers	schooldiscovery.com/
Educator's Reference Desk (Ask Eric)	www.eduref.org/
Learning Network For Teachers	teachervision.fen.com/
Lesson Plans Page.com	www.lessonplanspage.com/
National Geographic	nationalgeographic.com
Reading Rainbow	gpn.unl.edu/rainbow
Teachers.net	www.teachers.net

Resources for Teachers

Awesome Library	www.awesomelibrary.org/
Beaverton School District Leveled Books Database	www.beavton.k12.or.us
Book Spot	www.bookspot.com
California Electronic Learning Resources	clrn.org/search
Carol Hurst's Children's Literature Site	www.carolhurst.com/index.html

Creative Classroom	www.creativeclassroom.org/
Education Planet	www.educationplanet.com/
Education Week and Teacher Magazine	www.edweek.org/
Education World	www.educationworld.com/
Family Education	www.educationworld.com/At_Home/
International Reading Association	www.reading.org/
Kathy Schrock's Guide for Educators	schooldiscovery.com/schrockguide/ index.html
KIDPROJ Multicultural Calendar	www.kidlink.org/KIDPROJ/MCC/
National Board for Professional Teaching Standards	nbpts.org
National Council for the Social Studies	ncss.org
National Science Teachers Association	nsta.org
Reading A–Z	www.readinga-z.com
Sites for Teachers	www.sitesforteachers.com
SuperKids: Educational Software Review	www.superkids.com/
The Educator's Network	www.theeducatorsnetwork.com/

Resources for Children

Aesop's Fables Read	www.umass.edu/aesop
American Museum of Natural History's Ology	ology.amnh.org/
Arthur page	pbskids.org/arthur/
Astronomy for Kids	www.dustbunny.com
Babloo	www.babloo.com
Berenstain Bears	www.berenstainbears.com
Billy Bear's Playground	www.billybear4kids.com
Children's Storybook Online	www.magickeys.com/books/
Enchanted Learning	www.enchantedlearning.com
Eric Carle's website	www.eric-carle.com
Guys Read	www.guysread.com
Jan Brett's website	www.janbrett.com
Janet Stevens's website	www.janetstevens.com
Kids Click	sunsite.berkeley.edu/KidsClick!/
Kid's Space	www.kids-space.org
Laura Numeroff's website	www.lauranumeroff.com
Mem Fox's website	www.memfox.com
Monterey Bay Aquarium	www.montereybayaquarium.org/
NASA Kids	kids.msfc.nasa.gov
Peter Rabbit website	www.peterrabbit.com
Seussville	www.seussville.com/seussville
Storyline	www.bookpals.net/storyline
Zoom Astronomy	www.enchantedlearning.com/subjects/ astronomy/

SOFTWARE FOR KINDERGARTNERS AND THEIR TEACHERS

3D Froggy Phonics. (1998). Ingenuity Works Inc.
Alphabet Express. (1999). School Zone Interactive.

Easy Grade Pro. (2000). Orbis Software.
Eyewitness Children's Encyclopedia. (n.d.). Darling Kindersley Multimedia.
Hyperstudio. (2004). Sunburst Technology.
Jumpstart Advanced Kindergarten. (2003). Knowledge Adventure.
Jumpstart Kindergarten. (1999). Knowledge Adventure.
Jumpstart Phonics Learning System. (1999). Knowledge Adventure.
Kidspiration. (2001). Inspiration Software Inc.
Language First Program. (2002). LeapFrog School House.
Leap into Language. (2004). INNOVA Multimedia Ltd.
Millie and Bailey Kindergarten. (1999). Edmark.
Read, Write & Type. (2003). Learning Company.
Sound Reading CD. (2001). Sound Reading Solutions.
Start Write. (1999). Idea Maker Inc.
Storybook Weaver (2004). Learning Company.
Type to Learn Jr.: New Keys for Kids. (2001). Sunburst Technology.
Vowels: Short and Long. (1999). Sunburst Technology.

25 THEMES WITH BOOKS FOR KINDERGARTEN

Africa

Aardema, V. (1975). *Why mosquitoes buzz in people's ears.* New York: Dial.
Kurtz, J., & Kurtz, C. (2002). *Water hole waiting.* New York: Greenwillow Books.
Moss, M. (2000). *This is the tree.* LaJolla, CA: Kane/Miller.
Steptoe, J. (1987). *Mufaro's beautiful daughters.* New York: Morrow.
Swinburne. S.(1998). *Water for one, water for everyone: A counting book of African animals.* Riverside, NJ: Millbrook Press.

All about Me Books

Hamanaka, S. (1994). *All the colors of the Earth.* New York: Morrow.
Henkes, K. (1991). *Chrysanthemum.* New York: Scholastic.
Intrater, R. G. (1995). *Two eyes, a nose, and a mouth.* New York: Scholastic.
Kraus, R. (1971). *Leo the late bloomer.* New York: HarperCollins.
Wood, A. (1982). *Quick as a cricket.* Singapore: Child's Play.

Animals

Bancroft, H., & Van Gelder, R. G. (1997). *Animals in winter.* New York: HarperCollins.
Conrad, P. (1995). *Animal lingo.* New York: HarperCollins.
Ganeri, A. (1995). *Animals in disguise.* New York: Simon & Schuster.
Hickman, P. (2001). *Animals eating: How animals chomp, chew, slurp, and swallow.* Tonawanda, NY: Kids Can Press.
Jenkins, S. (2001). *Slap, squeak and scatter: How animals communicate.* Boston: Houghton Mifflin.

Australia

Base, G.(1983). *My grandma lives in Gooligulch.* New York: Abrams.
Fox, M. (1991). *Possom magic.* Orlando: Harcourt Brace.
Germein, K. (1999). *Big rain coming.* New York: Clarion Books.
Gray, S. (2001). *Australia.* Minneapolis: Compass Point Books.

Morin, P. (1998). *Animal dreaming: An Aboriginal dreamtime story.* New York: Harcourt Brace.

Bears

Butterfield, M. (1997). *Brown, fierce, and furry.* Austin, TX: Raintree Steck-Vaughn.
Fair, J. (1991). *Black bear magic for kids.* Milwaukee, WI: Gareth Stevens.
Galdone, P. (1973). *The three bears.* New York: Scholastic.
Gibbons, G. (2001). *Polar bears.* New York: Holiday House.
Helmer, D. (1997). *Black bears.* New York: Rosen.

Butterflies

Carle, E. (1971). *The very hungry caterpillar.* New York: Philomel.
Ehlert, L. (2001). *Waiting for wings.* New York: Harcourt.
Gibbons, G. (1989). *Monarch butterfly.* New York: Scholastic.
Heiligman, D. (1996). *From caterpillar to butterfly.* New York: HarperCollins.
Mitgutsch, A. (1972). *From egg to butterfly.* Minneapolis, MN: Carolrhoda Books.

Chicks, Ducks, and Eggs

Gibbons, G. (2001). *Ducks!* New York: Holiday House.
Gill, S. (2001). *The egg.* Watertown, MA: Charlesbridge.
Heller, R. (1981). *Chickens aren't the only ones.* New York: Penguin Books.
McCloskey, R. (1969). *Make way for ducklings.* New York: Viking Press.
Winer, Y. (2002). *Birds build nests.* Watertown, MA: Charlesbridge.

China

Bishop, C. H. (1938). *Five Chinese brothers.* New York: Scholastic.
Czernecki, S. (1996). *The cricket's cage: A Chinese folktale.* New York: Hyperion.
Flack, M. (2000). *The story about Ping.* New York: Grosset & Dunlap.
Louie, A. (1982). *Yeh-Shen: A Cinderella story from China.* New York: Philomel.
Mosel, A. (1989). *Tikki Tikki Tempo.* New York: Holt.

Colors

Bentley, D. (2003). *Goodnight sweet butterflies.* New York: Simon & Schuster
Hoban, T. (1987). *Is it red? Is it yellow? Is it blue?* New York: Morrow.
Lionni, L. (1994). *Little blue, and little yellow* New York: Morrow.
Lionni, L. (1997). *A color of his own.* New York: Bantam Doubleday Dell.
Seuss, Dr. (1996). *My many colored days.* New York: Knopf.

Dinosaurs

Lewis, J. (2001). *Dinosaur 123 ABC.* London: Tucker Slingsby.
Maynard, C. (1998). *The best book of dinosaurs.* New York: Kingfisher.
Mitton, T. (2002). *Dinosaurumpus!* New York: Scholastic.
Wood, A. J. (1998). *Countdown to extinction.* New York: Disney Press.
Zoehfeld, K. W. (2001). *Terrible Tyrannosaurus.* New York: HarperCollins.

Ecology

Fleming, D. (2000). *Where once there was a wood.* New York: Holt.
Garland, S. (1995). *The summer sands.* San Diego, CA: Harcourt.

Glaser, L. (2000). *Our big home: An Earth poem*. Riverside, NJ:. Millbrook Press.
Miller, D. (2000). *River of life*. Boston: Clarion Books.
Rauzon, M. J., & Bix, C. O. (1994). *Water water everywhere*. San Francisco: Sierra Club.

Families

Dotlich, R. (2002). *A family like yours*. Honesdale, PA: Boyds Mills Press.
Hausheir, R. (1997). *Celebrating families*. New York: Scholastic.
Pellegrini, N. (1991). *Families are different*. New York: Scholastic
Rylant, C. (1985). *The relatives came*. New York: Scholastic.
Skutch, R. (1995). *Who's in a family?* Berkeley, CA: Tricycle Press.

Five Senses

Adolph, A. (1989). *Chocolate dreams*. New York: Lothrop, Lee & Shepard.
Hewitt, S. (1999). *It's science! The five senses*. Danbury, CT: Children's Press.
McMillan, B. (1994). *Sense suspense: A guessing game for the five senses*. New York: Scholastic.
Miller, M. (1994). *My five senses*. New York: Simon & Schuster.
Moncure, J. B. (1997). *Clang, boom, bang: My five senses series*. Elgin, IL: Child's World.

Friends

Gainer, C. (1998). *I'm like you, you're like me*. Minneapolis: Free Spirit.
Hoban, L. (1967). *Will I have a friend?* New York: Aladdin.
Lobel, A. (1979). *Frog and Toad are friends*. New York: HarperCollins.
Payne, L. M. (1997). *We can get along*. Minneapolis: Free Spirit.
Pfister, M. (1992). *Rainbow fish*. New York: North-South Books.

Insects and Reptiles

Baher, K. (1995). *Hide and snake*. New York: Voyager Picture Books.
Nickle, J. (1999). *The ant bully*. New York: Scholastic.
Petie, H. (1975). *Billions of bugs*. Englewood Cliffs, NJ: Prentice-Hall.
Simon, S. (1999). *Crocodiles and alligators*. New York: HarperCollins.
Rockwell, A. (2001). *Bugs are insects*. New York: HarperCollins.

Mexico

Aardema, V. (1991). *Borreguita and the coyote: A tale from Ayutla, Mexico*. New York: Knopf.
Ancona, G. (1994). *The pi–ata maker*. Orlando, FL: Harcourt.
Coburn, J. (2000). *Domitila: A Cinderella tale from the Mexican tradition*. Fremont, CA: Shen's Books.
Grossman, P. (1994). *Saturday market* New York: HarperCollins.
Paulson, G. (1998). *The tortilla factory*. Orlando, FL: Harcourt.

Ocean Life

Andreae, G. (1998). *Commotion in the ocean*. Waukesha, WI: Little Tiger Press.
Gibbons, G. (1999). *Exploring the deep dark sea*. Boston: Little, Brown.
Lionni, L. (1973). *Swimmy*. New York: Random House.
Savage, S. (1997). *Animals of the ocean*. Chatham, NJ: Raintree/Steck Vaughn.
Seelig, T. L. (1999). *Ocean*. San Francisco: Chronicle Books.

Plants

Carle, E. (1991). *The tiny seed.* New York: Aladdin.
Ehlert, L. (1987). *Growing vegetable soup.* New York: Scholastic.
Gibbons, G. (1991). *Seed to plant.* New York: Scholastic.
Jordan H. (1992). *How a seed grows.* New York: Scholastic.
Kraus, R. (1972). *The carrot seed.* New York: HarperCollins.

Poetry and Rhyme

Douglas, V. (2002). *Mother Goose rhymes.* Boston: McGraw-Hill.
Fujikawa, G. (2002). *Mother Goose.* New York: Backpack Books.
Prelutsky, J. (1983). *The Random House book of poetry for young children.* New York: Random House.
Schenk de Regniers, B., & Moore, E. (Eds.).(1990). *Sing a song of popcorn: Every child's book of poems.* New York: Scholastic.
Strickland, D. S., & Strickland, M. R. (1996). *Families: Poems celebrating the African-American experience.* Honesdale, PA: Boyds Mills Press.

Post Office

Gibbons, G. (1997). *The post office book: Mail and how it moves.* New York: HarperCollins.
Keats, E. (1968). *Letter to Amy.*New York: Harper Trophy.
O'Tunnell, M. (2000). *Mailing May.* New York: Greenwillow Books.
Selway, M. (1992). *Don't forget to write.* Nashville, TN: Ideals Children's Books.
Thaler, R. (1994). *Never mail an elephant.* New York: Troll.

Rabbits

Evans, M. (1992). *Rabbit: A practical guide to caring for your rabbit.* London: DK Publishers.
Gibbons, G. (2000). *Rabbits, rabbits and more rabbits.* New York: Holiday House.
National Geographic. (1989). *Cottontails: Little rabbits of field and forest.* Washington, DC: Author.
Potter, B. (2002). *Peter Rabbit.* New York: Warne.
Ruis, M. (1987). *Habitats: Life underground.* New York: Barron's.

Seasons and Holidays

General Books about Seasons

Borden, L. (1991). *Caps, hats, socks and mittens: A book about four seasons.* New York: Scholastic.
Gibbons, G. (1996). *The reasons for the seasons.* New York: Holiday House.
Miller, D. (2000). *River of life.* Boston: Clarion Books.
Schnur, S. (2000). *Spring thaw.* New York: Viking Press.

Autumn

Fleming, D. (1997). *Time to sleep.* New York: Holt.
Hunter, A. (1996). *Possum's harvest moon.* New York: Houghton Mifflin.
Robbins, K. (1998). *Autumn leaves.* New York: Scholastic.
Russel, C. Y. (1997). *Moon festival.* Honesdale, PA: Boyds Mills Press.
Saunders, G. (1998). *Autumn.* Danbury, CT: Children's Press.

Spring

Adoff, A. (1997). *In for winter, out for spring*. New York: Harcourt Brace.
Daigneault, S. (1998). *Bruno springs up*. New York: HarperCollins.
Preller, J. (1994). *Wake me in spring*. New York: Scholastic.
Rylant, C. (1996). *Henry and Mudge in puddle trouble*. New York: Aladdin.
Spelter, J. (1999). *Lily and Trooper's spring*. Ashville, NC: Front Street Press.

Summer

Brown, M. W. (1993). *The summer noisy book*. New York: HarperCollins.
Hesse, K. (1999). *Come on, rain!* New York: Scholastic.
Lerner, C. (1996). *Backyard birds of summer*. New York: Morrow.
Maass, R. (1993). *When summer comes*. New York: Holt.
Sturges, P. (1995). *Rainsong snowsong*. New York: North-South.

Winter

Brown, M. W. (1994). *The winter noisy book*. New York: HarperCollins.
Carle, E. (1998). *The snowy day*. New York: Viking Press.
Ehlert, L. (1995). *Snowballs*. New York: Harcourt Brace.
Frank, J. (2003). *A chill in the air: Nature poems for fall and winter*. New York: Hyperion.
Shulevitz, U. (1998). *Snow*. New York: Farrar, Straus & Giroux.

Space

Barton, B. (1988). *I want to be an astronaut*. New York: Scholastic.
Branley, F. (1987). *The moon seems to change*. New York: HarperCollins.
Carle, E. (1999). *Papa, please get the moon for me*. New York: Little Simon.
Gibbons, G. (1987). *Sun up, sun down*. New York: Voyager Books.
Sims, L. (1996). *Exploring space*. Chatham, NJ: Raintree/Steck-Vaughn.

Trees

Jones, C. R. (1995). *The tree in the ancient forest*. Nevada City, CA: Dawn.
Lauber, P. (1994). *Be a friend to trees*. New York: HarperCollins.
Maestro, B. (1994). *Why do leaves change color?* New York: HarperCollins.
Marzollo, J. (1988). *I am a leaf*. New York: Scholastic.
Pfeffer, W. (1997). *A log's life*. New York: Simon & Schuster.

Weather

Barrett, J. (1978). *Cloudy with a chance of meatballs*. New York: Atheneum.
Gibbons, G. (1990). *Weather words and what they mean*. New York: Holiday House.
Martin, J. B. (1998) *Snowflake Bentley*. Boston: Houghton Mifflin.
Polacco, P. (1990). *Thundercake*. New York: Philomel.
Updike, J. (1999). *Child's calendar*. New York: Holiday House

SUPPLIERS OF LEVELED TEXT

Capstone Press	www.capstonepress.com
Celebration Press	www.pearsonlearning.com
Mondo	www.mondopub.com
National Geographic	www.nationalgeographic.com
Newbridge	www.newbridgeonline.com

Pearson Learning Group   www.pearsonlearning.com
Rigby   www.rigby.com
Sadlier   www.sadlier-oxford.com
Scholastic Books   www.scholastic.com
Steck-Vaughn   www.steck-vaughn.com
Sundance   www.sundancepub.com
Wright Group   www.WrightGroup.com

ADDITIONAL RESOURCES FOR UNIT ON DINOSAURS

Books

Aliki. (1981). *Digging up dinosaurs*. New York: HarperCollins.
Aliki. (1985). *Dinosaurs are different*. New York: HarperCollins.
Aliki. (1988). *Dinosaur bones*. New York: HarperCollins.
Aliki. (1990). *Fossils tell of long ago*. New York: HarperCollins.
Barton, B. (1990) *Bones, bones, dinosaur bones*. New York: HarperCollins.
Big book of dinosaurs. (1994). New York: DK Publishing.
Branley, F. M. (1989). *What happened to the dinosaurs?* New York: HarperCollins.
Brown, D. (2003). *Rare treasure: Mary Anning and her remarkable discoveries*. New York: Houghton Mifflin.
Carrick, C. (1986). *What happened to Patrick's dinosaurs?* New York: Clarion Books.
Carrick, C. (1989). *Big old bones: A dinosaur tale*. New York: Clarion Books.
Cole, J. (1995). *The Magic School Bus in the time of the dinosaur*. New York: Scholastic.
Dussling, J. (2000). *Dinosaur eggs*. New York: Scholastic.
Eye openers: Dinosaurs. (1991). London: DK Publishing.
Hennessy, B. G. (1999). *The dinosaur who lived in my backyard*. New York: Bt Bound.
Joyce, W. (1995) *Dinosaur Bob and his adventures with the family Lazardoro*. New York: Geringer.
Lindsay, W.(1988). *On the trail of incredible dinosaurs*. New York: DK Publishing.
MacLeod, E. (2001). *What did dinosaurs eat?: And other things you want to know about dinosaurs*. Toronto, ON, Canada: Kids Can Press.
Moss, J. (1997). *Bone poems*. New York: Workman.
Most, B. (1978). *If the dinosaurs came back*. New York: Harcourt Brace.
Most, B. (1984). *Whatever happened to the dinosaurs?* New York: Harcourt Brace.
Most, B. (1991). *Dinosaur named after me*. New York: Harcourt Brace.
Simpson, J. (1996). *Mighty dinosaurs*. New York: Time-Life Books.
Taylor, P. (1990). *Fossil*. New York: DK Publishing.
The visual dictionary of prehistoric life. (1995). New York: DK Publishing.
Yolen, J.(2000). *How do dinosaurs say goodnight?* New York: Scholastic.
Wahl, J. (2000). *The field mouse and the dinosaur named Sue*. New York: Cartwheel Books.
Whitfield, P. (1992). *Children's guide to dinosaurs and other prehistoric animals*. New York: Simon & Schuster.
Wilkes, A. (1994). *Big book of dinosaurs: A first book for young children*. New York: DK Publishing.

Series

Cohen, D. (2003). Discovering Dinosaurs Series. Mankato, MN: Bridgestone Books.
Matthews, R. (2003). First Library Series. New York: Heinemann.

Books for Guided Reading

The Wright Group
Dinosaur times
Dinosaurs
Geoffrey, the dinosaur
I dig dinosaurs
Dinosaur morning

Scholastic
Dinosaur eggs
Danny and the dinosaur

Sundance
Dinosaur reports
Dinosaur time

Miscellaneous Suppliers
Parish, P. (1974). *Dinosaur time.* New York: Harper & Row.
Thomson, R. *(2000). Dinosaur's day.* New York: Darling Kindersley.
Collins, M. (n.d.). *Dinosaurs.* New York: Mondo.
Benton, M. (2004). *The world of dinosaurs.* Boston: Kingfisher.

Videos

Dinosaur. VHS. Eyewitness 1995.
Magic School Bus: The Busasaurus. VHS. A Vision. 1999.

Book Clubs

Scholastic Book Clubs, Inc., Firefly (preschool), SeeSaw (K–1), Lucky (2–3), 2931 East McCarty Street, P.O. Box 7504, Jefferson City, MO 65102–7504; 800-724-6527.
TrollCarnival Book Club, P.O. Box 3730, Jefferson City, MO 65102-9610; 800-654-3037.
Trumpet Book Club, P.O. Box 7511, Jefferson City, MO 65102; 800-826-0110.

Children's Book Awards

Caldecott Medal. American Library Association, 50 East Huron Street, Chicago, IL 60611-2795
Children's Book Showcase. Children's Book Council, 12 West 37th Street, 2nd floor, New York, NY 10018-7480
Newbery Medal. American Library Association, 50 East Huron Street, Chicago, IL 60611-2795.

ALPHABET LETTER FORMATION

Letter Features

1. Line down
2. Slant back
3. Slant forward
4. Curve forward
5. Circle back (stop)
6. Big curve forward
7. Over
8. Across
9. Line down and curve back
10. Line down and curve forward
11. Little line back
12. Little line forward
13. Little line down
14. Curve back and curve back the other way
15. Itsy line in
16. Itsy slant forward
17. Itsy line across
18. Circle back line down
19. Hump (stop)
20. Dot
21. Big circle back
22. Little circle back
23. Little circle back stop
24. Little slant forward
25. Little slant back
26. Little circle forward
27. Little line down and curve forward
28. Itsy slant back
29. Little curve back and curve back the other way
30. Hump

Standard Directions for Alphabet Formation

A
Slant back
Slant forward
Over

B
Line down
Curve forward
Curve forward

C
Circle back
Stop

D
Line down
Big curve forward

E
Line down
Over
Over
Over

F
Line down
Over
Over

G
Circle back
Little line back

H
Line down
Line down
Over

I
Line down
Itsy line across
Itsy line across

J
Line down and curve back

K
Line down
Little slant back
Little slant forward

L
Line down
Over

M
Line down
Slant forward
Slant back
Line down

N
Line down
Slant forward
Line down

O
Big circle back

P
Line down
Curve forward

Q
Big circle back
Itsy slant forward

R
Line down
Curve forward
Little slant forward

S
Curve back and curve back the other
way

T
Line down
Across

U
Line down and
Curve forward

V
Slant forward
Slant back

W
Slant forward
Slant back
Slant forward
Slant back

X
Slant forward
Slant back

Y
Little line forward
Little line back
Line down

Z
Over
Slant back
Over

a
Little circle back
Little line down

b
Line down
Little circle forward

c
Little circle back stop

d
Little circle back
Line down

e
Little circle back stop
Itsy line in

f
Circle back line down
Across

g
Little circle back
Line down
Curve back

h
Line down
Hump

i
Little line down
Dot

j
Line down
Curve back (stop)
Dot

k
Line down
Itsy slant back
Itsy slant forward

l
Line down

m
Little line down
Hump
Hump

n
Little line down
Hump

o
Little circle back

p
Line down
Little circle forward

q
Little circle back
Line down
Curve forward

r
Little line down
Hump (stop)

s
Little curve back and curve back the
other way

t
Line down
Across

u
Little line down and curve forward
Little line down

v
Little slant forward
Little slant back

w
Little slant forward
Little slant back
Little slant forward
Little slant back

x
Little slant forward
Little slant back

y
Itsy slant forward
Little slant back

z
Little line forward
Little slant back
Little line forward

ELKA ALPHABET RECOGNITION TASKS

Name Writing and Letters-in-Name Recognition

DIRECTIONS FOR ADMINISTRATION AND PREPARATION OF MATERIALS

1. Name writing (materials: paper and pencil). "Write your name for me." If refusal, "Some children write like this [demonstrate scribble ☞], some write like this [demonstrate linear mock cursive ‿‿‿], some write like this [demonstrate mock letters ४४४], and some like this [write a name Lea]. You can write any way you want."

2. Name spelling (materials: none). "Tell me how to spell your name." Write letters on score sheet.

3. Letter identification (materials: letters of name typed and cut out, presented in random order). Example: James

"These are the letters in your name. Can you arrange the letters so they spell your name?" Write letter arrangement, order, and orientation on score sheet.

4. Name recognition (materials: child's name printed on card, two children's names from the classroom that do not begin with first letter in child's name printed on cards, one child's name from classroom—or another name—that does begin with the child's first name printed on card, all presented in random order).

"Show me your name. Can you tell me any of the other names?" Record whether child chooses his name or any mistakes. Record names child reads and any mistakes on score sheet.

5. Letter matching (materials: word card with child's name printed on it

cont.

from subtask 4 and letters from subtask 3; these materials should be the same size so that matching letters can be one-to-one as shown).

J	a	m	e	s
J	a	m	e	s

Write arrangement, order, and orientation of letters in matching on score sheet.

SCORE SHEET

I.   Name-writing task (circle description of signature)

scribble

linear mock cursive

separate symbols

separate symbols with one/two mock letters

all mock and recognizable letters

recognizable mock letters with few orientation difficulties

may have orientation difficulties

first name with conventional letters

first or first and last name with conventional letters and consistent letter sizing

2.   Name-spelling task

child spells: _____

does not respond

responds with only first letter

knows a few letters

knows most letters

spells name

3.   Letter identification task

Letters recognized: _____

Knows no, few, some, many, all letters in name

4.   Name recognition task

Child locates and reads own name.

Child locates name with same letter and reads as own.

Child refuses to read name.

Child reads one, two, three other names correctly.

Children reads some names correctly.

5.   Letter-matching task

Child matches letters: _____

All letters are matched without orientation difficulties

All letters are matched with orientation difficulties

Some letters are matched

Random order

Teachers can copy the entire page to administer the task to children. They point to letters across the lines of the text as they administer the task. A score sheet can be made by simply copying the administration form for each child. Teachers circle letters on the score sheet that children do not know. To administer the task, teachers say: "Some children know the names of alphabet letters. If you know the name of the letter I point to, you say it. Sometimes children don't know the name and you just say 'pass' if you don't know the name." Teachers point to each letter across the line of text. Teachers may want to abandon the assessment if children do know recognize the first eight letters.

O	X	T
S	A	M
B	P	I
W	Q	R
E	K	Z
F	H	C
N	L	J
U	G	V
D	Y	

Teachers can copy the entire page to administer the task to children. They point to letters across the lines of the text as they administer the task. A score sheet can be made by simply copying the administration form for each child. Teachers circle letters on the score sheet that children do not know. To administer the task, teachers say: "Some children know the names of alphabet letters. If you know the name of the letter I point to, you say it. Sometimes children don't know the name and you just say 'pass' if you don't know the name." Teachers point to each letter across the line of text. Teachers may want to abandon the assessment if children do know recognize the first eight letters.

o	s	x
w	i	c
j	y	p
f	k	z
e	m	r
t	n	v
u	l	a
g	b	h
d	q	

Alphabet Writing

_____   _____   _____   _____

_____   _____   _____   _____

_____   _____   _____   _____

_____   _____   _____   _____

_____   _____   _____   _____

_____   _____   _____   _____

_____   _____

Ask students to write their name on the top line. Then have students write one letter on each line in the following order:

O A H L
T E C I
Q U F M
X B W D
J V K N
P R S Y
G Z

ELKA CONCEPTS ABOUT PRINT TASKS

CAP: Concepts about Book Orientation, Directionality, and Letters and Words

Use *Too-Tall Paul, Too-Small Paul* (Hood, 1998).

Directions: "I'm going to show you a book and ask some questions about it."

1. Hold book out with spine toward the child. "Show me the front of this book."
   Score correct if child points to front of book.

2. "Show me the back of the book."
   Score correct if child points to back of book

3. Open the book to page 18 and lay book flat. "Point to the top of this page."
   Score correct if child points at the top of either page.

4. "Point to the bottom of this page."
   Score correct if child points at the bottom of either page.

5. "After I read this page [sweep hand down page 18], where do I read next?"
   Score correct if child points to page 19.

6. "After I read this page [sweep hand down page 19], where do I read next?"
   Score correct if child turns to page 20.
   If child does not point to page 20, but merely turns the page, ask:

7. "Which page do I read first?"
   Score correct if child turns to page 20 and points to that page in response to question #6.
   OR score correct if child points to page 20 in response to question #7.

8. (Remain on page 20). "Show me just one word on this page."
   Score correct if child clearly points to a single word.

9. "Show me the letter *S* on this page."
   Score correct if child points to either upper- or lower-case S.

cont.

10. "Let's suppose I was going to start reading this page. Point to exactly where I would start reading."

Score correct if child points to the first word in the top line of text (*Sometimes*)

OR score correct if child points to first word and sweeps finger across line of text.

11. "After I read this word [run finger under the word *Sometimes*], where do I read next?"

Score correct if child points to second word (*it's*)

OR score correct if child points to the second word and sweeps across the line.

12. "After I read this line [run finger under the first line of text], where do I read next?"

Score correct if child points to first word in second line of text (*It*)

OR score correct if child starts at that word and sweeps finger under the entire second line of text.

13. "Point to a long word on this page."

Score correct if child points to *Sometimes* or *Basketball*.

14. "Point to a short word on this page."

Score correct if child point to the words *to*, *be*, *so*, *It*, or *I*.

15. "Point to a word that has four letters."

Score correct if child points to the words *good*, *tall*, *when*, or *play*.

DIRECTIONS: The teacher introduces the text and talks with the child about his or her experiences with spiders, rain spouts, and what happens when it rains hard. Then the teacher reads the text, pointing to each word as he or she reads it. The teacher reads the text a second time, again pointing to each word as he or she says it and invites the child to say the text. The third time the teacher reads the text, he or she says, "Now you point to the words while I read the text. You read along with me." During this rereading the teacher guides children, pointing so that they do point to each word as that word is spoken. The assessment begins after these three practice readings. The teacher says, "Now you point to the words and say the poem. Start here [point to the first word in the title]." Two additional tasks are administered to analyze children's use of fingerpoint reading to locate and identify words. The teacher points to four words in the text (see the score sheet for identification of these four words) and says, "What is this word?" Then the teacher has children locate four words (the score sheet lists these words); the teacher says, "Can you find the word *spider*?" The teacher scores whether children identified or located the correct word.

The Itsy Bitsy Spider

cont.

The itsy bitsy spider
went up the water spout.

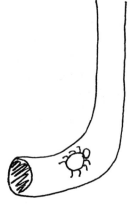

Down came the rain and
washed the spider out.

Out came the sun and
dried up all the rain.

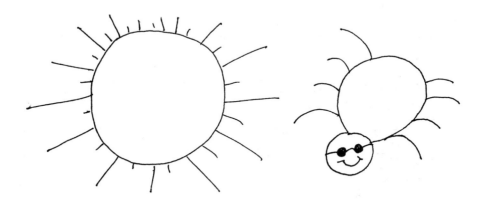

The itsy bitsy spider
went up the spout again.

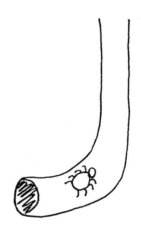

cont.

SCORE SHEET

Identify the following words:

____ spider

____ rain

____ out

____ up

Locate the following words:

____ spout

____ down

____ sun

____ the

Score: _____/8

ELKA PHONEMIC AWARENESS TASKS

APPENDIX E.1. Rhyme

To administer this task, teachers say: "We are going to look for rhyming words. These two words rhyme [show the picture of the *star* and the *jar*]. *Star, jar* rhyme. Now you say them. Now we will play a game of finding two pictures that rhyme. Here is how we do it." Teachers will point to the practice line of pictures and say: "*Fish, bug, dish.* Now you say them. I think *fish, dish* rhyme. You say them. Now it's your turn. I will say the pictures first, then you will say the pictures and find the two that rhyme." Children are shown 10 sets of three pictures, teachers say the picture names, and children repeat these words. Then children find the two words that rhyme. Teachers count the number of rhyming pairs children correctly identify. Children have mastered rhyme when they correctly match seven or more of the 10 rhyming items.

Demonstration

Practice

cont.

In the beginning-phoneme oddity task (MacLean, Bryant, & Bradley, 1987; Lonigan et al., 1999), children are shown three pictures. They must select the picture that does not have the same beginning sound as the other pictures. Teachers first demonstrate for children by saying: "We are going to play a game to find the word that does not start with the same sound as the other words. Listen as I say these words: *tent, fork, toe*. Now you say them. Now I am going to pick the word that does *not* sound like the other two. *Tent* and *toe* sound alike, but *fork* sounds different. I pick *fork*."

Teachers say the names of the pictures, children repeat the names of the pictures, and children select the word that does not sound the same as the other two pictures. There are a total of 18 items on this assessment; however, we recommend that teachers only use 10 items to assess this concept at the beginning of the year. Teachers score whether children identified correctly the picture that does not sound the same as the other two.

Demonstration

Practice

1.

2.

3.

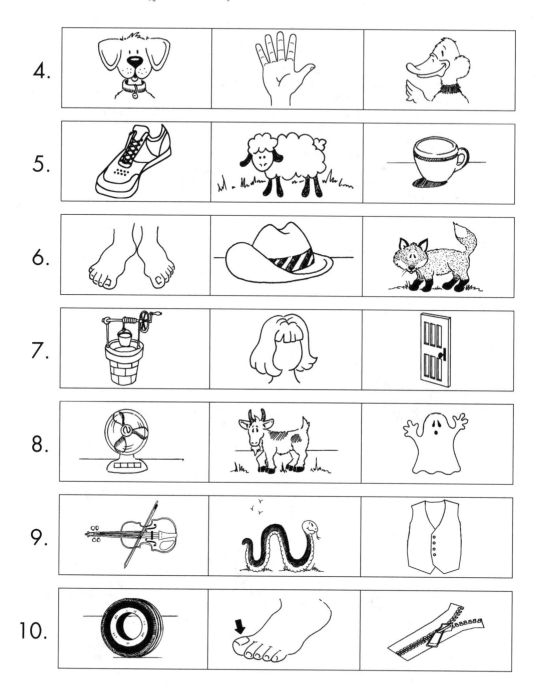

11.

12.

13.

14.

15.

16.

17.

18.

Isolating Beginning Phoneme Task

DIRECTIONS: "You are going to tell me the sound you hear at the beginning of words. Let me do this first one. The word is *paint*. I hear /p/ at the beginning of that word. Now you say /p/." This is an oral test. Teachers say the word and children say the beginning phoneme.

Demonstration

paint   /p/

Teacher says   Child responds

1.	junk	/j/	20.	dad	/d/
2.	fat	/f/	21.	thumb	/th/
3.	moon	/m/	22.	whistle	/wh/
4.	sun	/s/	23.	apple	/ă/
5.	van	/v/	24.	egg	/ĕ/
6.	wet	/w/	25.	igloo	/ĭ/
7.	nap	/n/	26.	otter	/ŏ/
8.	light	/l/	27.	ugly	/ŭ/
9.	rock	/r/	28.	apron	/ā/
10.	ship	/sh/	29.	eagle	/ē/
11.	baby	/b/	30.	ice	/ī/
12.	hat	/h/	31.	open	/ō/
13.	puppy	/p/	32.	unicorn	/ū/
14.	tire	/t/			
15.	kite	/k/			
16.	yell	/y/			
17.	ghost	/g/			
18.	zoo	/z/			
19.	chair	/ch/			

APPENDIX E.4. Isolating Ending Phoneme Task

DIRECTIONS: "You are going to tell me the sound you hear at the end of words. Let me do this first one. The word is *paint*. I hear /t/ at the end of that word. Now you say /t/." This is an oral test. Teachers say the word and children say the ending phoneme.

Demonstration

paint   /t/

Teacher says	Child responds
1. crab	/b/
2. bad	/d/
3. leaf	/f/
4. dig	/g/
5. rock	/k/
6. yell	/l/
7. ham	/m/
8. nap	/p/
9. moon	/n/
10. house	/s/
11. fat	/f/
12. buzz	/b/
13. wave	/v/
14. wish	/sh/
15. ouch	/ch/

Teachers say words segmented into syllables, onsets and rimes, or phonemes. Teachers say the first segment, pause 2 seconds, and then say the second segment. Teachers introduce the task by saying: "I am going to say a silly word, and you will tell me the real word I am trying to say. *Fire* [pause 2 seconds] *man*. The real word is *fireman*. Let's do another one. *Tooth* [pause 2 seconds] *brush*. That word is *toothbrush*. Now I'll say a silly word and you tell me the real word."

Demonstration

fire	man

Practice

tooth	brush

1.	foot	ball

2.	rain	bow

3.	birth	day

4.	sis	ter

5.	sciss	ors

6.	tr	ain

7.	b	at

8.	ch	in

9.	t	oy

10.	m	e

Segmenting Phonemes Task

Teachers demonstrate by saying: "I am going to say a word and then say each of its little bits of sound. Here is the first word: *tie*. You know, like 'Tie your shoes.' *Tie*. Now I'll divide it into its little bits of sounds /t/ /ie/. Here's another word. The word is *it*. You know, like "You are it." *It*. The little bits of sounds in *it* are /i/ /t/. Now it's your turn. I'll say the word and you tell me the little bits of sounds that you hear."

Demonstration

tie		/t/	/ī/

Practice

it		/ī/	/t/

	Teacher says	Child responds		
1.	toe	/t/	/ō/	
2.	up	/ŭ/	/p/	
3.	bee	/b/	/ē/	
4.	ape	/ā/	/p/	
5.	ten	/t/	/ĕ/	/n/
6.	pig	/p/	/ī/	/g/
7.	bag	/b/	/ă/	/g/
8.	dime	/d/	/ī/	/m/
9.	sheep	/sh/	/ē/	/p/

ELKA PHONICS TASKS

Children are shown a picture and then asked to select the letter (from a set of three letters) that the picture word begins with. Teachers first demonstrate by saying: "You are going to look at the picture, and then at the letters. You will say the letter that the picture word begins with. Look, this is a *sock*. I see the letters *L, B,* and *S.* The word *sock* begins with the letter *S.* Now it's your turn." Teachers say the name of each picture and then have the children say the letter that the picture word begins with. Teachers score children's attempts as correct or incorrect. There are a total of 18 items on this assessment, one item for each consonant letter. Teachers can use selected items from this assessment to determine whether children have learned letter–sound relationships taught.

Demonstration

	L	B	S
1.	N	L	F
2.	B	Q	M
3.	Z	T	J
4.	K	R	S

cont.

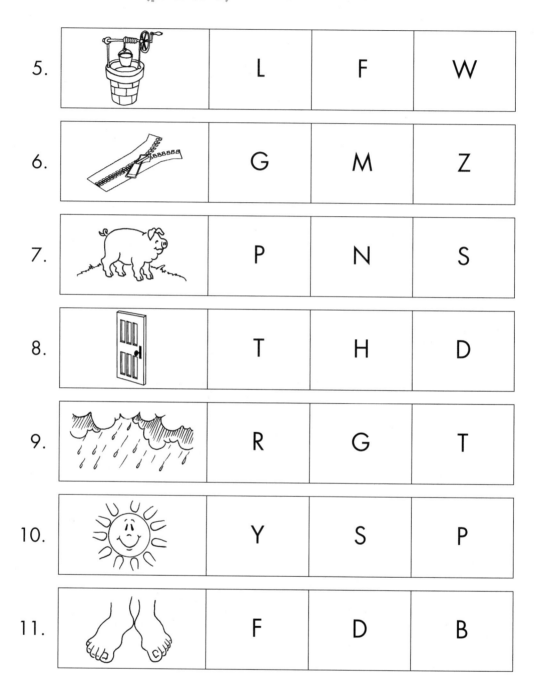

5.	L	F	W
6.	G	M	Z
7.	P	N	S
8.	T	H	D
9.	R	G	T
10.	Y	S	P
11.	F	D	B

12.		R	Y	M
13.		W	G	F
14.		N	T	Y
15.		S	R	H
16.		N	T	W
17.		Y	R	S
18.		B	F	V

APPENDIX F.2. Blending New Rhyming Words Task

Children are shown pictures and written words for five familiar rhyming words (*bat, net, lip, sock,* and *jump*). First, the teacher demonstrates reading a new rhyming word by saying: "Look at the picture of the *bat.* This word is *bat* [pointing to the word *bat*]. Here are some words that rhyme with *bat.* Look, all of these words end like *bat.* Here is the first word that I am going to read. It rhymes with *bat,* but instead of beginning with *b,* it begins with the letter *h. H* says /h/, so that word is *hat.* Let's try another one. The next word begins with *s* and *s* says [pause for the child to say /s/ or provide it if the child does not pronounce the phoneme]. So that word is *sat.* Now you try." The teacher points to the next word in the list and has the child read that word. If the child hesitates, the teacher can encourage the child to say the name of the first letter and its sound, then say the word. The teacher scores the item correct if the child correctly identifies the word.

Demonstration

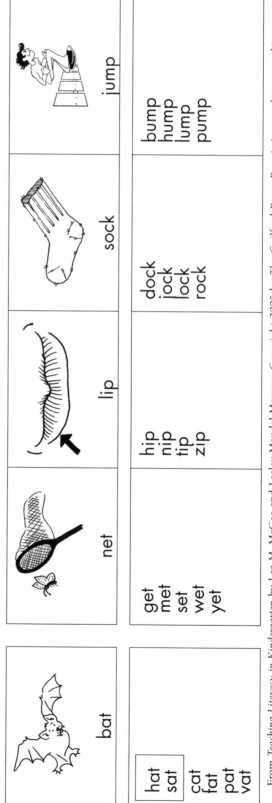

bat	net	lip	sock	jump

| hat
sat | get
met | hip
nip | dock
jock | bump
hump |
| cat
fat
pat
vat | set
wet
yet | tip
zip | lock
rock | lump
pump |

From *Teaching Literacy in Kindergarten* by Lea M. McGee and Lesley Mandel Morrow. Copyright 2005 by The Guilford Press. Permission to photocopy this page is granted to purchasers of this book for personal use only. See copyright page for details.

In this assessment children are shown words and asked to read them. The words all have three letters, include only short vowels, and are presented with the vowels mixed (rather than sorted into short-*a* words, etc.). Teachers use the administration sheet as a score sheet and mark words that children read correctly. Teachers will have children read the words, noting whether children know the word without decoding, know the correct phonemes, can hold phonemes in memory in order to blend the phonemes together, and can blend quickly enough to pronounce a word.

Words	Nonsense Words
cup	kot
ram	rud
tin	bip
bet	len
mop	fam
vet	
got	
sub	
job	
rag	
nut	
den	
vat	
peg	
zip	
had	
wit	
lot	
fun	
kin	

In this assessment children are shown words and are asked to read them. The words include only long vowels and are presented with the vowels mixed (rather than sorted into long-*a* words, etc.). Teachers use the administration sheet as a score sheet and mark words that children read correctly. Teachers will have children read the words, noting whether children know the word without decoding, know the correct phonemes, can hold phonemes in memory in order to blend the phonemes together, and can blend quickly enough to pronounce a word.

Words	Nonsense Words
hide	zay
bay	mone
joke	teef
seem	wate
wait	kide
boat	soad
feed	leat
gate	bime
meat	jool
rain	nute
pine	
vane	
note	
zoo	
cone	
keep	
dew	
load	
yule	

Consonant Phoneme and Letter–Sound Analysis Form

Consonant, Digraph, or Vowel	Isolate Beginning Phoneme	Isolate Ending Phoneme	Letter–Sound Match	Blend Rhyme	Decode Short-Vowel Words	Decode Short-Vowel Nonsense Words
b	baby	crab		bump	bet	bip
c				cat	cup	
d	dad	bad		dock	den	rud
f	fat	leaf		fat	fun	fam
g	ghost	dig		get	got	
h	hat			hump	him	
j	junk			jock	jet	
k	kite	rock		kip	kin	kot
l	light	yell		lump	lot	le
m	moon	ham		met	mop	fam
n	nap	moon		nip	nut	len
p	puppy	nap		pump	pat	bip
r	rock			rock	ram	rud
s	sun	house		set	sun	
t	tire	fat		tip	tin	kot
v	van	wave		van	vat	
w	wet			wet	win	
y	yell			yet	yet	
z	zoo	buzz		zip	zip	
ch	chair	ouch				
th	thumb	bath				
sh	ship	wish				
wh	whistle					

Vowel Analysis Form

Short Vowels

	Rhyme Family	Short-Vowel Words			Nonsense Words
/a/	vat	ram	rag	had	fam
/e/	yet	bet	peg	den	len
/i/	zip	tin	hit	wig	bip
/o/	rock	mop	got	job	kot
/u/	pump	cup	sub	fun	rud

Long Vowels

	Long-Vowel Words				Nonsense Words	
/a/	bay	gate	rain	vane	zay	wate
/e/	keep	meat	seem	tea	teef	leat
/i/	hide	tight	pine	ride	bight	kide
/o/	load	joke	note	cone	soad	mone
/u/ /oo/	dew	zoo	yule	pool	jool	nute

ELKA WRITING TASK
Invented Spelling List and Scoring Rubric

1 point   One letter represents a phoneme (not the first pho-
           neme); may include allowable unconventional matches
           d = trade, h = trade, j = trade, g = bug, t = steep,
           p = bug, p = steep

     OR

           One letter represents phoneme of first letter (including
           allowable matches)
           s = steep, c = steep, t = trade, b = bug, m = man,
           f = fit

2 points   Two letters with either the first or last letter or both
           hd = trade, tp = steep, mn = man, bg = bug, ft = fit,
           cp = steep, td = trade

3 points   First, last, and another letter with conventional or allow-
           able matches
           stp = stop

     OR

           First and last with incorrect vowel spelling
           bag = bug, men = man, beg = bug, min = man

     OR

           Correct long vowel included along with first and last
           sep = steep, tad = trade

     OR

           Blend spelled correctly
           tr = trade, st = steep

     OR

           Short-vowel word spelled correctly
           man, bug, fit

ELKA COMPREHENSION AND VOCABULARY TASK

RETELLING CHECKLIST FOR *OFFICER BUCKLE AND GLORIA* (RATHMAN, 1995)

_____ Officer Buckle knew lots of safety tips.
_____ He always thumb-tacked his safety tips on his bulletin board.
_____ Sometimes Officer Buckle shared his tips with students at Napville School.
_____ No one listened.
_____ The police department bought a dog named Gloria.
_____ One day Gloria went with Officer Buckle to Napville School.
_____ Gloria listened to Officer Buckle and obeyed his commands.
_____ Officer Buckle gave his safety tips with Gloria.
_____ The children sat up and listened.
_____ Gloria acted up where Officer Buckle could not see.
_____ Officer Buckle checked on Gloria.
_____ She sat at attention every time he looked.
_____ Officer Buckle got thank-you notes from the students at Napville.
_____ A picture of Gloria was on every note.
_____ All the schools around wanted to have Officer Buckle and Gloria.
_____ One day the news came and recorded the safety tips.
_____ Everyone cheered Officer Buckle and Gloria.
_____ Officer Buckle saw himself and Gloria on the news.
_____ He decided not to give any more speeches.
_____ He said, "No one looks at me.
_____ Students sent letters to Officer Buckle.
_____ Gloria went to the school by herself.
_____ Gloria didn't act out the safety tips.
_____ Everyone fell asleep.
_____ Napville School had its biggest accident ever.
_____ The principal fell.
_____ Officer Buckle thought of his best safety tip yet.
_____ Always Stick with Your Buddy.

Imagery or information in illustrations recalled

Past tense:	consistent	inconsistent	none	
Sequence:	correct	inconsistent	random	
Characters:	all names	some by name	no names	
Main events:	most	some	few	none
Setting:	most places	few	places	time
Overall summary statement:	yes	no		

REFERENCES

Anthony, J. L., Lonigan, C. J., Driscoll, K., Phillips, B. M., & Burgess, S. R. (2003). Phonological sensitivity: A quasi-parallel progression of word structure units and cognitive operations. *Reading Research Quarterly, 38,* 470–487.

Asher, J. (1982). *Learning another language through actions: The complete teachers' guidebook.* Los Gatos, CA: Sky Oaks.

Ashworth, M., & Wakefield, H.P. (1993). *Teaching the world's children: ESL for ages three to seven.* Markham, ON, Canada: Pippin.

Au, K.H. (2000). Multicultural factors and the effective instruction of students of diverse backgrounds. In A. E. Farstrup & S. J. Samuels (Eds.), *What research has to say about reading instruction* (3rd ed., pp. 392–413). Newark, DE: International Reading Association.

Barone, D. M., Mallette, M. H., & Xu, S. H. (2004). *Teaching early literacy: Development, assessment, and instruction.* New York: Guilford Press.

Bear, D., Invernizzi, M., Templeton, S., & Johnston, F. (2004). *Words their way: Word study for phonics, vocabulary, and spelling instruction* (3rd ed.). Columbus, OH: Merrill.

Beaver, J. (1997). *Developmental reading assessment.* Parsippany, NJ: Celebration Press.

Beck, I., & McKeown, M. (2001). Text talk: Capturing the benefits of read-aloud experiences for young children. *Reading Teacher, 55,* 10–20.

Beck, I. L., McKeown, M. G., & Kucan, L. (2002). *Bringing words to life: Robust vocabulary instruction.* New York: Guilford Press.

Behymer, A. (2003). Kindergarten writing workshop. *Reading Teacher, 57,* 85–88.

Bloodgood, J. W. (1999). What's in a name?: Children's name writing and literacy acquisition. *Reading Research Quarterly, 34,* 342–367.

Bodrova, E., & Leong, D. (1998). Scaffolding emergent writing in the zone of proximal development. *Literacy Teaching and Learning, 3,* 1–18.

Bodrova, E., Leong, D., Paynter, D., & Hughes, C. (2001). *Scaffolding literacy development in the kindergarten classroom.* Aurora, CO: Mid-continent Research for Education and Learning.

Brown, K.J. (2003). What do I say when they get stuck on a word?: Aligning teachers' prompts with students' development. *Reading Teacher, 56*(8), 720–733.

Byrne, B., & Fielding-Barnsley, R. (1991). Evaluation of a program to teach phonemic awareness to young children. *Journal of Educational Psychology, 83,* 451–455.

Clay, M. M. (1990). *The early detection of reading difficulties* (3rd ed.). Portsmouth, NH: Heinemann.

Clay, M. M. (1993a). *The early detection of reading difficulties* (4th ed.). Portsmouth, NH: Heinemann.

Clay, M. M. (1993b). *An observation survey of early literacy achievement.* Portsmouth, NH: Heinemann.

Cummins, J. (1989). *Empowering minority students.* Sacramento: California Association for Bilingual Education.

Dickinson, D. K., & Smith, M. W. (1994). Long-term effects of preschool teachers' book readings on low-income children's vocabulary and story comprehension. *Reading Research Quarterly, 29,* 104–122.

Donovan, C. (2001). Children's development and control of written story and informational genres: Insights from one elementary school. *Research in the Teaching of English, 35,* 394–447.

Donovan, C., & Smolkin, L. (2002). Considering genre, content, and visual features in the selection of trade books for science instruction. *Reading Teacher, 55,* 502–520.

Duke, N. K. (2000). Print environments and experiences offered to first-grade students in very low- and very high-SES school districts. *Reading Research Quarterly, 35,* 456–457.

Duke, N. K., & Kays, J. (1998). "Can I say 'once upon a time'?": Kindergarten children developing knowledge of information book language. *Early Childhood Research Quarterly, 13,* 295–318.

Duke, N. K., & Purcell-Gates, V. (2003). Genres at home and at school: Bridging the known to the new. *Reading Teacher, 57,* 30–37.

Echevarria, J., Vogt, M., & Short, D. (2000). *Making content comprehensible for English language learners: The SIOP model.* Boston: Allyn & Bacon.

Ehri, L., & Sweet, J. (1991). Finger-point reading of memorized text: What enables beginners to process the print. *Reading Research Quarterly, 26,* 442–462.

Feldgus, E., & Cardonick, I. (1999). *Kid writing: A systematic approach to phonics, journals, and writing workshop.* Bothell, WA: Wright Group.

Froebel, F. (1974). *The education of man.* Clifton, NJ: Kelly.

Gibson, E. J., Gibson, J. J., Pick, A.D., & Osser, H. (1962). A developmental study of discrimination of letter-like forms. *Journal of Comparative Physiological Psychology, 55,* 897–906.

Gunning, T. G. (2003). *Creating literacy instruction for all children* (4th ed.). Boston: Allyn & Bacon.

Hadaway, N. L., Vardell, S. M., & Young, T. A. (2002). *Literature-based instruction with English language learners, K–12.* Boston: Allyn & Bacon.

Hannon, J. (1999). Talking back: Kindergarten dialogue journals. *Reading Teacher, 53,* 200–203.

Hargrave, A. C., & Senechal, M. (2000). A book reading intervention with preschool children who have limited vocabularies: The benefits of regular reading and dialogic reading. *Early Childhood Research Quarterly, 15,* 75–90.

Hickman, P., Pollard-Durodola, S., & Vaughn, S. (2004). Storybook reading: Improving vocabulary and comprehension for English-language learners. *Reading Teacher, 57*(8), 720–730.

Hildreth, G. (1936). Developmental sequences in name writing. *Child Development, 7,* 291–303.

International Reading Association and National Association for the Education of Young Children. (1998). Learning to read and write: Developmentally appropriate practices for young children. *Reading Teacher, 52,* 193–216.

Intrater, R. (1995). *Two eyes, a nose, and a mouth.* New York: Scholastic.

Johnston, R. S., Anderson, M., & Holligan, C. (1996). Knowledge of the alphabet and explicit awareness of phonemes in pre-readers: The nature of the relationship. *Reading and Writing: An Interdisciplinary Journal, 8,* 217–234.

Krashen, S. (1985). *Principles and practices in second language acquisition.* Oxford, UK: Pergamon Press.

Leslie, L., & Caldwell, J. (2001). *Qualitative Reading Inventory–3.* New York: Addison Wesley Longman.

Lester, H. (1998). *Tacky in trouble.* New York: Scholastic.

LeVine, J. (2002). Writing letters to support literacy. *Reading Teacher, 56,* 232–234.

Lonigan, C. J., Burgess, S. R., Anthony, J. L., & Baker, T.A. (1998). Development of phonological sensitivity in 2- to 5-year-old children. *Journal of Educational Psychology, 90,* 294–311.

Loughlin, C. E., & Martin, M. D. (1987). *Supporting literacy: Developing effective learning environments.* New York: Teachers College Press.

Maclean, M., Bryant, P., & Bradley, L. (1987). Rhymes, nursery rhymes, and reading in early childood. *Merrill-Palmer Quarterly, 33,* 255–281.

McCarrier, A., Pinnell, G. S., & Fountas, I. C. (2000). *Interactive writing: How language and literacy come together, K–2.* Portsmouth, NH: Heinemann.

McGee, L. M., & Richgels, D. J. (1989). "K is Kristen's": Learning the alphabet from a child's perspective. *Reading Teacher, 43,* 216–225.

McGee, L. M., & Richgels, D. J. (2004). *Literacy's beginnings: Supporting young readers and writers* (4th ed.). Boston: Allyn & Bacon.

Montessori, M. (1965). *Spontaneous activity in education.* New York: Schocken Books.

Moore, G. (1986). Effects of the spatial definition of behavior settings on children's behavior: A quasi-experimental field study. *Journal of Environmental Psychology, 6*(3), 205–231.

Morris, D., Bloodgood, J., Lomax, R., & Perney, J. (2003). Developmental steps in learning to read: A longitudinal study in kindergarten and first grade. *Reading Research Quarterly, 38,* 302–328.

Morris, D., & Slavin, R. (Eds.). (2003). *Every child reading.* Boston: Allyn & Bacon.

Morrow, L. M. (1985). Retelling stories: A strategy for improving children's comprehension, concept of story structure and oral language complexity. *Elementary School Journal, 85,* 647–661.

Morrow, L. M. (1990). Preparing the classroom environment to promote literacy during play. *Early Childhood Research Quarterly, 5,* 537–554.

Morrow, L. M. (1992). The impact of a literature-based program on literacy achievement, use of literature, and attitudes of children from minority backgrounds. *Reading Research Quarterly, 27,* 250–275.

Morrow, L. M., O'Connor, E. M., & Smith, J. (1990). Effects of a story reading program on the literacy development of at-risk kindergarten children. *Journal of Reading Behavior, 20*(2), 104–141.

Morrow, L. M., & Rand, M. (1991a). Preparing the classroom environment to promote literacy during play. In J. F. Christie (Ed.), *Play and early literacy development* (pp. 141–165). Albany: State University of New York Press.

Morrow, L. M., & Rand, M. (1991b). Promoting literacy during play by designing early childhood classroom environments. *Reading Teacher, 44,* 396–405.

Morrow, L. M., & Smith, J. K. (1990). The effects of group size on interactive storybook reading. *Reading Research Quarterly, 25,* 213–231.

Morrow, L. M., & Tracey, D. H. (1996). Instructional environments for language and learning: Considerations for young children. In J. Flood, S. B. Heath, & D. Lapp (Eds.), *Handbook for literacy educators: Research on teaching the communicative and visual arts* (pp. 475–485). New York: Macmillan.

Morrow, L. M., & Weinstein, C. S. (1986). Encouraging voluntary reading: The impact of a literature program on children's use of library centers. *Reading Research Quarterly, 21,* 330–346.

Murray, B. A. (1998). Gaining alphabetic insight: Is phoneme manipulation skill or identity knowledge causal? *Journal of Educational Psychology, 90*(3), 461–475.

Murray, B. A., Stahl, S. A., & Ivey, M. G. (1996). Developing phoneme awareness through alphabet books. *Reading and Writing: An Interdisciplinary Journal, 8,* 306–322.

Neuman, S. B., & Roskos, K. (1990). The influence of literacy-enriched play settings on preschoolers' engagement with written language. In J. Zutell & S. McCormick (Eds.), *Literacy theory and research: Analyses from multiple paradigms* (pp. 179–187). Chicago: National Reading Conference.

Neuman, S. B., & Roskos, K. (1992). Literary objects as cultural tools: Effects on children's literacy behaviors in play. *Reading Research Quarterly, 27*(3), 202–225.

Neuman, S. B., & Roskos, K. (1993). Access to print for children of poverty: Differential effects of adult mediation and literacy-enriched play settings on environmental and functional print tasks. *American Educational Research Journal, 30,* 95–122.

Notari-Syverson, A., O'Connor, R. E., & Vadasy, P. F. (1998). *Ladders to literacy: A preschool activity book.* Baltimore: Brookes.

Orellana, M. E., & Hernandez, A. (1999). Talking with the walk: Children reading urban environmental print. *Reading Teacher, 51,* 612–619.

Pappas, C. C., & Barry, A. (1997). Scaffolding urban students' initiations: Transactions in reading information books in the read-aloud curriculum. In N. J. Karolides (Ed.), *Reader response in elementary classrooms: Quest and discovery* (pp. 215–236). Mahwah, NJ: Erlbaum.

Parkes, B. (2000). *Read it again!: Revisiting the shared reading.* Portland, ME: Stenhouse.

Paris, A. H., & Paris, S. G. (2003). Assessing narrative comprehension in young children. *Reading Research Quarterly, 38*(1), 36–76.

Piaget, J., & Inhelder, B. (1969). *The psychology of the child.* New York: Basic Books.

Purcell-Gates, V., & Dahl, K. (1991). Low-SES children's success and failure at early literacy learning in skills-based classrooms. *Journal of Reading Behavior, 23,* 1–34.

Purcell-Gates, V., McIntyre, E., & Freppon, P. A. (1995). Learning written storybook language in school: A comparison of low-SES children in skills-based and whole language classrooms. *American Educational Research Journal, 32,* 659–685.

Reese, E., & Cox, A. (1999). Quality of adult book reading affects children's emergent literacy. *Developmental Psychology, 35*(1), 20–28.

Reutzel, D. R., & Cooter, R. B. (2004). *Teaching children to read: Putting the pieces together* (4th ed.). Upper Saddle River, NJ: Pearson/Merrill/Prentice-Hall.

Reutzel, D. R., & Wolfersberger, M. (1996). An environmental impact statement: Designing supportive literacy classrooms for young children. *Reading Horizons, 36*(3), 266–282.

Rhodes, L., & Natheson-Mejia, S. (1992). Anecdotal records: A powerful tool for ongoing literacy assessment. *Reading Teacher, 45,* 502–509.

Richgels, D. J. (1995). A kindergarten sign-in procedure: A routine in support of written language learning. In K. A. Hinchman, D. J. Leu, & C. K. Kinzer (Eds.), *Perspectives on literacy research and practice* (pp. 243–254). Chicago: National Reading Conference.

Richgels, D. J. (2001). Invented spelling, phonemic awareness, and reading and writing instruction. In S. B. Neuman & D. K. Dickinson (Eds.), *Handbook of early literacy research* (pp. 142–155). New York: Guilford Press.

Richgels, D. J. (2002). Informational texts in kindergarten. *Reading Teacher, 55,* 586–595.

Richgels, D. J., Poremba, K. J., & McGee, L. M. (1996). Kindergartners talk about print: Phonemic awareness in meaningful contexts. *Reading Teacher, 49,* 632–642.

Ritchie, S., James-Szanton, J., & Howes, C. (2003). Emergent literacy practices in early childhood classrooms. In C. Howes (Ed.), *Teaching 4- to 8-year-olds* (pp. 71–92). Baltimore: Brookes.

Ritterskamp, P., & Singleton, J. (2001). Interactive calendar. *Reading Teacher, 55,* 114–116.

Rusk, R., & Scotland, J. (1979). *Doctrines of the great educators.* New York: St. Martin's Press.

Schickedanz, J. A. (1993). Designing the early childhood classroom environment to facilitate literacy development. In B. Spodek & O.N. Saracho (Eds.), *Yearbook in early childhood education: Vol. 4. Language and literacy in early childhood education.* New York: Teachers College Press.

Schickedanz, J. A. (1998). What is developmentally appropriate practice in early literacy?: Considering the alphabet. In S. Neuman & K. Roskos (Eds.), *Children achieving: Best practices in early literacy* (pp. 20–35). Newark, DE: International Reading Association.

Schickedanz, J. A. (2003). Engaging preschoolers in code learning: Some thoughts about preschool teachers' concerns. In D. M. Barone & L. M. Morrow (Eds.), *Literacy and young children: Research-based practices* (pp. 121139). New York: Guilford.

Sipe, L. (2002). Talking back and taking over: Young children's expressive engagement during storybook read-alouds. *Reading Teacher, 55,* 476–483.

Smolkin, L. B., & Donovan, C. A. (2001). "Oh excellent, excellent question!": Developmental differences and comprehension acquisition. In C. C. Block & M. Pressley (Eds.), *Comprehension instruction: Research-based best practices* (pp. 140–157). New York: Guilford Press.

Snow, C. E., Burns, M. S., & Griffin, P. (Eds.). (1998). *Preventing reading difficulties in young children.* Washington, DC: National Academy Press.

Stahl, S. A., & Murray, B. A. (1994). Defining phonological awareness and its relationship to early reading. *Journal of Educational Psychology, 86*(2), 221–233.

Stein, N. L., & Glenn, C. G. (1979). An analysis of story comprehension in elementary school children. In R. O. Freedle (Ed.), *Advances in discourse processes, Vol. 2: New directions in discourse processing* (pp. 53–120). Norwood, NJ: Ablex.

Tabors, P. O. (1997). *One child, two languages: A guide for preschool educators of children learning English as a second language.* Baltimore: Brookes.

Ukrainetz, T. A., Cooney, M. H., Dyer, S. K., Kysar, A. J., & Harris, T. J. (2000). An investigation into teaching phonemic awareness through shared reading and writing. *Early Childhood Research Quarterly, 15,* 331–355.

van den Broek, P. (2001). *The role of television viewing in the development of reading comprehension.* Ann Arbor, MI: Center for the Improvement of Early Reading Achievement.

Villaume, S. K., & Wilson, L. C. (1989). Preschool children's explorations of letters in their own names. *Applied Psycholinguists, 10,* 283–300.

Vygotsky, L. S. (1978). *Mind in society: The development of higher psychological processes.* Cambridge, MA: Harvard University Press.

Wasik, B. A., & Bond, M. A. (2001). Beyond the pages of a book: Interactive book reading and language development in preschool classrooms. *Journal of Educational Psychology, 93*(2), 243–250.

Weinstein, C. S., & Mignano, A. J., Jr. (2003). *Elementary classroom management* (3rd ed.). Boston: McGraw-Hill.

Whitehurst, G. J., & Lonigan, C. J. (2001). Emergent literacy: Development from prereaders to readers. In S. B. Neuman & D. K. Dickinson (Eds.), *Handbook of early literacy research* (pp. 11–29). New York: Guilford Press.

Wood, D., Bruner, J., & Ross, G. (1976). The role of tutoring in problem solving. *Journal of Child Psychology and Psychiatry, 17*(2), 89–100.

Wylie, R. E., & Durrell, D. D. (1970). Teaching vowels through phonograms. *Elementary English, 47,* 787–791.

Xu, S. H., & Rutledge, A. L. (2003). Chicken starts with ch!: Kindergarteners learn through environmental print. *Young Children, 58,* 44–51.

Yaden, D., Smolkin, L., & Conlon, A. (1989). Preschoolers' questions about pictures, print convention, and story text during reading aloud at home. *Reading Research Quarterly, 24,* 188–214.

Yopp, H. K., & Yopp, R.H. (2000). Supporting phonemic awareness development in the classroom. *Reading Teacher, 54,* 130–143.

CHILDREN'S LITERATURE

Aigner-Clark, J. (2001). *Baby Einstein: Language nursery*. New York: Cartwheel Books.

Alborough, J. (2001). *Duck in a truck*. New York: HarperCollins.

Allen, M. (1999). *Top job, Mom!: Dr. Maggie's phonics readers: A new view*. Cypress, CA: Creative Teaching Press.

Atkins, J. (1999). *Mary Anning and the sea dragon*. New York: Farrar Straus Giroux.

Barton, B. (1981). *Building a house*. New York: Puffin Books.

Barton, B. (1989). *Dinosaurs, dinosaurs*. New York: Crowell.

Beall, P. C., & Nipp, S. H. (1999). *Wee sing in the car*. New York: Price Stern Sloan.

Brenner, B. (1972). *The three little pigs*. New York: Random House.

Brett, J. (1987). *The three bears*. New York: Putnam.

Briggs, R. (1970). *Jim and the beanstalk*. New York: Coward-McCann.

Brown, M. (1942). *The runaway bunny*. New York: Harper & Row.

Brown, M. (1947). *Goodnight, moon*. New York: Harper & Row.

Brown, M. (1990). *Arthur's pet business*. New York: Little, Brown.

Burningham, J. (1993). *Mr. Gumpy's motor car*. New York: Thomas Y. Crowell.

Buxton, J. (1997). *My bike*. Bothell, WA: Wright Group.

Canizares, S., & Chessen, B. (1998). *From egg to robin*. New York: Scholastic.

Caple, K. (2000). *Well done, worm!* Cambridge, MA: Candlewick Press.

Carle, E. (1984). *The very busy spider*. New York: Philomel.

Carle, E. (1986). *The grouchy ladybug*. New York: Harper & Rowe.

Carlson, N. (1988). *I like me!* New York: Penguin Books.

Carrick, C. (1983). *Patrick's dinosaurs*. New York: Clarion Books.

Christelow, E. (1989). *Five little monkeys jumping on the bed*. New York: Clarion Books.

Connelly, L. (1988). *Bears, bears, everywhere*. Cypress, CA: Creative Teaching Press.

Cowley, J. (1989). *Yuck soup*. Bothell, WA: Wright Group.

Cowley, J. (1999). *Mrs. Wishy Washy*. New York: Wright Group.

Craft, R. (1991). *The day of the rainbow*. Illustrated by Niki Daly. New York: Puffin Books.

Crews, D. (1985). *Freight train*. New York: Puffin Books.

dePaola, T. (1988). *The legend of the Indian paintbrush*. New York: Alladin.

DK Multimedia. *Eyewitness virtual reality: Dinosaur hunter*. New York: DK Publishing.

DK Publishing. (1995). *The visual dictionary of prehistoric life*. New York: DK Publishing.

Dunn, J. (1976). *The little duck*. New York: Random House.

Eastman, P. D. (1961). *Go dog, go*. New York: Random House.

Educational Insights. (1990). *Phonics readers*. Carson, CA: Author.

Edwards, P. (1998). *Warthogs in the kitchen.* New York: Hyperion.

Ehlert, L. (1995). *Snowballs.* Orlando, FL: Harcourt Brace.

Flack, M. M. (1932). *Ask Mr. Bear.* New York: Macmillan.

Fleming, D. (1991). *In the tall, tall grass.* New York: Holt.

Fleming, M. (2000). *Autumn leaves are falling.* Illustrated by Melissa Sweet. New York: Scholastic.

Fletcher, N. (1993). *See how they grow: Penguins.* New York: Dorling Kindersley.

Fontanel, B. (1989). *The penguin: A funny bird.* Watertown, MA: Charlesbridge.

Galdone, P. (1968). *Henny Penny.* New York: Clarion Books.

Galdone, P. (1972). *The three bears.* New York: Scholastic.

Gelman, R. G. (1993). *More spaghetti, I say.* New York: Scholastic.

Gibbons, F. (1999). *Mama and me and the Model T.* New York: Morrow.

Greenfield, E. (1975). *Me and Nessie.* Illustrated by Moneta Barnett. New York: Crowell.

Guarino, D. (1989). *Is your mama a lama?* Illustrated by Steven Kellogg. New York: Scholastic.

Hall, Z. (2000). *Fall leaves fall!* Illustrated by Shari Halpern. New York: Scholastic.

Harrison, C. (1998). *Dinosaurs everywhere!* New York: Scholastic.

Harste, J., & Goss, J. (1993). *It didn't frighten me!* Pinellas Park, FL: Willowisp.

Hazen, B. S. (1983). *Tight times.* New York: Picture Puffins.

Henderson, P. (1998). *Colors at the zoo.* New York: Sadlier-Oxford.

Hoff, S. (1958). *Danny and the dinosaur.* New York: Harper & Row.

Hood, S. (1998). *Too-tall Paul, too-small Paul.* Brookfield, CT: Millbrook Press.

Hutchins, P. (1968). *Rosie's walk.* New York: Macmillan.

Kennedy, J. (1991). *Teddy bears' picnic.* New York: Simon & Schuster.

Izawa, T. (1968). *Goldilocks and the three bears.* New York: Grosset & Dunlap.

Jeunesse, G., & Delafosse, C. (1995). *Houses.* New York: Scholastic.

Keats, E. J. (1971). *Over in the meadow.* New York: Scholastic.

Kovalski, M. (1987). *The wheels on the bus: An adaptation of the traditional song.* New York: Little, Brown.

Maestro, B. (1994). *Why do leaves change color?* New York: HarperCollins.

Martin, B. Jr. (1967). *Brown bear, brown bear, what do you see?* Illustrated by E. Carle. New York: Holt, Rinehart and Winston.

Martin, R. (1985). *Foolish rabbit's big mistake.* New York: G. P. Putman's Sons.

Maslen, B. L. (1994). *Bob books for beginning readers.* New York: Scholastic.

Mayes, K. E. (2002). *Things that go.* Boston: Sundance.

McKissack, P. (1988). *Mirandy and Brother Wind.* New York: Knopf.

Minarik, E. H. (1996). *A kiss for Little Bear.* New York: Harper & Row.

Most, B. (1994). *How big were the dinosaurs?* New York: Harcourt Brace.

Murphy, S. J. (2000). *Beep beep, vroom vroom!* New York: HarperCollins.

Osborne, M. P. (1992). *Dinosaurs before dark.* New York: Random House.

Phonics Readers. (1990). *A cat nap.* Carson, CA: Educational Insights.

Pienkowski, J. (1980). *Dinnertime.* Los Angeles, CA: Price/Stern/Sloan.

Plourde, L. (1997). *Pigs in the mud in the middle of the rud.* New York: Blue Sky Press.

Polacco, P. (1990). *Thundercake.* New York: Philomel.

Pomery, D. (1996). *One potato: A counting book of potato prints.* New York: Harcourt.

Potter, B. (1902). *The tale of Peter Rabbit.* New York: Scholastic.

Prince, S. (1999). *Playing.* Littleton, MA: Sundance.

Pruett, D. (1991). "I'm a mean old dinosaur." In *Dinosaurs.* Monterey, CA: EvanMoor.

Rathman, P. (1995). *Officer Buckle and Gloria.* New York: G.P. Putman's Sons.

Reber, D. (2001). *My favorite letters.* Illustrated by Karen Craig. New York: Simon Spotlight/Nickleodeon.

Riley, L. (1997). *Mouse mess.* New York: Scholastic.

Robbins, K. (1998). *Autumn leaves.* New York: Scholastic.

Roche, D. (1999). *Can you count ten toes?: Count to 10 in 10 different languages.* Boston: Houghton Mifflin.

Ruwe, M. (1989). *Ten little bears.* Illustrated by D. Hockerman. Glenview, IL: Scott Foresman.

Scholastic. (2000). *Phonics ready readers.* New York: Author.

Sendak, M. (1962a). *Chicken soup with rice.* New York: Scholastic.

Sendak, M. (1962b). *Pierre.* New York: HarperCollins.

Seuss, Dr. (Theodore Giesel). (1963). *Hop on Pop.* New York: Random House.

Shaw, N (1986). *Sheep in a Jeep.* New York: Houghton Mifflin.

Sykes, J. (1997). *Dora's eggs.* Wauwatosa, WI: Little Tiger Press.

Sloan, P., & Sloan, S. (1994). *We went to the zoo.* Boston: Sundance.

Sloan, P., & Sloan, S. (1996). *Family work and fun.* Boston: Sundance.

Sokoloff, M. L. (1997). *Discovering dinosaurs.* New York: Sadlier.

Stevens, J. (1995). *Tops and bottoms.* New York: Harcourt Brace.

Stojic, M. (2002). *Hello world!: Greetings in 42 languages around the globe.* New York: Scholastic.

Stuart, M. (2001). *Who can run fast?* New York: Sadlier-Oxford.

Taback, S. (1997). *There was an old lady who swallowed a fly.* New York: Viking.

Thomson, R. (2000). *A dinosaur's day.* New York: Dorling Kindersley.

Thorpe, K. (2000). *Snowbound.* Illustrated by Mel Grant. New York: Simon Spotlight/Nickelodeon.

Tolhurst, M. (1991). *Somebody and the three Blairs.* New York: Scholastic.

Wadsworth, O. (1992). *Over in the meadow: An old counting rhyme.* New York: Scholastic.

Wells, R. (1981). *Timothy goes to school.* New York: Puffin Books.

Wells, R. (2000). *Noisy Nora.* New York: Puffin Books.

Williams, V. B. (1982). *A chair for my mother.* New York: Greenwillow Books.

Wood, A. (1992). *Silly Sally.* New York: Harcourt.

World Book's young scientist: Vol. 6. Animals. (1991). Chicago: World Books.

Yolen, J. (1987). *Owl moon.* New York: Philomel.

Ziefert, H. (1996). *Where is my baby?* Brooklyn, NY: Handprint Books.

INDEX

Page numbers followed by *f* indicate figure.

Alphabet books
  English language learners and, 128, 133–134
  list of, 179
  overview, 73–74
  shared-reading techniques and, 72–74, 75
  See also Books
Alphabet knowledge
  assessment of, 151–155, 152*f*, 154*f*, 201–206
  developmental phases and, 119*f*–120*f*
  expectations regarding, 44–46, 45*f*
  letter formation, 195–198
  national standards and, 148*f*
  phonics and, 48–49
  reading aloud and, 91*f*
  shared-reading techniques and, 90
  small-group instruction and, 95, 98–99, 110*f*
  as a year-end goal, 93*f*
Alphabet-writing task, 155, 201–206. *See also* Assessment
Anecdotal notes, 172. *See also* Assessment
Art, 12, 16
Art center
  example of, 9
  interactive read-alouds and, 72
  managing work in, 112
  overview, 32
  See also Centers, learning
Assessment
  alphabet recognition and writing, 45–46, 151–155, 152*f*, 154*f*, 201–206
  comprehension and vocabulary, 152*f*, 167–168, 239

concepts about print, 152*f*, 155–156, 209–214
  example of, 4
  overview, 146–147, 148*f*–150*f*, 150–151, 174–175
  phonemic awareness, 152*f*, 156–158, 217–225
  phonics, 152*f*, 158–161, 229–236
  planning for and selecting, 174
  selecting children for small groups and, 94
  spelling, 152*f*, 166–167*f*
  text reading, 152*f*, 161–163*f*, 164*f*–165*f*, 165–166
  via observation, 171–174, 173*f*
  via work samples, 168–171, 170*f*
  writing, 152*f*, 166–167*f*, 237
Audio books, 28
Awareness and exploration stage of development. *see also* Development
  matching instruction with, 117
  overview, 116

Basal reading programs. *See* Core reading programs
Beginning phoneme oddity task, 157. *See also* Assessment
Behavior, 25–26
Benchmarks, 147, 148*f*–150*f*. *See also* National standards
Big books
  list of, 180–181
  overview, 30

shared-reading techniques and, 74–75, 77–79
    See also Books
Biographies, 30. *See also* Books
Blending
    assessment of, 158, 159–160
    small-group instruction and, 100–101, 101–
        102, 108, 110*f*
Blending new rhyming words task, 159–160.
    See also Assessment
Blending syllables, onset/rimes, and phoneme
    task, 158. *See also* Assessment
Block center
    example of, 3, 8
    overview, 32
    See also Centers, learning
Book orientation
    assessment of, 155–156
    concepts regarding, 50
Books
    concepts regarding, 50–51
    English language learners and, 128, 129*f*,
        130, 133–134, 135*f*, 136*f*–138
    genres of, 58–60, 59*f*
    introducing in an interactive read-aloud,
        66–67
    levels of, 109
    in the library corner, 29–31
    list of, 179–184, 186–192
    multiple readings of, 70–72, 76
    reading aloud and, 91*f*
    shared-reading techniques and, 72–79, 74–
        75, 80*f*–82*f*

Caldecott Medal, 29. *See also* Books
CAP: Concepts about Book Orientation,
        Directionality, and Letters and Words,
        155–156. *See also* Assessment
CDs, books on, 28
Center time
    example of, 8–9*f*, 12, 15–16, 21, 23
    managing work during, 34–35, 111–113*f*
    See also Centers, learning
Centers, learning
    example of, 2–3
    furniture arrangement and, 35–37, 36*f*
    managing work in, 4, 34–35, 111–113*f*
    overview, 31–32
    preparing, 26–34
Chapter books, 30. *See also* Books
Charts, 74–75, 77–79
Classroom environment
    examples of, 2–3, 37–38

furniture arrangement and, 35–37, 36*f*
importance of, 24–26
preparing, 26–34
scheduling and, 38
    See also Learning centers
Closing circle, 12–13, 16, 18, 21, 23
Coding system in library, 27. *See also* Library
        corner
Community
    dramatic play center and, 33
    English language learners and, 131
Comprehensible input, 132
Comprehension
    assessment of, 152*f*, 167–168, 239
    English language learners and, 126
    interactive read-alouds and, 65, 68–69
    multiple readings of a book and, 70–71
    overview, 53–55*f*, 56*f*–57*f*
    reading aloud and, 89–90, 91*f*
    as a year-end goal, 93*f*
Computer center
    example of, 8
    managing work in, 112
    resources, 184–186
    See also Centers, learning
Computers, in the writing area, 31
Concept books, 128. *See also* Books
Concepts about print, books, and words
    assessment of, 152*f*, 155–156, 209–
        214
    developmental phases and, 116, 117
    national standards and, 148*f*
    overview, 50–51
    reading aloud and, 91*f*
    shared-reading techniques and, 77–79, 80*f*–
        82*f*
    as a year-end goal, 93*f*
Consonant letter–sound associations
    assessment of, 159, 160
    expectations regarding, 47–48
    See also Phonics
Consonant letter–sound matching task, 159.
        See also Assessment
Consonant phoneme and letter–sound analy-
        sis form, 160. *See also* Assessment
Continuants, 100. *See also* Phonemic aware-
        ness
Cookbooks, 30. *See also* Books
Cooperative play, 25–26
Copying, 58–60, 59*f*
Core reading programs, 113–114
Craft books, 30. *See also* Books

Culture
  becoming familiar with, 131–132
  family literacy and, 139
Curriculum integration, 1

Decodable books, 106–107. *See also* Books
Decoding
  assessment of, 160
  developmental phases and, 120*f*
  national standards and, 149*f*
  small-group instruction and, 95, 106–109
Decoding long-vowel words task, 160. *See also* Assessment
Decoding short-vowel words task, 160. *See also* Assessment
Development
  differentiated instruction and, 115–118
  English language learners and, 126, 127*f*, 128, 129*f*, 130
  See also Development of literacy
Development of literacy
  assessment of, 146–147, 148*f*–150*f*, 150–151
  environment and, 25
  family involvement and, 138–141, 142*f*–144*f*, 144–145
  matching instruction with, 117–118
  phases of, 116
  See also Development
Dialogue journals, 88–89
Differentiated instruction
  English language learners and, 125–126, 127*f*, 128, 129*f*, 130–134, 135*f*, 136*f*–138
  family involvement and, 138–141, 142*f*–144*f*, 144–145
  overview, 115–118, 145
  See also Small-group reading instruction
Dinosaur theme
  example of, 6–23, 9*f*, 10*f*
  list of books, 191–192
Directionality of print
  assessment of, 155–156
  concepts regarding, 50
  cultural considerations to, 133
  shared-reading techniques and, 80*f*
Dora's Eggs (Sykes), 66
Dramatic play center
  example of, 3, 9
  interactive read-alouds and, 72
  overview, 25, 32–34
  pretend writing and, 58*f*

year-end goals and, 93*f*
See also Centers, learning

Early literacy knowledge assessment tasks (ELKA)
  alphabet recognition and writing, 151–155, 152*f*, 154*f*, 201–206
  comprehension and vocabulary, 152*f*, 167–168, 239
  concepts about print, 152*f*, 155–156, 209–214
  overview, 151, 152*f*
  phonemic awareness, 152*f*, 156–158, 217–225
  phonics, 152*f*, 158–161, 229–236
  spelling, 152*f*, 166–167*f*
  text reading, 152*f*, 161–163*f*, 164*f*–165*f*, 165–166
  writing, 152*f*, 166–167*f*, 237
  See also Assessment
Early reading and writing phase of development, 116, 119*f*–120*f*. *See also* Development
Echo reading, 97, 103, 110*f*
ELL interactive read-aloud procedure, 134, 135*f*, 136*f*–137. *See also* English language learners; Interactive read-alouds
Emergent writing, 86, 87. *See also* Writing
Encouraging remarks, 121
End-of-the-year goals, 92–93*f*
English language learners
  audio books and, 28
  challenges related to, 125–126, 127*f*, 128, 129*f*, 130–134, 135*f*, 136*f*–138
  instruction and, 145
Environment, classroom
  examples of, 2–3, 37–38
  furniture arrangement and, 35–37, 36*f*
  importance of, 24–26
  preparing, 26–34
  scheduling and, 38
  See also Learning centers
Example of a kindergarten classroom
  environment and, 37–38
  overview, 1–5, 23
  small-group instruction and, 95–97
  a typical week in, 6–23, 9*f*, 10*f*, 20*f*
Expectations in kindergarten
  of English language learners, 125–126
  overview, 43–52, 45*f*, 48*f*, 49*f*, 52*f*
  small-group instruction and, 92–93*f*
  text reading, 161
  year-end goals, 92–93*f*

Experimentation phase of development, 116.
    See also Development
Explaining why events, 69
Exploration stage of development
    matching instruction with, 117
    overview, 116
    See also Development

Fables, 30. *See also* Books
Fairy tales, 29. *See also* Books
Family
    English language learners and, 131–132
    involving, 138–141, 142*f*–144*f*, 144–145
Family literacy, 139
Fantasy books, 30. *See also* Books
Fingerpoint reading
    assessment of, 155–156, 155–156
    developmental phases and, 116, 117–118,
        119*f*–120*f*
    overview, 50–51, 73–74
    reading aloud and, 91*f*
    running records and, 165–166
    shared-reading techniques and, 79, 81*f*–82*f*
    small-group instruction and, 103–104, 104–
        106, 110*f*
    as a year-end goal, 93*f*
Fluency
    decoding and, 107–108
    leveled books and, 109
Folktales, 30. *See also* Books
Furniture arrangement, 35–37, 36*f*. *See also*
    Classroom environment

Genres, 58–60. *See also* Books
Goals, year-end, 92–93*f*
Group reading instruction
    kid writing and, 87
    overview, 4–5, 9–10
    reading aloud and, 63–64, 64–72
    See also Interactive read-alouds; Small-
        group reading instruction
Guided book introduction, 97, 103, 104–105,
    110*f*, 111*f*
Guided fingerpoint reading
    developmental phases and, 118
    small-group instruction and, 104–106, 110*f*
    See also Fingerpoint reading
Guided invented spelling. *See* Kid writing
Guided reading instruction, 93, 106–109,
    111*f*
Guided shared reading
    developmental phases and, 117

small-group instruction and, 103–104,
    110*f*
    See also Shared-reading techniques
Henny Penny (Galdone)
    comprehension and, 68
    multiple readings of, 70–71
    vocabulary and, 67–68
High-frequency words, 108–109

Independent writing, 60*f*–61. *See also* Writing
Individualized Education Plans (IEPs), 124–
    125
Inference, 69
Informational books
    English language learners and, 134
    genres elements of, 59–60
    interactive read-alouds and, 71–72
    introducing in an interactive read-aloud,
        66–67
    overview, 29
    retelling of, 52
    See also Books
Instruction
    assessment and, 4, 174–175
    English language learners and, 125–126,
        127*f*, 128, 129*f*, 130–134, 135*f*, 136*f*–
        138
    family involvement and, 138–141, 142*f*–
        144*f*, 144–145
    matching with developmental phases, 117–
        118
    national standards and, 147, 148*f*–150*f*
    overview, 145
    scaffolding as, 118, 120–125
    in small groups, 92–109, 93*f*
    See also Differentiated instruction; Group
        reading instruction; Small-group read-
        ing instruction
Instruction, differentiated
    English language learners and, 125–126,
        127*f*, 128, 129*f*, 130–134, 135*f*, 136*f*–
        138
    family involvement and, 138–141, 142*f*–
        144*f*, 144–145
    overview, 115–118, 145
    See also Small-group reading instruction
Instruction, group
    kid writing and, 87
    overview, 4–5, 9–10
    reading aloud and, 63–64, 64–72
    See also Interactive read-alouds; Small-
        group reading instruction

Instruction, small-group
  core reading programs and, 113–114
  developmental phases and, 117
  example of, 4–5, 9–10, 13–15, 17, 19–20,
    22
  kid writing and, 87
  managing, 109, 110f–111f, 111–113f
  overview, 92, 114
  teaching conventions in, 92–109, 93f
  See also Differentiated instruction; Group
    reading instruction
Instructional level, 161
Integration of curriculum, 1
Interactive read-alouds
  big books and, 74
  English language learners and, 134, 135f,
    136f–137
  informational books and, 71–72
  list of books, 180–181, 181–182
  multiple readings of a book and, 70–72
  overview, 63, 64–72, 89–90, 91f
  year-end goals and, 93f
  See also Read-alouds
Interactive writing, 84–85, 90
Invented spelling
  assessment of, 166, 169
  developmental phases and, 116, 117–118,
    119f–120f
  independent writing and, 60–61
  national standards and, 149f
  overview, 85–89f, 88f, 90
  as a year-end goal, 93f
  See also Spelling; Writing
Isolating beginning and ending phonemes
  task, 157–158. See also Assessment

Joke books, 30. See also Books
Journal writing, 87–89, 88f. See also Writing

Kid writing
  example of, 60f–61
  overview, 85–89f, 88f, 90
  See also Writing
Knowledge, prior, 68–69

Language development, 126, 127f, 128, 129f,
    130, 145. See also Development
Language play books, 75–77, 180. See also
    Books
Learning
  developmental phases in, 116
  environment and, 24–25

Learning centers
  example of, 2–3
  furniture arrangement and, 35–37, 36f
  managing work in, 4, 34–35, 111–113f
  overview, 31–32
  preparing, 26–34
Letter formation, 98–99, 195–198
Letter identification, 98–99. See also Alphabet
    knowledge
Letter–sound associations. See also Phonics
  cultural considerations to, 132–133
  developmental phases and, 117–118
  expectations regarding, 47–48
  national standards and, 149f
  shared-reading techniques and, 90
  small-group instruction and, 101–102
Letter-study area, 31. See also Literacy center
Letters, concepts regarding
  national standards and, 148f
  overview, 50
Leveled texts
  assessment and, 161
  resources, 190–191
  small-group instruction and, 109
  See also Books
Library corner
  interactive read-alouds and, 72
  overview, 27–31
Listening center, 112. See also Centers, learn-
    ing
Literacy center
  example of, 2, 8
  furniture arrangement and, 37
  overview, 25, 27, 27–28, 31–32
  See also Centers, learning
Literacy development
  assessment of, 146–147, 148f–150f, 150–
    151
  environment and, 25
  family involvement and, 138–141, 142f–
    144f, 144–145
  matching instruction with, 117–118
  phases of, 116
  See also Development
Literacy-rich environment, 26–34. See also
    Classroom environment

Magazines, 30. See also Books
Math, 11–12, 15, 22–23
Math center, 3, 8, 32. See also Centers, learn-
    ing
Me and Neesie (Greenfield), 54–55f, 56f–57f

Memorization
    fingerpoint reading and, 73–74
    pretend reading and, 50–51
    shared-reading techniques and, 90
    small-group instruction and, 104
Miscue analysis, 162–163, 165f. See also Assessment
Modeling, 123–124
Montessori education, 25
Morning meeting, 7–8, 13, 16–17, 18–19, 21–22
Movies, books that tie into, 138
Multiple readings of a book
    interactive read-alouds and, 70–72
    language play books and, 76
    See also Books
Music, 12
Music center
    furniture arrangement and, 37
    overview, 32
    See also Centers, learning

Name-writing and letters-in-name recognition
    assessment, 152–153, 154f. See also Assessment
Narrative composition analysis form, 168, 169f, 170–171. See also Assessment
Narratives, 59. See also Books
National standards
    assessment and, 146–147, 148f–150f, 150–151, 175
    core reading programs and, 113–114
Newspapers, 30. See also Books
Nursery rhymes
    overview, 29
    shared-reading techniques and, 72–74
    See also Books

Observational assessment, 171–174, 173f. See also Assessment
Officer Buckle and Gloria (Rathman)
    overview, 30
    using in assessing comprehension, 167–168
    See also Books
Onset
    assessment of, 158
    overview, 46
    small-group instruction and, 100–101
    See also Phonological awareness
Open-ended questioning, 121–122. See also Questions
Oral comprehension, 51–52f. See also Comprehension

Outdoor environment, 26–27, 32. See also Centers, learning; Classroom environment
Owl Moon (Yolen), 51–52f, 53f

Parents. See Family
Participation books, 30. See also Books
Pattern books, 73–74. See also Books
Peer interactions, 25–26
Phonemes, 47
Phonemic awareness
    alphabet books and, 75
    assessment of, 152f, 156–158, 217–225
    compared to phonics, 47
    developmental phases and, 117–118, 119f–120f
    expectations regarding, 46–47
    national standards and, 149f
    reading aloud and, 91f
    shared-reading techniques and, 90
    small-group instruction and, 95, 99–101, 110f
    as a year-end goal, 93f
Phonics
    alphabet books and, 75
    assessment of, 152f, 158–161, 229–236
    expectations regarding, 47–50, 48f, 49f
    national standards and, 149f
    overview, 90
    shared-reading techniques and, 81f–82f
    small-group instruction and, 95, 101–102
    as a year-end goal, 93f
Phonological awareness, 46–47
Picture concept books, 29. See also Books
Picture storybooks
    English language learners and, 137
    overview, 29
    See also Books
Pictures, 137–138
Play, dramatic
    example of, 3, 9
    interactive read-alouds and, 72
    overview, 25, 32–34
    pretend writing and, 58f
    year-end goals and, 93f
    See also Centers, learning
Pocket charts
    displaying the daily schedule and, 128
    reading aloud and, 91f
    shared-reading techniques and, 78–79, 80f–82f
    small-group instruction and, 96–97, 110f

Poetry, 30. *See also* Books
Portfolios, 147
Posters, 28
Predictable literature
  English language learners and, 130, 133–134
  overview, 30–31
  See also Books
Prediction, 69
Pretend reading
  memorization and, 73–74
  overview, 50–51
  as retelling, 52, 53*f*
Pretend writing, 58*f*. *See also* Writing
Print, concepts regarding
  assessment of, 152*f*, 155–156, 209–214
  developmental phases and, 116, 117, 119*f*–120*f*
  national standards and, 148*f*
  overview, 50–51
  reading aloud and, 91*f*
  shared-reading techniques and, 77–79, 80*f*–82*f*, 90
  as a year-end goal, 93*f*
Print in the classroom, 26–27. *See also* Classroom environment
Print tracking
  concepts regarding, 50
  as a year-end goal, 93*f*
Prior knowledge, 68–69
Props, storytelling, 28

Questions
  interactive read-alouds and, 68–69
  scaffolding and, 121–122, 123

Read-alouds
  developmental phases and, 117
  English language learners and, 133–134, 135*f*, 136*f*–137
  example of, 12–13, 16, 18, 21, 23
  interactive, 64–72
  list of books, 182–184
  overview, 63–64, 89–90, 91*f*
  shared-reading techniques and, 72–79
  See also Interactive read-alouds
Reading, developmental phases in, 116, 119*f*–120*f*
Reading expectations, 43–52, 45*f*, 48*f*, 49*f*, 52*f*
Reading, fingerpoint
  assessment of, 155–156, 155–156
  developmental phases and, 116, 117–118, 119*f*–120*f*

overview, 50–51, 73–74
reading aloud and, 91*f*
running records and, 165–166
shared-reading techniques and, 79, 81*f*–82*f*
small-group instruction and, 103–104, 104–106, 110*f*
as a year-end goal, 93*f*
Reading of text
  assessment of, 152*f*, 161–163*f*, 164*f*–165*f*, 165–166
  national standards and, 149*f*
  small-group instruction and, 95, 102–109
Reading, pretend
  memorization and, 73–74
  overview, 50–51
  as retelling, 52, 53*f*
Reading strategies, 53–55*f*, 56*f*–57*f*
Realistic literature, 29–30. *See also* Books
Record keeping, 45
Repetitive books, 73–74. *See also* Books
Retelling of stories
  comprehension and vocabulary and, 51–52*f*, 53*f*, 167–168
  year-end goals and, 93*f*
Rhyme task, 156–157. *See also* Assessment
Rhyming books, 75–77. *See also* Books
Rhyming words
  assessment of, 159–160
  developmental phases and, 117–118
  expectations regarding, 46–47
  phonics and, 49
  reading aloud and, 91*f*
  shared-reading techniques and, 72–74, 76
  small-group instruction and, 110*f*
  See also Phonological awareness
Riddle books, 30. *See also* Books
Rime
  assessment of, 158
  overview, 46
  small-group instruction and, 100–101
  See also Phonological awareness
Routines
  kid writing and, 86–89*f*, 88*f*
  scheduling and, 38–42, 39*f*, 40*f*, 41*f*
  shared writing and, 82–84, 83*f*
Running records
  overview, 4, 161
  using, 162–163*f*, 164*f*, 165*f*–166
  See also Assessment

Scaffolding
  overview, 118, 120–125

with special-needs children, 124–125
  See also Instruction
Scheduling
  during center time, 34–35
  displaying the daily schedule, 128
  example of, 5
  overview, 38–42, 39*f*, 40*f*, 41*f*
Science center
  example of, 3, 8, 9*f*, 10*f*
  furniture arrangement and, 37
  overview, 32
  See also Centers, learning
Segmenting
  assessment of, 158
  small-group instruction and, 100–101
Segmenting phonemes task, 158. *See also* Assessment
Shared-reading techniques
  list of books, 180–181
  overview, 64, 72–79, 80*f*–82*f*, 90
  small-group instruction and, 103–104
  See also Read-alouds
Shared writing, 79, 82–84, 83*f*, 85*f*, 90
Sign-in procedure
  alphabet knowledge and, 46
  overview, 39–40*f*
Skills, assessment of, 146–147, 148*f*–150*f*, 150–151. *See also* Assessment
Small-group reading instruction
  core reading programs and, 113–114
  developmental phases and, 117
  example of, 4–5, 9–10, 13–15, 17, 19–20, 22
  kid writing and, 87
  managing, 109, 110*f*–111*f*, 111–113*f*
  overview, 92, 114
  teaching conventions in, 92–109, 93*f*
  See also Differentiated instruction; Group reading instruction
Social studies center
  furniture arrangement and, 37
  overview, 32
  See also Centers, learning
Special-needs children, 124–125
Spelling
  assessment of, 152*f*, 166–167*f*, 169
  national standards and, 149*f*
  small-group instruction and, 108–109
  writing and, 58–60, 59*f*
  See also Invented spelling
Spelling, invented
  assessment of, 166, 169

developmental phases and, 116, 117–118, 119*f*–120*f*
  independent writing and, 60–61
  national standards and, 149*f*
  overview, 85–89*f*, 88*f*, 90
  as a year-end goal, 93*f*
  See also Spelling; Writing
Spelling scoring rubric, 166. *See also* Assessment
Standards
  assessment and, 146–147, 148*f*–150*f*, 150–151, 175
  core reading programs and, 113–114
Step Up technique, 83*f*. *See also* Shared writing
Storytelling, 28, 139
Strategies for reading
  assessment of, 146–147, 148*f*–150*f*, 150–151
  overview, 53–55*f*, 56*f*–57*f*
Students, 94
Syllable awareness
  assessment of, 158
  expectations regarding, 46
Syntactic patterns, 138
Systematic direct instruction, 95

Tapes, books on, 28
Television, books that tie into, 138. *See also* Books
Testing, 174. *See also* Assessment
Text reading
  assessment of, 152*f*, 161–163*f*, 164*f*–165*f*, 165–166
  national standards and, 149*f*
  small-group instruction and, 95, 102–109
Thematic backpacks, 144
Themed dramatic play center, 33–34. *See also* Centers, learning; Dramatic play center
Themes
  books related to, 186–190, 191–192
  overview, 114
Thinking, levels of, 53–55*f*, 56*f*–57*f*
Tight Times (Hazen), 29–30. *see also* Books
Time management, 34–35. *See also* Scheduling
Total physical response (TPR), 126, 128
Tracking print
  concepts regarding, 50
  as a year-end goal, 93*f*
Traditional literature, 29. *See also* Books

Upper-case and lower-case alphabet recognition tasks, 154–155. *See also* Assessment

Visual aids, 137–138
Vocabulary
  assessment of, 152*f*, 167–168, 239
  developmental phases and, 120*f*
  English language learners and, 126, 134,
    136*f*–137
  expectations regarding, 51–52*f*
  interactive read-alouds and, 65, 67–68, 71–72
  multiple readings of a book and, 70–71
  reading aloud and, 89–90, 91*f*
  shared-reading techniques and, 72–73
  as a year-end goal, 93*f*
Vowel analysis form, 160–161. *See also* Assessment
Vowel-first decoding, 108. *See also* Decoding

Websites, 184–185
Whole-group instruction
  kid writing and, 87
  reading aloud and, 63–64, 64–72
  See also Small-group reading instruction
Why Do Leaves Change Color (Maestro), 66–67
Why events, 69
Word families, 101–102
Word reading, 95
Word recognition prompts, 105, 108, 110*f*, 111*f*
Word study
  national standards and, 149*f*
  small-group instruction and, 95, 98–102, 104
Word-study area, 31. *See also* Literacy center
Word wall
  example of, 2–3
  overview, 26

Words, concepts regarding
  national standards and, 148*f*–149*f*
  overview, 50–51
  shared-reading techniques and, 80*f*–82*f*
Work samples, 168–171, 170*f*
Workbench center, 32. *See also* Centers,
  learning
Write On technique
  overview, 84, 85*f*
  small-group instruction and, 99
  See also Shared writing
Writing
  assessment of, 152*f*, 166–167*f*, 237
  developmental phases in, 116, 119*f*–120*f*
  English language learners and, 138
  interactive, 84–85
  kid writing and, 85–89*f*, 88*f*
  in kindergarten, 57–61, 58*f*, 59*f*, 60*f*
  of letters, 98–99
  national standards and, 149*f*–150*f*
  shared, 79, 82–84, 83*f*
  small-group instruction and, 95, 98–102
Writing area, 31. *See also* Literacy center
Writing center, 2–3, 8. *See also* Centers,
  learning
Writing expectations, 43–52, 45*f*, 48*f*, 49*f*,
  52*f*
Writing, pretend, 58*f*. *See also* Writing
Writing workshop
  example of, 11, 15, 17–18, 20*f*–21, 22
  overview, 89*f*

Year-end goals, 92–93*f*